Améfrica in Letters

Améfrica in Letters

Literary Interventions from Mexico to the Southern Cone

Edited by Jennifer Carolina Gómez Menjívar
Afterword by Mamadou Badiane

Vanderbilt University Press
Nashville, Tennessee

Copyright 2022 Vanderbilt University Press
All rights reserved
First printing 2022

Cover image: *La Luna*, by Alberta "Betty" Nicolás

Library of Congress Cataloging-in-Publication Data
Names: Gómez Menjívar, Jennifer Carolina, editor.
Title: Améfrica in letters : literary interventions from Mexico to the Southern Cone / edited by Jennifer Carolina Gómez Menjívar.
Description: Nashville, Tennessee : Vanderbilt University Press, [2022] | Series: Hispanic issues ; [46] | Includes bibliographical references and index.
Identifiers: LCCN 2022007209 (print) | LCCN 2022007210 (ebook) | ISBN 9780826505132 (paperback) | ISBN 9780826505149 (hardcover) | ISBN 9780826505156 (epub) | ISBN 9780826505163 (pdf)
Subjects: LCSH: Latin American literature—Black authors—History and criticism. | Latin American literature—African influences. | Latin American literature—20th century—History and criticism. | Latin American literature—21st century—History and criticism. | Identity (Psychology) in literature. | Black people—Latin America—Intellectual life. | LCGFT: Literary criticism. | Essays.
Classification: LCC PQ7081.7.B55 A59 2022 (print) | LCC PQ7081.7.B55 (ebook) | DDC 860.089/9608--dc23/eng/20220708
LC record available at https://lccn.loc.gov/2022007209
LC ebook record available at https://lccn.loc.gov/2022007210

HISPANIC ISSUES
Nicholas Spadaccini, Founding Editor
Ana Forcinito, Executive Editor
Luis Martín-Estudillo, Executive Editor
Megan Corbin, Managing Editor
William Viestenz, Associate Managing Editor
Sophia Beal, Osiris A. Gómez, Associate Editors
Carolina Julia Añón Suárez, Ariel Arjona,
Collin Diver, Tim Frye, Javier Zapata Clavería,
Assistant Editors

*ADVISORY BOARD / EDITORIAL BOARD
Rolena Adorno (Yale University)
Román de la Campa (Unversity of Pennsylvania)
David Castillo (University at Buffalo)
Jaime Concha (University of California, San Diego)
Tom Conley (Harvard University)
Estrella de Diego Otero (Universidad Complutense de Madrid)
Nora Domínguez (Universidad de Buenos Aires)
William Egginton (Johns Hopkins University)
Brad Epps (University of Cambridge)
Edward Friedman (Vanderbilt University)
Wlad Godzich (University of California, Santa Cruz)
Antonio Gómez L-Quiñones (Dartmouth College)
Hans Ulrich Gumbrecht (Stanford University)
*Carol A. Klee (University of Minnesota)
Germán Labrador Méndez (Princeton University)
Eukene Lacarra Lanz (Universidad del País Vasco)
Raúl Marrero-Fente (University of Minnesota)
Kelly McDonough (University of Texas at Austin)
Walter D. Mignolo (Duke University)
*Louise Mirrer (The New-York Historical Society)
Mabel Moraña (Washington University in St. Louis)
Alberto Moreiras (Texas A & M University)
Bradley J. Nelson (Concordia University, Montreal)
Michael Nerlich (Université Blaise Pascal)
*Francisco Ocampo (University of Minnesota)

Antonio Ramos-Gascón (University of Minnesota)
Jenaro Talens (Universitat de València)
Miguel Tamen (Universidade de Lisboa)
Noël Valis (Yale University)
Teresa Vilarós (Texas A & M University)
Santos Zunzunegui (Universidad del País Vasco)

CONTENTS

ACKNOWLEDGMENTS   ix

INTRODUCTION. Black Writing on the Latin American Mainland: Disruptions to the Prose of Multiculturalism   1
JENNIFER CAROLINA GÓMEZ MENJÍVAR

PART I. AFRO POETICS

1. Language and the Construction of Gendered Identities in Afro-Mexican *Corridos* or Ballads   25
   PAULETTE A. RAMSAY

2. A Post-Ethnic/Racial Futurescape in Wingston González's *cafeína MC*   42
   JUAN GUILLERMO SÁNCHEZ MARTÍNEZ

3. Antonio Preciado: Ecuador's Afrocentric Poet   68
   MICHAEL HANDELSMAN

PART II. LETTERED OUTLIERS

4. Transatlantic Routing and Rooting in Quince Duncan's *Kimbo*   83
   GLORIA ELIZABETH CHACÓN

5. The Palimpsestic Afro-Panamanian Woman in Melanie Taylor Herrera's *Camino a Mariato*   97
   ÁNGELA CASTRO

6. Black Lives Matter in Brazil: Cidinha da Silva's *#Parem de nos matar*   109
   ELISEO JACOB

PART III. INTELLECTUAL SONAR

7. Other Forests: The Afro-Brazilian Literary Archive 129
   ISIS BARRA COSTA

8. Dismantling Coloniality via the Vocabulary of
   Afro-Chilean and Afro-Puerto Rican Music-Dance 150
   JUAN EDUARDO WOLF

9. Xiomara Cacho Caballero: Linguistic Heritage and
   Afro-Indigenous Survivance on Roatán 170
   JENNIFER CAROLINA GÓMEZ MENJÍVAR

10. Reclaiming Lands, Identity, and Autonomy:
    Rapping Youth in Rural Chocó, Colombia 194
    DIANA RODRÍGUEZ QUEVEDO

    AFTERWORD. *Racial Encounters in the Americas
    in Times of Black Lives Matter* 219
    MAMADOU BADIANE

CONTRIBUTORS 237
INDEX 243

◆ ACKNOWLEDGMENTS

This book owes everything to the Afrodescendant writers across Amérfica whose work in Indigenous and Creole languages—and in the official languages of Spanish, Portuguese, French, English of the nations they inhabit—constitutes an account of Black life, thought, joy, sorrow, and resistance that is nothing less than a hemispheric cultural patrimony. In this vein, I would like to especially thank the writers who penned the letters we literary critics engage with in this volume: Lélia Gonzalez, Cidinha da Silva, Xiomara Cacho Caballero, Quince Duncan, Wingston González, Antonio Preciado, Melanie Taylor Herrera, the Afro-Mexican lyricists of *corridos*, the Afro-Chilean troupes Sociedad Religiosa de Morenos Hilario Ayca and Compañía de don Andrés Baluarte, and the Afro-Puerto Rican and Afro-Colombian artists Grupo de Rap Infantil and Renacientes. I am also enormously grateful to Centro Cultural Cimarrón in El Ciruelo, Oaxaca (Mexico) for the work they do on multiple platforms to give Afro-Mexican artists their due recognition and for putting me in contact with Alberta "Betty" Hernández Nicolás (Albert Nicolás), whose work graces this cover. Betty, your artwork is not just an outstanding contribution to this volume, but also a beautiful testament to the ancestral tradition you honour therein. Our hearts are filled with gratitude to you for granting us permission to feature "La luna" on the cover of this volume and to share your artist biography with its readers.

To the team of contributors who defied the challenges posed by a global pandemic to participate in this project: thank you for your commitment to this undertaking and for charting new paths for our field with your incisive and reflective contributions. To those whose encouragement and thoughtful feedback shaped this volume from start to finish: the anonymous peer reviewers, Luis Martín-Estudillo, Sophia Beal, Ana Forcinito, Zach Gresham, Kristen Hadley, Lindsey Jungman, Nicolás Ramos Flores, Nicholas Spadaccini, and David Syring, my sincerest gratitude to you all for your critical input and guidance at so many different phases of the process. To Mamadou Badiane: your work on negrismo and négritude inspired me early in my career and your ongoing work on transcontinental Black letters has led our field into ground-breaking terrain; thank you for writing the afterword to this volume. To my colleagues at the University of North Texas, especially Tamara Brown, Steven Cobb, and Harry Benshoff: thank you for nurturing this project by providing me with a strong and productive academic home in which to bring all its elements together. To those who have enriched my approach to the Afro-Indigenous letters and intellectual histories of the mainland: Ileana Rodríguez, bell hooks, Arturo Arias, Dorothy Mosby, and Beatriz Cortez, I will always be grateful to you for what you have taught me through your work and your example.

This book is dedicated to the next generation of letter-readers, especially Ezra, Nazareth, Noel, Max, Willie, Amelia, and Camila. To my partner in love for letters, William Salmon: everything.

◆ INTRODUCTION

Black Writing on the Latin American Mainland

Disruptions to the Prose of Multiculturalism

Jennifer Carolina Gómez Menjívar

Was race or class responsible for the marginalization of Black and Indigenous peoples in Latin America? By the last four decades of the twentieth century, the "rosy vision of racial democracy" that the intelligentsia of the region had long upheld—and used to distinguish the region as a counterpoint to the notably segregated United States—was beginning to cloud.[1] It was becoming evident that discussions about exclusion needed to shift from economic factors to racism. Within the political space opened by the Cuban Revolution, Black and Afrodescendant intellectuals in the 1960s and 1970s were able to highlight inequities that could not be reduced to micro-economics or explained by Dependency Theory.[2] The global emergence of "new 'Black' movements aimed at combating racial discrimination that prevented the full integration of Black and brown people into national life" bolstered activism in Brazil, Panama, and Colombia that then spread to Latin American countries with relatively smaller Black populations.[3] Sandinista Nicaragua, for example, adopted constitutional reforms to validate the multiracial republic by recognizing its minority communities on its Caribbean coast.[4] In 1988, constitutional reform in Brazil led to the recognition of the ancestral rights of quilombos. Many other countries followed suit, as constitutional reforms in

Bolivia, Colombia, Ecuador, Guatemala, and Honduras provided collective rights for their Black and Afrodescendant populations.

In the introduction to his landmark book, *Black Writing, Culture, and the State in Latin America*, Jerome Branche stresses the need to apprehend and appreciate "the voices of those (enslaved) subjects who were ab initio not held to be part of the colonial cluster of *vecinos* or *colonos*," a condition that "implied a multilateral suffocation of their subjectivity." In effect, it took "fully five hundred years after the Columbus landing, with the new constitutions of the post-dictatorial period of the 1990s, for some Latin American states to recognize the retrograde slave-era content of the term *negro* that designated these subjects, to attempt to dislodge them from the social debasement and stigma of forced labor, or to recognize their essential citizenship."[5] Since then, activists have demanded legislative changes and, importantly, state accountability to Black and Afrodescendant populations in all the nations across this vast space. The *Conferencia Regional Preparatoria de las Américas contra el Racismo, la Xenofobia y las Formas Conexas de Intolerancia* (Regional Preparatory Conference of the Americas Against Racism, Xenophobia, and Related Forms of Intolerance), held in Santiago de Chile in 2000, marked a turning point in Afro-Latin American intellectual history and cultural production. Significantly, it was at this meeting that the term "Afrodescendants" was adopted by attendees. As Cristian Alejandro Báez Lazcano states in his reflections of the meeting:

> So many terms had been imposed by the colonizers to describe us: *negro, zambo, mulato, zambaigo, moreno*. With the term Afrodescendant, we get to define ourselves as "people of African origin who were brought as slaves during colonial times and who historically have been victims of racism, racial discrimination and slavery, with the consequent denial of their human rights, experiencing conditions based on marginalization, poverty and exclusion that are expressed through the profound social and economic inequality under which they live," in the words of the Declaration of Santiago.[6]

The term "Afrodescendant" had legal and political implications, as it cemented the belongingness of Black peoples to the Americas. Implicit in this adoption of a regional identity was also a sense of nation-specific historical presence. Not only were Black communities comprised of Afrodescendants, but they were simultaneously Afro-Chilean, Afro-Mexican, Afro-Costa Rican, and so forth. Thus, the overarching term "Afrodescendant" did not preclude Black peoples from asserting cultural differences across nations. The effect of this change in nomenclature and assertion of civil rights was further strengthened at the 2001

World Conference against Racism, Racial Discrimination, Xenophobia and Related Intolerance, held in Durban, where the Durban Declaration and Programme of Action was adopted. The document consisted of recommendations to strengthen an international human rights framework targeting racism and xenophobia against Afrodescendants worldwide.[7] Thus, from the 1960s to the 2010s, these marginalized communities went from being invisible to being recognized as political subjects with a firm claim to civil rights and equality in their respective nations. Their countries went from being agents of racism to being held accountable for systemic and historical racism and exclusion.

A new cycle of discourse gained traction on the heels of this consistent activism, highlighting structural racism and the demand for new scholarly approaches to Black experience in the region, specifically for the *producción de nuevos saberes,* or the creation of new ways of knowing.[8] Correspondingly, research on Afrodescendance and racism grew in those four decades. The increased attention to Black social and political movements spread across the Americas. In Latin America, this led to a critical assessment of the colonial period and coloniality in texts such as: *África en América Latina* (1979), *Afrodescendencia en el Ecuador: Raza y género desde los tiempos de la colonia* (2001), *Rutas de esclavitud en América Latina* (2001), *Afroamérica: La ruta del esclavo* (2006), and *La influencia de la cultura africana en el Perú colonial: Las poblaciones afrodescendientes de América Latina y el Caribe* (2012).[9] Mirroring scholarly interventions from the disciplines of history, anthropology, and sociology, the field of Afro-Latin American literary criticism was enriched by "the research of noted critics; proliferation of artistic works by Black and Hispanophone writers; publication of three important journals; application of new critical methodologies for interpreting literature; and studies that focus on single countries and individual writers," as Miriam DeCosta-Willis writes in her preface to the second edition of her groundbreaking volume, *Blacks in Hispanic Literature: Critical Essays.*[10] Literary critics working with this body of literature, DeCosta-Willis goes on to explain, have been shaped by Black aesthetic precepts, New Criticism, culturalism, new historicism, postcolonialism, and even new media studies.

The Latin American literary canon does indeed include a handful of Afrodescendant writers—we know, for example, that the seminal poet Rubén Darío was an Afrodescendant and Nicolás Guillén's poetry is included in virtually any literary anthology. However, the themes of the great Black writers who have been ignored fall outside of the canon and have thus not been assembled in the literary compendiums that form our discipline. This anthology brings together new research on Black literary history in the crucial period of the late twentieth and early twenty-first century—a timeframe that saw the consolidation of Black power movements and human rights struggles across the Americas. It proposes the conceptualizations of hemispheric Blackness and exchanges with theories of Indigeneity and decolonization as timely methodologies through which scholars can examine the voluminous Black literatures of the region. It also makes overtures to the impact of the digital turn on Amefrican letters, specifically on what Brazilian anthropologist Goli Guerreiro refers to as the "third diaspora," understood as the contemporary digital circuit of communication that connects Black peoples across geographic divides on a worldwide scale. Concomitantly, it examines the production of letters in the domains of music, poetry, and prose to more thoroughly engage with their circulation and consumption on traditional print and digital platforms among this third diaspora. The core assertion of the analyses presented is that the Black letter writers examined here have left an enduring legacy on *Améfrica*, particularly on its mainland. Though they have been often overlooked, they have produced, and often single-handedly distributed, a voluminous catalog of letters that challenges the overarching theme of mestizo-imagined multiculturalism that remains entrenched in many of Latin America's national histories and publishing venues.

Afrodescendant Letter Writers in *Améfrica*

Following independence, national elites erected literary traditions that promoted the order, progress, and ideologies they perceived to be fundamental to their new republics. Their visions for the nation states they ruled depended on the folklorization of Indigenous peoples and on the erasure of Black peoples within their borders. In Central America, for example, "eliminating black-identified racial categories and granting manumission to the last slaves in the Captaincy General of Guatemala set the stage for romantic representations of black peoples in Central American letters, for they could only be apprehended and subjected to representation in the elsewhere of 'fiction' as Afrodescendance ceased to be a *fact* of Central American reality and instead passed into *fictions*."[11] As Doris Sommer writes in her reflections on Afrodescendant writers in the context of the national literatures of the region: "Afrodescendant writers and readers were the black sheep of national hybrid families, and many were understandably skeptical about ending racism with mere rhetoric."[12] These conditions influenced the way that Black characters would be situated in plots that were produced and circulated in mainstream literary channels. National literary networks effectively prevented Black counterplots—which were, by definition, outside of established frames and racial democratic discourse—from being effectively "read."

As those of us who study Latin America know all too well, 1959 was a watershed year in the region. The Cuban Revolution was a political turning point, but it was also a literary turning point. When the Casa de las Américas was founded in 1959, it ushered a new era in the Spanish-language literatures of the Caribbean and the Latin American mainland. Established first as a literary prize and equipped with a publishing arm after 1960, Casa de las Américas cemented a circuit of literary production, circulation, and reception driven by "a guiding notion of solidarity based on the cultural values and elements of a common heritage that unite the nations of Latin America and the Caribbean."[13] While dictatorships on the Latin American mainland led to a repression of homegrown literary and socio-political theories, the Casa de las Américas harbored the region's exiled writers and critics. Yet, it must also be admitted that Blackness continued to be seen as a divisive discourse and that "black groups formed during 1974 and 1975 to discuss literature produced by African and African American writers, scholars, and activists. These groups were repressed by police and never re-formed."[14] This happened at a time when, paradoxically, Casa de las Américas was publishing texts written by prize-winning Afro-Caribbean authors such as Nicolás Guillén, C. R. James, and Kamau Brathwaite. Arguably, the parameters of revolutionary thought "permitted" certain Black writers to produce and remain in circulation in leftist Caribbean and Latin American circles, while delimiting the types of literary readings that could be given to such texts.[15]

Twenty years after Cuba, the Nicaraguan Revolution led to the demise of the Somoza Dynasty and to a similar cultural revitalization. The projects that emerged in Nicaragua differed from those established in Cuba in scale and scope, though not in their passion for grassroots cultural production and distribution. Sandinista Minister of Culture, Ernesto Cardenal, reflected on the change brought about by the revolution in an interview held ten years into Sandinista governance:

> Culture is now—as I was saying—the patrimony of all the people; the people have spontaneously created their "casas de cultura" and the vast proportion of the activities conducted there: music, theater, handicrafts, dance, and poetry. For example, many poetry workshops have been created by workers and peasants and by soldiers and police who write good modern poetry. Their poetry is influenced by Ezra Pound, William Carlos Williams, and by Chinese, Japanese, Greek, and Latin poetry. Also, many peasant and worker theatrical groups have been created.[16]

Cultural expressions of social criticism and protest developed as a concomitant and then a central mode of resistance in the armed struggle against Somoza, multiplying the sectors in which cultural production was born.

No longer a mode of expression that was property of the elite, literature in both Cuba and Nicaragua began to be steadily produced, published, and read by the masses. There was an important difference between the two contexts, however. Although the ideology of the Cuban Revolution dictated that "there would be no more black Cubans or white Cubans, only revolutionary Cubans destined to become New Men," Afro-Cuban writing remains vigorous and varied from the onset of the Cuban revolution to the present day.[17] Despite prejudice and censorship, writings such as Walterio Carbonell's *Cómo surgió la cultura nacional* and films by Black intellectuals such as Sara Gómez and Nicolás Guillén Landrían demanded "critical reflection on the persistence of marginality and racism in revolutionary Cuba, even if the socialist government had undertaken significant legislative, economic, and pedagogic efforts to eradicate them."[18] The possibilities available to Black Nicaraguan writers and authors were much narrower during the ten-year duration of the Sandinista government and in its aftermath. The reimagined Nicaraguan nation kept the aperture to its intellectual networks open just enough for notable author David McField and painter June Beer to enter, while keeping them just at the threshold. As Juliet Hooker observes, Sandinismo "generally did not acknowledge the presence of black Nicaraguans and costeños. Moreover, in the few instances when their presence was noted, they were often identified as potentially divisive agents of imperial foreign powers such as Britain and the United States."[19] Nicaragua's historically marginalized Black communities were added to the country's post-revolutionary cartographic and demographic analyses, but they were still enveloped in economically-rooted discussions of inequality. This then placed limits on what Nicaraguan Afrodescendants (and Indigenous communities) could express about the racism they continued to experience, and it also restricted the "acceptable" themes that Black intellectuals could express in their writing and other creative endeavors. Poignantly, color-blind socioeconomic analyses carried well into the twenty-first century. In a sharp indictment on the historical racism of his country, Nicaraguan novelist Sergio Ramírez wrote that in Nicaragua "lo negro sigue intolerable, en un sentido tácito. De eso no se habla. Un silencio sepulcral cae alrededor de su presencia en nuestra historia" (Blackness continues to be intolerable, in a tacit manner. It is not to be discussed. A sepulchral silence falls around its presence in our history).[20] Black peoples were enslaved, and racial hierarchies were established in the Americas from north to south, but the quincentennial legacy of Blackness has been both officially and extra-officially denied in Nicaragua and in many other countries in the mainland.

The Nicaraguan Revolution truly transformed the pattern of cultural production and even encouraged a taste for defiant content and genres in the Central

American isthmus and beyond. However, Black intellectual production from Latin America has continued to be excised from the "representative" Latin American literary canon and is often perceived as a boutique area of interest—despite decades of scholarly work on the subject and trailblazing anthologies like *The Afro-Hispanic Reader and Anthology* (2018) compiled by Paulette A. Ramsay (featured in this volume) and Antonio D. Tillis. Writing from the United States, literary critic Richard L. Jackson makes a solid case in his extensive scholarly oeuvre—*The Black Image in Latin American Literature* (1976), *Black Writers in Latin America* (1978), *The Afro-Spanish American Author* (1980), *The Afro-Spanish American Author II* (1989), *Black Writers and the Hispanic Canon* (1997), *Black Writers and Latin America: Cross Cultural Affinities* (1998), and *Black Literature and Humanism in Latin America* (2008)—for the magnificence of Hispanophone Black writing. As his work makes clear, many other Black voices besides those of Darío and Guillén merit a place in the canon and warrant increased circulation in the region's intellectual circles. The brilliant writing that Jackson explores highlights Black imagination and narrative deftness on a scale on par with, if not surpassing, that of their white and mestizo Latin American "admitted" literary counterparts. Richard L Jackson, along with other critics, such as Michael Handelsman (also featured in this volume), Martin Lewis, Laurence Prescott, Ian Smart, and Lorna Williams, highlight the vibrancy of the compendium of Afrodescendant writing. Together, their analyses make it clear that the exclusion of Black writers from their rightful place in Latin American letters is not due to a deficiency in skill or output. It is, to use the term popularized by Jesús Martín-Barbero, the effect of historical racism in the "mediations" at play in Latin American culture industries.

What Black writers, especially those in mainland Latin America, whether writing in Portuguese or Spanish, continue to experience and observe is concisely described by Lélia Gonzalez in her essay, "A Categoria Político-Cultural de Amefricanidade" (1988): "Já no caso das sociedades de origem latina, temos o racismo disfarçado ou, como eu o classifico, o *racismo por denegação*. Aqui prevalecem as 'teorias' de miscigenação, da assimilação e da 'democracia racial'. A chamada América Latina que, na verdade, é muito mais ameríndia e amefricana do que outra coisa, apresenta-se como o melhor exemplo de racismo por denegação" (In the case of societies of Latin origin, we have disguised racism or, as I term it, racism by denial. Here, the "theories" of miscegenation, assimilation and "racial democracy" prevail. The so-called Latin America, which, in fact, is much more Amerindian and Amefrican than anything else, manifests itself as the best example of racism by denial).[21] As a hemispheric issue, "O racismo latinoamericano é suficientemente sofisticado para manter negros e índios na condição de segmentos subordinados no interior das classes mais exploradas" (Latin American racism is sufficiently sophisticated to keep Black and Indigenous peoples in the condition of subordinate segments within the most exploited classes).[22]

In Gonzalez's appraisal, "Améfrica" emerges as an ethno-geographic system of reference for Black peoples in the Americas from south to north, while her theorization of "Amefricanity" is the lived experience that connects Black peoples in this hemisphere. Gonzalez explains:

> As implicações políticas e culturais da categoria de Amefricanidade ("*Amefricanity*") são, de fato, democráticas; exatamente porque o próprio termo nos permite ultrapassar as limitações de caráter territorial, linguístico e ideológico, abrindo novas perspetivas para um entendimento mais profundo dessa parte do mundo onde ela se manifesta: A AMÉRICA e como um todo (Sul, Central, Norte e Insular). Para alem de seu carater puramente geográfico, a categoria de Amefricanidade incorpora todo um processo histórico de intensa dinâmica cultural (adaptação, resistência, reinterpretação e criação de novas formas) que e afrocentrada.[23]

> *The political and cultural implications of the category of Amefricanity are, in fact, democratic; precisely because the term itself allows us to overcome territorial, linguistic, and ideological limitations, unlocking new perspectives for a deeper understanding of that part of the world where it manifests itself: AMERICA, as a whole [South, Central, North, and the Caribbean Basin]. In addition to its purely geographical character, the category of Amefricanity incorporates an entire historical process of intense cultural dynamics (adaptation, resistance, reinterpretation and creation of new forms) that is Afro-centered.*

Writing from the southern shores of Améfrica in the last decades of the twentieth century, Gonzalez opens an intellectual space by insisting on Amefricanity as that which flourished and was structured during the centuries marked with the presence of Black peoples in this hemisphere.[24] Those centuries, she poignantly argues, gave rise to successive waves of cultural resistance and to alternative means of free social organization in multiple coordinates and in multiple moments in time. While neither the critics in these chapters nor the authors they examine use the term "Améfrica," their work nonetheless fulfils the task of recognizing this hemisphere as the same ethno-geographic system of exchange and rebellion against the invisibility and subjection of Black, Indigenous, and Afro-Indigenous peoples. Their engagement with the concept of "mediations" is likewise implicit in their conversations with the: "gigantesco trabalho de dinâmica cultural que não nos leva para o lado do atlântico, mas que nos traz de la e nos transforma no que somos hoje: *amefricanos*" (gigantic labor of cultural dynamics that does not take us to the other side of the Atlantic, but brings us away from there and transforms us into what we are today: *Amefricans*).²⁵ These chapters speak to hemispheric Blackness, and, in their distinct yet interconnected methodologies, they bring into focus Black writing that challenges the myth of rosy racial democracy, understood today as "multiculturalism," in many of Améfrica's Hispanophone and Lusophone contexts.

Writing Against Multiculturalism

Between the period of the 1960s and today, critics from a variety of disciplines challenged the assumption that liberal multiculturalist paradigms would grant Afrodescendants (or Indigenous peoples) equitable space in national agendas. In her discussion about the multicultural turn that Nicaragua took in the 1990s, Juliet Hooker writes:

> Mestizo multiculturalism appears to recognize racial and cultural diversity in a way that older variants of mestizo nationalism did not. Whereas diversity is recognized, a hierarchy among diverse constituent identities is asserted. Because mestizo multiculturalism retains the idea of the nation as mestizo, it does not create an alternate multicultural identity; instead, like its predecessors, it discourages the assertion of "subnational" racial/cultural identities except insofar as they are contributors to this overarching national identity.²⁶

The festivals and holidays that were meant to celebrate the cultural diversity of the ethnic groups within Latin America's republics failed to generate an overhaul of the centuries of exclusion faced by minority ethnic communities. The disjuncture between ceremony and practice has ushered a new wave of mobilization, targeting the very language used to frame ethno-linguistic communities, as well as political actors from the margins. In her study on the subject, *Liberalism at its Limits* (2009), Ileana Rodríguez draws on examples from Guatemala, Colombia, and Mexico to argue that, in these societies, state-sanctioned mass murder and campaigns of terror and genocide reveal the extent to which liberal concepts have become inoperative and no longer capable of explaining new forms of violence or accounting for a wide variety of cultural conflicts. Importantly, she claims, "women and ethnic groups are agents of both material and discursive disruptions; they are both social actors of and figures and tropes in the discourse. In the twenty-first century, they disturb the prose of multiculturalism in the rhetoric of nation."[27] As both Hooker and Rodríguez suggest, the brand of multiculturalism espoused by several republics in Latin America was devised to preserve the nation states and its hierarchies. Failing to conform to such rhetoric within neoliberal contexts is perceived as a threat to governability and stability.

Several of the following contributions address violence and Afrodescendant writers' responses to state-imposed and state-sanctioned violence in their ancestral lands. In exploring this counter-multiculturalist strain of writing and criticism, the volume also explores the question of what has happened as the multiculturalist rhetoric espoused across Latin America fails to result in the inclusion of Afrodescendant authors on equal footing with *mestizo* authors. Specifically, several of the contributions engage with two questions: What is the nature of democracy and the literary sphere? What allows marginal Afrodescendant writers to make the transition from their own vernacular forms to mainstream Latin American audiences? Inroads have been made as Black critics in the region gather to discuss, for instance, the United Nations's International Decade for People of African Descent (2015–2024), which was eagerly adopted by many Latin American countries. As Rosa Campoalegre Septien writes, this call for a decade to celebrate Afrodescendants ushers in age-old challenges, not the least of which is the tendency for nation states to stall the momentum of Afrodescendant movements. As such, amplifying constitutional rights implies the need to remain alert to mechanisms of domination, as well as modes of resistance to them.[28]

Traditional histories of Black letters in Latin America have been devised with a geographic focus on the Caribbean. Critics have thus missed out on both Black writing in mainland Latin America and on writing that was penned after the tidal wave of multiculturalism led to the rise of Afrodescendant *and* Indigenous intellectual paradigms to counter the diluted inclusion of minority communities. Hence, the present volume approaches Black writing through the discussions that have emerged in minority intellectual circuits. This anthology is not alone in its assessment on the dual Afrodescendant–Indigenous objective to harness and direct discourse about and for ethnic minorities across Latin America. Catherine Walsh observes in *Pedagogías decoloniales: Prácticas insurgentes de resistir, (re)existir y (re)vivir*:

> The political, epistemic and existential insurgency of these movements, together with Afro-descendant organizations, would change the course and project in Latin America of the previous thought transformation and revolution; from here and

on, the struggle is not simply or predominantly a class struggle but a struggle for decolonization led, organized and largely envisioned by the racialized peoples and communities that have been suffering, resisting and surviving coloniality and domination. It is this resurgence and insurgency placed at the current junctures of not only these two countries but also at the continental level, which provoke and inspire new reflections and pedagogical considerations and, at the same time, new re-readings around the historical problem of the (de)humanization and (de)colonization.[29]

Controlling the narrative in all arenas, including literary circles, involves adopting language that goes beyond the standard economic analysis that has been available. Moreover, it takes a historical assessment of the effects of colonization, coloniality, and, yes, even nationhood, in shaping the marginalized experiences of Afrodescendant and Indigenous peoples. This emergence of ethnic minority voices has been insurgent in and of itself, as it implies introducing into intellectual circles discussions that have previously been circumscribed by terms like *inclusion* and *multiculturalism*.

This volume highlights the Black writers from the mainland who participated and are participating in creating a counter-multiculturalist literary history of América. To capture a sense of the variety of their contributions, this book spans Mexico, Central America, the Andes, and the Southern Cone—highlighting the trans-continental nature of the legacy of Black writing and its impact beyond national boundaries.[30] As the critics featured here attest, Afrodescendant authors have produced writings that are forceful testaments to the disjunction between multiculturalism and the lived experience of Black peoples across América's mainland. With this in mind, I caution readers and critics of this volume not to expect a tame request for inclusion in literary canons. Rather, the critical work collected here engages with the ways that Afrodescendant writers affirm their engagement while contesting national frameworks and devising alternative literary networks. The letters that they pen comprise a counterpublic sphere that demands reconstitution and reformulation of the societies in which they and other Afrodescendants reside.

A Black Trans-Continental Agenda

This anthology is divided into three parts, which mark historical progressions in the production and receptions of texts. Part I, Afro Poetics, analyzes the construction of Black subjectivities that disrupt frameworks of happy multiculturalism. The contributions in this section thus examine how Black writers avail themselves of the concept of the public sphere to critique monolithic representations of nation and citizen. The letters and *letras* (lyrics) that critics examine in this section highlight Afrodescendant resistance as authors think of Latin American literature *en clave afro* (encoded in blackness). The undercurrent of this section is Black writers' resistance to national renditions or literary expectations of what it means to be Black in Latin America. They do so with careful attention to the aesthetic qualities of the text and, importantly, to the responses they anticipate from their readers.

In "Language and the Construction of Gendered Identities in Afro-Mexican *Corridos* or Ballads," Paulette A. Ramsay examines the relationship between language and performance in the legitimization of masculine identities. The *corrido* is a musical folk ballad that dramatizes different aspects of Mexican history. It is normally associated with the Mexican Revolution, but, as Ramsay illustrates, the Black narrators of the *corridos* from Costa Chica use the genre to challenge the status quo; to disparage political leadership; to promote themselves as capable, confident men who are concerned with promoting a culturally nationalist agenda; to destabilize the hegemonic masculinity of the society; and to demonstrate the power of the Afrodescendant masculinity that they are performing and promoting. Ramsay's examination of the Costa Chican *corrido* poetics exposes the intricate ways in which speech and ideology work together to present listeners, or readers, with a conception of Black gender that is omitted from *mestizo*-centered narratives of Mexican masculinity. All the discursive language strategies—irony, diction, tone, register, syntax—accentuate a particular identity, one associated with Black men's power.

In the second chapter, "A Post-Ethnic/Racial Futurescape in Wingston González's *cafeína MC*," Juan Guillermo Sánchez Martínez focuses on the experimental poetry of Guatemala's most prolific Garífuna author. The two questions that guide his analysis are: is literary creativity a place where groupness and racial or ethnic classifications are currently being contested? And, how should literary critics "study" Garífuna expressions that are suspicious about academic discourses on Blackness and Indigeneity? The entry point for an answer to these questions is the observation that, despite González's Afro-Indigenous origins, Afrodescendance is not a central feature of his verses. Instead, his poetry demonstrates evidence of the tension between the transnational history of Garífuna peoples, self-representation, and the multiple possibilities in reading this body of work. These possibilities materialize as readers engage with the poet's play with popular culture and his building of a regional imaginary around places frequented by a generation who lives between Lake Atitlán, Guatemala City's main square, Tegucigalpa, San Salvador, and the Caribbean. The reader's chosen itinerary becomes a "journey" in which the choices made reveal the reader's own expectations of Black identity. The possibilities for itineraries surpass the writer's own intentions.

The section closes with "Antonio Preciado: Ecuador's Afrocentric Poet," in which Michael Handelsman observes that a source of strife common to many Black writers is their struggle to affirm and legitimize their intellectual and artistic relevance to all readers within the so-called Lettered City without minimizing their Afrodescendance as a vital source of their humanity or whitening their experience and content to be considered contributors to the regional or national literary tradition. Focusing on one of Ecuador's most prolific writers, Handelsman argues that Antonio Preciado understands the noxious implications of being categorized as Black by members of the literary world, the majority of whom are not Afrodescendants. The racist history that constitutes one of the principal pillars of coloniality as a hegemonic system has constructed dehumanizing images of Afrodescendants, leading Preciado to assume the responsibility of deconstructing longstanding stereotypes by affirming his own totality as a human being through writing that is nonetheless encoded in Blackness.

Part II, Lettered Outliers, examines the disruption that contemporary Black prose causes within national literary traditions, particularly because of Black writers' direct challenges to nation states. The chapters in this section demonstrate that both ideological violence and institutional violence are gendered and racialized, and that both forms of violence continue to pose a threat to Black peoples across Améfrica. The contributions explore how Black writers navigate the contractual relationship between citizens and nation states, throwing into relief the violence and elements that shred the fabric of social life. Examining the work of three key Black authors in context, the chapters articulate the forms and platforms that authors engage with to create literary outliers that uncompromisingly refuse ascription into multicultural rhetorics.

Gloria Elizabeth Chacón opens this section with "Transatlantic Routing and Rooting in Quince Duncan's *Kimbo*," which focuses on the fifth novel of Costa Rica's most versatile Black author. The essay centers the novel's use of oral storytelling and spirituality that disrupts Costa Rica's homogeneity and, at the same time, establishes Costa Rica's connection to Africa and the Antilles. The essay demonstrates how *Kimbo* counters the idea that Costa Rica is a democratic exception in Central America by underlining state violence against Blackness. Concomitant to this national demystifying, she argues that the Anancy folktales and the persistence and prevalence of the ancestors undermine Catholicism as the dominant religion. In doing so, Duncan's novel roots the Afro-Costa Rican community to the nation's body and establishes its links to multiple diasporas. Chacón highlights two main threads that underlie Duncan's critique of violence against Black men in Costa Rica: the author's weaving of Anancy folktales onto the Costa Rican national fabric to center cultural continuity, as well as his evocation of *samamfo* to affirm African ancestors in Costa Rica and their role in strengthening the Limonese community.

In the second contribution, "The Palimpsestic Afro-Panamanian Woman in Melanie Taylor Herrera's *Camino a Mariato*," Ángela Castro explores a novel that portrays the lives of thirteen Afro-Panamanian women. She argues that the novel engages with feminist theories of agency and intersectionality while conjuring the figure of a palimpsestic twentieth-century Afro-Panamanian woman, a subject that cannot be entirely defined due to the continuous reappearance of her overlayed identities. The identities of the female protagonists in the novel resist being disentangled, as they live in a constant state of a palimpsestic convolutedness. The text itself reflects this technique, as *Camino a Mariato* emerges as a palimpsestic novel in which unrelated texts are involved, entangled, and interwoven, thereby interrupting and inhabiting each other. In subject and matter, then, *Camino a Mariato* represents the complexity of the Afro-Panamanian woman, as well as the convolutedness of race in twentieth-century Panama.

Eliseo Jacob contributes the last essay in this section: "Black Lives Matter in Brazil: Cidinha da Silva's #*Parem de nos matar*." Recent years have seen the rise of concerns about anti-Black racism, and the genocide of Black populations in the peripheral communities of Brazil's major urban areas has become a focus in the works of contemporary Afro-Brazilian writers. Cidinha da Silva, a prominent Afro-Brazilian public intellectual, has published academic studies, short stories, and *crônicas* (chronicles) on issues related to racism, social inequality, and Black empowerment. Jacob uses the theory of necropolitics, or the physical and social death of the Black body, to frame da Silva's chronicles and to better understand Black genocide in Brazil. While da Silva covers a wide range of social issues in her book, including police brutality, poverty, and Black beauty, all the chronicles in #*Parem de nos matar* center around the question of the social, cultural, and political value of Afro-Brazilians in contemporary society, thus creating an opening for discussions about political mobilization and social empowerment in the face of state violence and repression.

Part III, Intellectual Sonar, evaluates post-1959 literary strategies as revolutionary techniques within the arsenal of Black intellectual history. The section engages with debates across the intellectual spheres, thereby crossing the linguistic and disciplinary boundaries that, prior to 1959, separated Black intellectual traditions. The contributions in this section are interested in examining how texts by Black authors conceptualize literary labor and how they conceive of writing as a practice that can rearrange disciplinary boundaries and the lines that define literary movements, all in order to expand the reach of Black letters.

This section opens with a reflection on poetics and their ramifications for critics' ability to listen to and study Black writing in Améfrica. In "Other Forests: The Afro-Brazilian Literary Archive," Isis Barra Costa finds that literary paradigms are organizing structures that inform the construction, reception, and legitimation of literary artifacts. The essay is a reflection on the "exiled" forms of the Brazilian literary canon—namely the Afro-Brazilian or, more specifically, the Bantu-Catholic oral poetics. Barra Costa demonstrates that, when formulating other literary paradigms, concepts beyond nation and ethnicity (such as other identitarian propositions, religious groups, and cultural regions) must be situated as necessary axes. To understand the Afro-Brazilian literary production not as a modality of the Brazilian canon but as a tradition with its own epistemological paradigms and cosmovisions, she proposes outlining a different interpretative structure. It is from the historic study of the Afro-Brazilian literary formation, from the root of Orature and its poetic and political unfoldings, that we can start thinking of Afro-Brazilian literature in its own transcontinental diasporic tradition.

The second contribution, "Dismantling Coloniality via the Vocabulary of AfroAfro-Chilean and Afro-Puerto Rican Music-Dance," inspects the intersections between Black writing and theories of decoloniality, generally associated with Indigenous writing and experience. Juan Eduardo Wolf examines the specific features of several genres of Afrodescendant music-dance in two different cultural contexts: the Chilean Andes and the Puerto Rican coast. He describes how the Afrodescendant communities in these contexts interacted with both the colonizers and Indigenous populations to create a wide range of music-dance expressions that contain Afrodescendant aesthetics and values. These Afrodescendant aesthetics and values offer alternatives to their colonialist counterparts that continue to reproduce the exclusion and inequality that Afrodescendant and Indigenous communities face in Latin America. Thus, the question that guides Wolf's analysis is: how can the vocabulary of Afrodescendant music-dance help to dismantle Latin American coloniality?

Next, "Xiomara Cacho Caballero: Linguistic Revitalization and Afro-Indigenous Survivance on Roatán," attends to the linguistic implications of the Garifuna writer's oeuvre. In this chapter, Jennifer Carolina Gómez Menjívar observes that Garifuna peoples were among the last to be recognized as Indigenous in the Central American isthmus and examines their unique place in the region's predominantly monolingual Hispanophone literary production. The essay puts Cacho Caballero's writing in conversation with Indigenous theories of survivance, arguing that to the risk of language and cultural loss, Cacho Caballero responds with her own theory of words—printed, recited, spoken, lived, and most recently, distributed online—as a healing point of departure for her Afro-Indigenous community. The analysis places Cacho Caballero within a hemispheric conversation about linguistic, political, and cultural resistance in which many of Améfrica's Indigenous peoples are participating.

The volume closes with "Reclaiming Lands, Identity, and Autonomy: Rapping Youth in Rural Chocó, Colombia," in which Diana Rodríguez Quevedo finds that Colombia has the largest number of internally displaced people (IDPs) in the world. In Colombia, IDPs are primarily Afrodescendant, Indigenous, and mestizo peasants, yet the phenomenon of forced displacement has affected the entire Colombian population. Memory is a key element in the formulation of history and in the processes of reparation, land restitution, and regaining of autonomy. Denouncing injustices and reclaiming a collective identity are at the forefront of the songs by the young Afro-Colombian peasant (rural) rappers Renacientes and Grupo de Rap Infantil. Their lyrics highlight collective experiences of resistance and self-determination after returning to their land—the Chocó region in the Colombian Pacific coast—in the late 1990s. Both groups appropriate rap music as a tool to relate accounts and denounce the causes and effects of forced displacement, while transforming their experiences and knowledge into social and political discourses. Rodríguez Quevedo analyzes the connection between the lyrics and the settings in which they are created and performed in relation to the land—rural aquatic territories—and its material and symbolic wealth: strategic political location, biodiversity, and African diasporic culture in contrast to decades of social and racial marginalization.

Literary Futurities

Both the primary texts and the criticism presented in this volume are not shaped within the celebratory "inclusion" paradigm informed by multiculturalism. Black letters in this region are often produced outside of the principal venues available in the authors' countries and are rarely put in circulation in the *ferias literarias* (literary festivals) or concerts in the region. After all, the letters of Améfrica rarely adhere to hegemonic literary and musical patterns, themes, and approaches. These conditions notwithstanding, the Afrodescendant writers of the Latin American mainland have fashioned letters that reflect on numerous historical and theoretical conditions of possibilities. This corpus of Black literary works is related to embodied legacies of Black resistance and contributes to Afrodescendant authors' arsenal of decolonized national rhetorical theory. The letters examined herewith not only evidence a clear rupture with the discourses of *mere* inclusion that have prevailed in the field of Latin American literatures and cultures, but they also shed light on the mechanisms at play when Afrodescendance is invoked only to be silenced in the echo chamber of multiculturalism.

From 1959 to the present day, Black letter writers in Améfrica have not assumed *a priori* scripts in their literary engagements. Elite-centered literary histories and even "global music" labels have flattened complex, multilayered Black letter-writing endeavors. Nonetheless, the production of Black letters from the margins *for* Black readers also in the margins represents an important resistance to Black peoples' historical exclusion from national and regional letter archives. The contestation from below evidenced in all of the Black letters examined in this volume has been, without a shadow of a doubt, a constant response to the elitism of the lettered circles and exclusion from *lo popular*. At best, the existing mainstream networks created spaces for *escritura negra permitida,* the kind that sought admittance at the risk of parodying mestizo imaginaries of Blackness and barring insurgent Black writing. At worst, they foreclosed the possibility of producing, circulating, and distributing Black letters on the Latin American mainland. It is time for a better appraisal of Améfrica's letters.

NOTES

1. Paulina L. Alberto and Jesse Huffnung-Garskof, " 'Racial Democracy' and Racial Inclusion: Hemispheric Histories," in *Afro-Latin American Studies: An Introduction*, eds. Alejandro de la Fuente and George Reid Andrews (Cambridge: Cambridge University Press, 2018), 264.
2. While it is beyond the scope of this introduction to discuss Dependency Theory, I direct the reader to the landmark book by Fernando Henrique Cardoso and Enzo Faletto, *Dependencia y desarrollo en América Latina: Ensayo de interpretación sociológica* (Buenos Aires: Siglo Veintiuno Editores, 1971). For an analysis of the literary implications of the theory written during the same time period, see Jean's Franco's "Dependency Theory and Literary History: The Case of Latin America," *Minnesota Review* 5, no. 1 (1975): 65–80.
3. George Reid Andrews, *Afro-Latin America, 1800–2000* (New York: Oxford University Press, 2004), 182.
4. Juliet Hooker, " 'Beloved Enemies': Race and Official Mestizo Nationalism in Nicaragua," *Latin American Research Review* 40, no. 3 (2005): 14. For a full discussion of the multicultural model adopted in Nicaragua, see Juliet Hooker's chapter on the subject in

Race and the Politics of Solidarity (New York: Oxford University Press, 2009), 129–166.
5. Jerome Branche, ed., *Black Writing, Culture, and the State in Latin America* (Nashville: Vanderbilt University Press, 2015), 1.
6. Cristian Alejandro Báez Lazcano, "Reflections on the Afro-Chilean Social Movement," *ReVista: Harvard Review of Latin America* 17, no. 2 (2018): 34.
7. Alejandro de la Fuente and George Reid Andrews, eds., *Afro-Latin American Studies: An Introduction* (Cambridge: Cambridge University Press, 2018), 20.
8. Aurora Vergara Figueroa and George Reid Andrews, "Introducción a los estudios afrolatinoamericanos," Afro-Latin American Research Institute at the Hutchins Center, Harvard University, accessed January 28, 2022, https://certificadoalari.fas.harvard.edu/módulos-y-docentes-curso-introducción-los-estudios-afrolatinoamericanos-1.
9. Several notable titles likewise appeared in the United States, though they primarily circulated in Anglophone contexts. Given that the present anthology focuses on Latin America and texts in Spanish have limited circulation among Anglophone readers, I have chosen to highlight landmark titles written in Spanish in the body of this introduction. I thus use this endnote to direct the reader to several notable texts written in English aside from those cited throughout this introduction: Lowell Gudmundson and Justin Wolfe, eds., *Blacks and Blackness in Central America: Between Race and Place* (Durham: Duke University Press, 2010); Jean Rahier, ed., *Black Social Movements in Latin America: From Monocultural Mestizaje to Multiculturalism* (New York: Palgrave Macmillan, 2012); Petra R. Rivera-Rideau, Jennifer A. Jones, and Tianna S. Paschel, eds., *Afro-Latin@s in Movement: Critical Approaches to Blackness and Transnationalism in the Americas* (New York: Palgrave Macmillan, 2016); Tianna S. Paschel, *Becoming Black Political Subjects: Movements and Ethno-racial Rights in Colombia and Brazil* (Princeton: Princeton University Press, 2016); Juliet Hooker, *Theorizing Race in the Americas: Douglass, Sarmiento, Du Bois, and Vasconcelos* (Oxford: Oxford University Press, 2017); and Kwame Dixon and Ollie A. Johnson III, eds., *Comparative Racial Politics in Latin America* (New York: Routledge, 2018).
10. Miriam DeCosta-Willis, *Blacks in Hispanic Literature: Critical Essays*, 2nd ed. (Baltimore, MD: Black Classic Press, 2011).
11. Jennifer Carolina Gómez Menjívar, "Passing into Fictions: Blackness, Writing and Power in the Captaincy General of Guatemala," *Chasqui: Revista de 'esarrollo latinoamericana* 45, no. 1 (2016): 104.
12. Doris Sommer, "Literary Liberties. The Authority of Afrodescendant Authors," in *Afro-Latin American Studies: An Introduction*, eds. Alejandro de la Fuente and George Reid Andrews (Cambridge: Cambridge University Press, 2018), 322.
13. Pamela Maria Smorkaloff, *Readers and Writers in Cuba: A Social History of Print Culture, 1830s–1990s* (New York: Garland Publishing, 1997), 131.
14. Andrews, *Afro-Latin America*, 184.
15. For more on Casa de las América's impact on literary production in the region, see George Lamming's "Creating and Independent Caribbean Culture," *The Black Scholar* 15, no. 3 (1984): 2–7; Joseph R. Pereira's "The Influence of the Casa de Las Américas

on English Caribbean Literature," *Caribbean Quarterly* 31, no. 1 (1985): 93–103; and Judith A. Weiss's *Casa de las Américas: An Intellectual Review in the Cuban Revolution* (Madrid: Editorial Castalia, 1977).
16. Ernesto Cardenal, Michael T. Martin, and Jeffrey Franks, "On Culture, Politics, and the State in Nicaragua: An Interview with Padre Ernesto Cardenal, Minister of Culture," *Latin American Perspectives* 16, no. 2 (1989): 128.
17. Odette Casamayor-Cisneros, "Imagining the 'New Black Subject': Ethical Transformations and Raciality in the Post-Revolutionary Cuban Nation," in *Black Writing and the State in Latin America*, ed. Jerome Branche (Nashville: Vanderbilt University Press, 2015), 64.
18. Ibid., 66.
19. Hooker, "Beloved Enemies," 27.
20. Sergio Ramírez, *Tambor olvidado* (San José, Costa Rica: Santillana, 2008) 11, 51.
21. Lélia Gonzalez, "A Categoria Político-Cultural de Amefricanidade," *Tempo Brasileiro* 92/93 (1988): 72. Translation mine.
22. Ibid., 75.
23. Ibid., 76.
24. Ibid, 79.
25. Ibid., 79.
26. Hooker, "Beloved Enemies," 16.
27. Ileana Rodríguez, *Liberalism at its Limits: Crime and Terror in the Latin American Cultural Text* (Pittsburgh: University of Pittsburgh Press, 2009), 3.
28. In Campoalegre Septien's words: "Los avances de la Declaración del Decenio Internacional de los Pueblos Afrodescendientes, hace aflorar peligros históricos: el principal de ellos es contrarrestar la acción política de los movimientos afrodescendientes. De modo, que abrir nuevos espacios y ampliar el sistema de derechos tutelados, implica estar alertas a no solo a los mecanismos de dominación, sino a las estrategias de resistencia ante ellos." Rosa Campoalegre Septien and Karina Bidaseca, eds., *Más allá del decenio de los pueblos afrodescendientes* (Buenos Aires: CIPS, Centro de Investigaciones Psicológicas y Sociológicas, 2017), 29.
29. Walsh, Catherine E., ed., *Pedagogías decoloniales: Prácticas insurgentes de resistir, (re)existir y (re)vivir* (Quito, Ecuador: Abya Yala, 2013), 30–31.
30. Based on recent work in transcontinental Black Indigenous Studies, including Tiffany Lethabo King's *The Black Shoals*, there is a strong relationship between Black and Indigenous ways of knowing that contributes to decolonization projects and needs to be further explored. See King, *The Black Shoals: Offshore Formations of Black and Native Studies* (Durham: Duke University Press, 2019).

WORKS CITED

Alberto, Paulina L. and Jesse Huffnung-Garskof. " 'Racial Democracy' and Racial Inclusion: Hemispheric Histories." In *Afro-Latin American Studies: An Introduction*, edited by Alejandro de la Fuente and George Reid Andrews, 282–335. Cambridge: Cambridge University Press, 2018.

Andrews, George Reid. *Afro-Latin America, 1800–2000*. New York: Oxford University Press, 2004.

Branche, Jerome, ed. *Black Writing, Culture, and the State in Latin America*. Vanderbilt University Press, 2015.

Campoalegre Septien, Rosa, and Karina Bidaseca, eds. *Más allá del decenio de los pueblos afrodescendientes*. Buenos Aires: CIPS, Centro de Investigaciones Psicológicas y Sociológicas, 2017.

Cardenal, Ernesto, Michael T. Martin, and Jeffrey Franks. "On Culture, Politics, and the State in Nicaragua: An Interview with Padre Ernesto Cardenal, Minister of Culture." *Latin American Perspectives* 16, no. 2 (1989): 124–133.

Cardoso, Fernando Henrique, and Enzo Faletto. *Dependencia y ̓esarrollo en América Latina: Ensayo de interpretación sociológica*. Buenos Aires: siglo XXI editores, 1971.

Casamayor-Cisneros, Odette. "Imagining the 'New Black Subject': Ethical Transformations and Raciality in the Post-Revolutionary Cuban Nation." In *Black Writing and the State in Latin America*, edited by Jerome Branche, 61–82. Nashville: Vanderbilt University Press, 2015.

DeCosta-Willis, Miriam. *Blacks in Hispanic Literature: Critical Essays*. 2nd ed. Baltimore, MD: Black Classic Press, 2011.

De la Fuente, Alejandro, and George Reid Andrews, eds. *Afro-Latin American Studies: An Introduction*. Cambridge: Cambridge University Press, 2018.

Dixon, Kwame, and Ollie A. Johnson III, eds. *Comparative Racial Politics in Latin America*. New York: Routledge, 2018.

Fernández-Rasines, Paloma. *Afrodescendencia en el Ecuador: Raza y género desde los tiempos de la colonia*. Quito, Ecuador: Editorial Abya Yala, 2001.

Franco, Jean. "Dependency Theory and Literary History: The Case of Latin America." *Minnesota Review* 5, no. 1 (1975): 65–80.

Gómez, Rina Cáceres, ed. *Rutas de la esclavitud en África y América Latina*. San José, Costa RIca: Editorial Universidad de Costa Rica, 2001.

Gómez Menjívar, Jennifer Carolina. "Passing into Fictions: Blackness, Writing and Power in the Captaincy General of Guatemala." *Chasqui: Revista de literatura latinoamericana* 45, no. 1 (2016): 97–112.

Gonzalez, Lélia. "A Categoria Político-Cultural de Amefricanidade." *Tempo Brasileiro* 92/93 (1988): 69–81.

Gudmundson, Lowell, and Justin Wolfe, eds. *Blacks and Blackness in Central America: Between Race and Place*. Durham: Duke University Press, 2010.

Guerreiro, Goli. *Terceira diáspora, culturas negras no mundo atlântico*. Salvador: Corrupio, 2010.

Hooker, Juliet. " 'Beloved Enemies': Race and Official Mestizo Nationalism in Nicaragua." *Latin American Research Review* 40, no. 3 (2005): 14–39.

———. *Race and the Politics of Solidarity*. Oxford: Oxford University Press, 2009.

———. *Theorizing Race in the Americas: Douglass, Sarmiento, Du Bois, and Vasconcelos*. Oxford: Oxford University Press, 2017.

Hübner, Nico. *La influencia de la cultura africana en el Perú colonial*. Munich, Germany: GRIN Verlag, 2011.

Jackson, Richard L. *The Afro-Spanish American Author: An Annotated Bibliography of Criticism*. New York: Garland Publishing, 1980.

———. *The Afro-Spanish American Author II: The 1980s: An Annotated Bibliography of Recent Criticism*. West Cornwall, CT: Locust Hill Press, 1989.

———. *The Black Image in Latin American Literature*. Albuquerque: University of New Mexico Press, 1976.

———. *Black Literature and Humanism in Latin America*. Athens: University of Georgia Press, 2008.

———. *Black Writers and Latin America: Cross Cultural Affinities*. Washington, DC: Howard University Press, 1998.

———. *Black Writers and the Hispanic Canon*. New York: Twayne Publishers, 1997.

———. *Black Writers in Latin America*. Albuquerque: University of New Mexico Press, 1978.

King, Tiffany Lethabo. *The Black Shoals: Offshore Formations of Black and Native Studies*. Durham: Duke University Press, 2019.

Lamming, George. "Creating an Independent Caribbean Culture." *The Black Scholar* 15, no. 3 (1984): 2–7.

Lazcano, Cristian Alejandro Báez. "Reflections on the Afro-Chilean Social Movement." *ReVista: Harvard Review of Latin America* 17, no. 2 (2018): 34–37.

Martín-Barbero, Jesús. *Communication, Culture, and Hegemony: From the Media to Mediations*. London: Sage Publications, 1993.

Moreno Fraginals, Manuel, ed. *África en América Latina*. Buenos Aires: siglo XXI editores, 1977.

Montiel, Luz M. Martínez. *Afroamérica: La ruta del esclavo*. Ciudad Universitaria, Mexico: Editorial UNAM, 2006.

Paschel, Tianna S. *Becoming Black Political Subjects: Movements and Ethno-racial Rights in Colombia and Brazil*. Princeton: Princeton University Press, 2016.

Pereira, Joseph R. "The Influence of the Casa de Las Americas on English Caribbean Literature." *Caribbean Quarterly* 31, no. 1 (1985): 93–103.

Rahier, Jean, ed. *Black Social Movements in Latin America: From Monocultural Mestizaje to Multiculturalism*. New York: Palgrave Macmillan, 2012.

Ramsay, Paulette, and Antonio D. Tillis. *The Afro-Hispanic Reader and Anthology*. Kingston, Jamaica: Ian Randle Publishers, 2018.

Ramírez, Sergio. *Tambor olvidado*. San José, Costa Rica: Santillana, 2008.

Rivera-Rideau, Petra R., Jennifer A. Jones, and Tianna S. Paschel, eds. *Afro-Latin@s in Movement: Critical Approaches to Blackness and Transnationalism in the Americas*. New York: Palgrave Macmillan, 2016.

Rodríguez, Ileana. *Liberalism at its Limits: Crime and Terror in the Latin American Cultural Text*. Pittsburgh: University of Pittsburgh Press, 2009.

Smorkaloff, Pamela Maria. *Readers and Writers in Cuba: A Social History of Print Culture, 1830s–1990s*. New York: Garland Publishing, 1997.

Sommer, Doris. "Literary Liberties. The Authority of Afrodescendant Authors." In *Afro-Latin American Studies: An Introduction*, edited by Alejandro de la Fuente and George Reid Andrews, 319–347. Cambridge: Cambridge University Press, 2018.

Vergara Figueroa, Aurora, and George Reid Andrews. "Introducción a los estudios afrolatinoamericanos." Afro-Latin American Research Institute at the Hutchins Center. Harvard University. Accessed January 28, 2022. https://certificadoalari.fas.harvard.edu/módulos-y-docentes-curso-introducción-los-estudios-afrolatinoamericanos-1.

Walsh, Catherine E., ed. *Pedagogías decoloniales: Prácticas insurgentes de resistir, (re)existir y (re)vivir*. Quito, Ecuador: Abya Yala, 2013.

Weiss, Judith A. *Casa de las Américas: An Intellectual Revuew in the Cuban Revolution*. Madrid: Editorial Castalia, 1977.

Zapata Silva, Claudia. *Intelectuales indígenas en Ecuador, Bolivia y Chile: Diferencia, colonialismo y anticolonialismo*. Quito, Ecquador: Abya Yala, 2013.

Part I: Afro Poetics

◆ CHAPTER 1

Language and the Construction of Gendered Identities in Afro-Mexican *Corridos* or Ballads

Paulette A. Ramsay

In the 1960s, while feminist linguists studied the centrality of language in the construction of feminine identities, the role of language in the construction of masculine identities was ignored. The first call to correct this inexactitude was made by linguist Dell Hymes, who declared that a focus on women brings to light an aspect of language in social life that has its counterpart for men, demonstrating that "men's language needs study too."[1] Since then, particularly in the field of social sciences, greater attention has been given to masculinity and its intersections with language and gender-related issues. Several studies were conducted in the late twentieth century that have established that language informs the construction of gender identities. They also demonstrated that men use language differently from women to project particular images and impressions of themselves, thus describing male behavior and presenting man as the representative of humanity.

Indeed, language is indispensable in shaping and legitimizing particular masculine identities, because language is also crucial to performance. Moreover, it is generally agreed that language is central in every social situation. Sally Johnson and Ulrike Hanna Meinhof assert that this is so because both masculinity and femininity are "social processes dependent upon systematic restatement, a process which is referred to as 'performing gender' or doing identity work."[2] Of course, language refers not just to the spoken word but also to other aspects of language usage, which may provide an indication of the gendered identities being projected and the specialized ways these identities are presented. Johnson and Hanna Meinhof further claim that "language does not simply mirror gender, it helps constitute it, it is one of the means by which gender is enacted."[3] Other studies also suggest that even language usage in the workplace supports the position that men and women use language in different manners. Men's speech often supports traditional constructions of gender roles that hold men as authority figures, while women exercise their authority by using language strategies that create a symmetrical alignment (that is, they downplay their authority). Men use language strategies that create and maintain an asymmetrical alignment, the alignment that is traditionally associated with authority.[4]

This chapter will explore the construction of masculinity among Afro-Mexican males through a discussion of a collection of Afro-Mexican *corridos*. The *corrido* is a musical folk ballad that dramatizes different aspects of Mexican history, although it is primarily associated with the portrayal of events linked to the Mexican Revolution. The *corridos* that will be analyzed have been confirmed by Miguel Angel Gutiérrez, a specialist in Afro-Mexican cultural expressions, as productions of the Afro-Mexican region of Costa Chica. Many of them were published as part of an album entitled *Traigo una flor hermosa y mortal* (1995), but this chapter also includes those collected from other sources, including "Pedro el Chicharón" and "La gallinita," which were taken from John McDonald's *Poetry and Violence* and *¡Corrido!*, respectively. The *corridos* are very well known in the black communities of Costa Chica, and Jameelah S. Muhammad has emphatically impressed the popularity of these cultural forms practiced in Black communities.[5]

One major caveat to much of the scholarly representation so far is that the performance of masculinity by Afro-Mexican males in the *corrido* can hardly be considered a single subordinated form or only a response to the masculinity of oppressive white or *mestizo* governments and groups. On the contrary, the *corridos* assume several shades of complexity when examined in the light of how Afro-Mexican male figures interact with Afro-Mexican female figures, who are also marginalized under the same oppressive systems and sometimes further marginalized by the black men with whom they are in relationships.

Important to the examination of the *corridos* are studies of the construction of masculine identities in popular songs produced in similar cultural contexts. These studies include the work of Caribbean scholars, such as Kenneth Ramchand and Gordon Rohlehr, who have discussed the construction of masculinity in popular forms in the Caribbean, including the Trinidadian calypso. The calypso is a traditional form of music that developed as a form of protest against British rule and combines European and African beats. Ramchand further points to the expression of masculinity in Trinidad as being "historically linked with the figure of the bad-john"—a figure associated with marginalized existence in the ghetto or lower-class Afro-Trinidadian life—or "persons repeatedly flouting colonial attempts to regulate and civilize them."[6] Gordon Rohlehr further contends that, in the Caribbean, "the underclass, which tends to be criminalized by elite groups constructs masculinity in terms of resistance, rebellion aggressiveness, toughness and the style and the reputation that are inseparable from any ethnic or violent performance."[7] The discourse of masculinity in the Afro-Mexican *corrido* is similarly constructed on the basis of a particular cultural and historical context of marginalization and, as a consequence, depicts individuals who feel compelled to challenge the status quo and invert power positions.

In the Afro-Mexican *corrido* or ballad the spoken/sung word is important for showing how ideology and speech work together to create the identity that male performers want to project or perform. Rhetorical analysis indicates that both the Afro-Mexican male protagonists within the *corridos,* as well as the male narrators of the *corridos,* use a particular repertoire to challenge the status quo, disparage political leadership, and promote themselves as competitive, capable, and confident men. In turn, these men are concerned with promoting a culturally nationalist agenda to privilege members, destabilize the hegemonic masculinity, and demonstrate that the new masculinity they perform and promote is essentially concerned with exhibiting power. Examination of the language in the *corridos* exposes the intricate ways in which speech and ideology work together to create a particular identity or masculinity. All the discursive language strategies—irony, diction, tone, register, syntax—accentuate a particular identity, one associated with power.

In the *corrido*, the direct speech of the Afro-Mexican male figures is forceful and in consonance with the agenda to project men who assert their subjectivity and agency and who exercise power over others to counteract and modify actions that they consider injurious to themselves as Afro-Mexican male subjects. These particular *corridos* refer to authority figures, such as the government or federal troops, who often wield power over Afro-Mexican communities. Many disparaging statements are made to depict these federal troops as weak despite their positions in society. Male voices make authoritarian statements and depict themselves as exhibiting masculine traits like fearlessness and bravery. For instance, Pedro el Chicharrón (Pedro the Crackling), the protagonist in the following *corrido* by the same name, states his categorical dismissal of the perceived might of government troops:

Voy a cantar un corrido
me permitan su atención,

de esos hombres pocos nacen,
hombres de mucho valor,
el que nace no se logra
como Pedro el Chicharrón,
el que nace no se logra
como Pedro el chicarrón.

Ese Pedro el Chicharrón
era hombre y no se rajaba,
que si el gobierno le caiba
con el gobierno peleaba,
le decía a sus compañeros
que hasta risa le causaba
le decía a sus compañeros
que hasta risa le causaba.

Bajaba Zeta Martínez
A rumbo de Espinalillo:
"Voy a ver al Chicharrón
que lo quiero para amigo,
me lo encargó el comandante
que lo quiere muerto o vivo,
me lo encargó el comandante
que lo quiere muerto o vivo."

Cuando el general llegó
Pedrito estaba sentado,
estaba cuidando las armas
un ladito de la puerta,
y de todito el parque
que lo estaba asoleando.
y de todito el parque
que lo estaba asoleando.

Le contesta el Chicharrón:
"Dejes de estar molestando,
lárguese con esas armas
ya no me esté usted enfadando,
no vaya a venir el diablo

no vaya a estar achuchando,
no vaya a venir el diablo
no vaya a estar achuchando.

I will sing a corrido / give me your attention; / few men like these are born / men of great resolve; / those who are born don't last, / like Pedro el Chicharrón, / those who are born don't last / like Pedro el Chicarrón, // That Pedro el Chicharrón / was tough and wouldn't back down; / if the government fell upon him / with the government he would fight; / he was saying to his companions / that it just made him laugh, / he was saying to his companions / that it just made him laugh. // Zeta Martínez came down / on his way to Espinalillo: / "I am going to see Chicharrón; / I want him to be my friend; / the commander gave me the job / he wants him dead or alive, / the commander gave me the job / he wants him dead or alive." // When the general arrived / Pedrito was sitting down, / taking care of his weapons, / just beside the door, / and all of his ammunition / was drying in the sun, / and all of his ammunition / was drying in the sun. // Chicharrón answers Him: / "Stop making trouble here; / get out of here with those weapons / and quit making me angry; / I hope the devil doesn't come / and make me lose patience, / I hope the devil doesn't come / and make me lose patience.

Even despite being outnumbered by government troops who are determined to annihilate him, El Chicharrón confronts them with language that indicates his contempt of government soldiers and police and projects himself as fearless, authoritative, and in control of the situation. His fearless attitude is also corroborated by the language that the narrators employ to characterize him:

Otro día por la mañana
su compadre lo invitó:
"Vamos a echarnos un trago
pero con ordenamiento,
ahora que estás desarmado
te ayudo en tu sentimiento,
ahora que estás desarmado
te ayudo en tu sentimiento"

Luego sacó su cerrojo
también su reglamentaria,
y le decía a su compadre:

"De eso ya ni diga nada,
voy a tirar de balazos
por si acaso hay emboscada,
voy a tirar de balazos
por si acaso hay emboscada."

Allí dijo su compadre
Al llegar a la cantina:
"Que nos a sirvan una copa
de mescal o de tequila."
El Chicharrón pensativo
porque ya lo presentía,
El Chicharrón pensativo
porque ya lo presentía,

Pedro al sentir el balazo
dio la vuelta y luego dijo:
"Ya me chingastes, compadre
salte a matarte conmigo,
con esta reglamentaria
van a ser siete contigo,
con esta reglamentaria
van a ser siete contigo."

The next day in the morning / his compadre invited him out: / "Let's go and have a drink / but in an orderly way; / now that you are disarmed / I'll help you through your trouble, / now that you are disarmed / I'll help you through your trouble." // Then he took out his Mauser, / also his forty-five Luger, / and he was telling his compadre: / "Don't even speak about that; / I am going to fire some shots / just in case there is an ambush, / I am going to fire some shots / just in case there is an ambush." // There his compadre told him / on arriving at the cantina: / "Serve us each a drink / of mescal or of tequila." / Chicharrón was full of thought / because he knew what was coming, / Chicharrón was full of thought / because he knew what was coming, // When Pedro felt the bullet / he turned around and then spoke: / "Now you have screwed me, compadre; / come over and let's have it out, / with this forty-five Luger / it'll be seven bullets for you, / with this forty-five Luger / it'll be seven bullets for you."

Much of the language in *corridos* is related to how the protagonist perceives himself. Thus, Pedro el Chicharrón behaves and speaks as if he is in control, even after policemen riddle him with bullets. Connell has addressed this matter of self-attribution—a subjective sense of being either masculine or feminine—stating that the matter of individuals attributing certain qualities to themselves reflects an understanding of masculine identity in the context.[8] Indeed, Pedro el Chicharón remains defiant and confrontational, even as he writhes in pain from the bullets embedded in his body. His feeling of invisibility is undeniable as he challenges the Federal troops to duel with him.

Ethnic pride and loyalty to the community are strong traits attributed to the male hero, who is usually seen protecting his people. This is reflected in the regional language used in the *corridos*. The expressive arrangements of some lexical items and metaphors seem to be unique to Afro-Mexican speech, as is seen in "El Zanatón" in the phrases: "no saberse tantear" (they didn't know how to fend for themselves); "porque los traiban de encargo" (because they were giving them a hard time); "no zanatilla sin pluma" (not a zanatilla without plumes); and "ya me chingastes" (now you have screwed me). The use of non-standard lexical and syntactic forms projects images of males who share a particular linguistic code, which itself indicates the extent to which a protagonist understands his community. According to Johnson and Hanna Meinhof, "this use of language which carries connotations of strength, masculinity and confidence in defying linguistic and social condition is important in establishing particular masculine identities."[9] In the *corridos*, loyalty to community is an important masculine trait exhibited by the hero character and augmented by the use of the community's language.

Language that suggests fearlessness in the face of organized oppression and the use of violence by government forces is also apparent in "La gallinita" (Little Chicken). The hero figure announces his presence to the soldiers, who have been sent to capture him, by firing gunshots at them. He thus makes it clear that he is not a coward but one who will go to any length to protect himself and defend his position. This same commitment to community is seen in the case of Fan (Juan) Chanito, the "Rooster of Costa Chica," who oversees weapons in the town of San Nicolás and keeps Juchitán and Huehuetán from stealing. The government sends him ammunition and supplies, until they turn on him and send men to ambush him one December night. The Rooster of Costa Chica, however, chooses death, rather than betray the trust of the community he has devoted himself to protect:

> Eran las siete de la noche
> Juan estaba en la ramada
> Pero lo estaban espiando
> con las armas preparadas

Vinieron dice escopetas
y un calibre 30-30
vinieron dos de cerrojo
y una 380.

Le hicieron unos disparos
pero ¡ay, con gran enojo!
Ay, luego que Fan vivo
Le quitaron el cerrojo.

Ya no quisieron tirarle
pensaron que estaba muerto,
pero Fan estaba vivo
tenía los ojos abiertos.

La gente se amontonaba
donde Fan estaba herido,
preguntó por sus muchachos
que si ya estaba reunidos.

Ay, luego que se reunieron
Él les tendió una mirada,
Adiós muchachos queridos
No me sirvieron pa' nada

Será que ya se me acerca
o ya se me arranca el alma,
cuídense los más que puedan
y hagan las cosas con calma.

Será que ya se me acerca
el corazón me palpita,
ya se muere Fan Rodríquez
el gallo de Cosa Chica.

Su mujer lo acariciaba
y estrechándolo en sus brazos,
ya se muere Fan Chanito
tiene cuarenta balazos

Cuando al fin cerró sus ojos
como cuando están dormidos,
ya se muere Fan Rodriguez

Ya me voy a despedir
el corazón se me agita,
ya se muere Fan Chanito
el gallo de Costa Chica.

It was seven o'clock at night / Juan was in the arbor / but they were watching him / with their guns ready // They came with shotguns / and a 30-30 calibre rifle / two bolt action rifles came / and a 380. // They shot several times / but, with great fury! / Because Fan was still alive / they took away the bolt. // They no longer wanted to shoot him, / they thought he was dead, / but Fan was still alive / his eyes were open. // The people gathered / where Fan was wounded / they asked for his boys / if they had already met. // Then, after they met / he gave them a look, / Goodbye beloved friends / You did not serve me in vain // Maybe the time is drawing near / or my soul is being ripped out, / take the best care of yourselves / and do things with calm. // Maybe the time is drawing near / my heart is pounding / Fan Rodríguez is dying / the rooster of Costa Chica. // His wife caressed him / and while stretching him out in her arms / Fan Chanito dies / shot forty times // When at last he closed his eyes / as when one is asleep / Fan Rodríguez dies // I'm going to say goodbye / my heart is pounding / Fan Chanito is dead / the rooster of Costa Chica.

The hero is undoubtedly a "sacrificial lamb," facing death without trepidation or cowardice. The cogent and compelling metaphor "el gallo de Costa Chica" (the rooster of Costa Chica) not only intimates Juan's lack of faint-heartedness but also implies an unmatched sexual prowess.

Language choice in "El corrido de los Zapatistas de San Nicolás" is marked by poignant diction, strong metaphors, and sharp similes designed to dismiss and disparage leadership positions and the efforts of leaders to oppress and overpower Afro-Mexican guerilla troops as ineffective and weak. The weapons of the *carrancistas* are dismissed as useless toys. The Afro-Mexicans do not need to resort to trench warfare, as they can face the enemy head on. The valiant hero figure, El Zanatón, is presented as a predatory animal who can hunt his prey for a meal: "El Zanatón los buscaba como cosa de comer" (El Zanatón looked for them like he would eat them alive). The efforts of his opponents are presented as the weak actions of "birds" while El Zanatón declares his past feats: "He toreado toros bravos" (I have fought fierce bulls). The language of contempt used to show how the protagonists conduct themselves is, indeed, very graphic.

In the *corridos*, forceful and potent language is employed for the purpose of raising political awareness or consciousness. Indeed, political consciousness can only be achieved through powerful political vocabulary, phrases, and language. Davis Graber outlines five purposes of political language: disseminating information, agenda setting, interpreting, linking, and preparing for the future and past.[10] Without question, close and serious scrutiny of the *corridos* reveals that the language they employ fulfills these purposes, as the *corridos* provide detailed and explicit information about the confrontation and clashes with government troops by all opponents. It cannot escape notice that the language used is "inflated" and provides detailed characterizations of the central characters in terms of "reason," "location," "process," and "time."

"Pedro el Chicharrón" (Pedro the Crackling) powerfully depicts these five uses. The name of the protagonist not only suggests his complexion—*chicharrón* is a colloquial term used in Latin America to refer to a person with very dark skin—but also suggests a level of egotism, arrogance, and self-certainty. *Chicharrón* also implies toughness, like the toughness of the pork skin when it is overdone, and the language depicting his feats graphically captures his character in consonance with these insinuations. There is no doubt that his role and character are intended to overthrow the status quo and to confront oppression with bravery. This *corrido* provides his past confrontations, his intentions to put an end to his challenges, and celebrates his victory.

Similarly, the well-known *corrido* "La gallinita" (Little Chicken) reveals the five uses of political language. It commences with the presentation of information about the protagonist's audacity and dauntless spirit, and then the second stanza announces his agenda:

Me voy a Azoyú Guerrero
a ver a un familiar,
y también al comandante
que me quiere desarmar.

I'm going to Azoyú Guerrero / to see a relative, / and also the commander / who wants to disarm me.

The information conveyed about his mission indicates that the action he intends to undertake in his encounter with the *comandante* is confrontational and conflictual in nature. The graphic and explicit language provides details of how he initiates the confrontation with his use of violence. The language helps, furthermore, to depict him as a fearless character who places no value on his life but revels in his reputation as "un valiente" (a brave man) who never surrenders to anyone. Language also effectively delineates an idealized confrontation in which the protagonist, *La Gallinita*, defeats the *comandante* and his men without much difficulty: "a los primeros balazos la policía corrió . . . el comandante está muerto . . . la gallinita lo mató" (at the first shots the policemen ran . . . the commander is dead . . . the little chicken killed him). The *corrido* closes with language that reinforces his bravery, with the connotation that he will continue to be this fearless defender of his honor, and with the unmistakable understanding that the agenda set at the beginning has been fulfilled: "la gallinita mató a un gallo" (the little chicken has killed a rooster). The direct juxtaposition of *gallinita* and *gallo* renders his achievement even more awe-inspiring and dramatic.

Furthermore, the language of the *corridos* may be characterized as political because it is a language of power, which employs exaggeration to present the Afro-Mexican political community members as invincible and to project the important political needs of the community. To this end, the poetic voices employ name-calling strategies to influence the listener's judgement of their oppressors and to seduce the listeners into condemning the government representatives who would oppress the Afro-Mexican community. The language of the *corrido* is also a language of "illusion" and "ambiguity" because the strengths of the male protagonists who are projected are not necessarily real.

The way Afro-Mexican male protagonists express themselves suggests their determination to exercise their rights. In other words, they do not simply listen and allow themselves to be spoken to, but they decide to participate by actively contributing to the situation in which they find themselves. They demonstrate in this way their right to defend themselves, giving support to the assertion that "the right to speak depends on the right to be in the situation and the right to engage in particular kinds of speech activities in that situation."[11]

Norman Fairclough argues that language helps to maintain power relations in society. As a result, there is always a connection between language usage and the ideology of oppression, as the more powerful in society often use language to legitimize power relations.[12] Undoubtedly, the linguistic attributes of the *corridos* suggest an understanding on the part of Afro-Mexican narrators and characters of how language is used to maintain the social order and, more importantly, how it can be used to create change. Consequently, these narrators invert power relations by appropriating very powerful words and expressions to communicate their own ideology of self-definition and to tip the balance of power in their favor by employing a discourse of power. They use language as a forceful alternative to the established or conventional discourse type, in which army personnel, police officers, and people who are used to maintaining the power relations in conversations issue the orders to Afro-Mexican male representations. As a result, they create an oppositional discourse, or an "anti-language," which dismantles the unequal relations and distributions of power.

Problematizing Masculinity in the *Corrido*

Notwithstanding the skillful use of language to promulgate a particular understanding of Afro-Mexican maleness, the overt representations of masculinity in the *corridos* are problematic because the *corridos* often present masculine characteristics as the standard of human behavior in the Afro-Mexican community. With its emphasis on fighting and violence in which men are involved, the philosophical value system of the *corridos* is essentially masculinist. In other words, the social construction of masculine identity in the *corridos* is embedded in, or influenced by, sexism and patriarchy.

Of course, it cannot go unnoticed that the *corridos* have been, for the most part, written, narrated, and sung by men. The central characters in this musical genre are males, and the females who appear in them occupy minor roles in which they are often disparaged. All perceptions and portrayals of the world of the Afro-Mexicans, as well as images of women in the society being represented, are presented from the male perspective, as John McDowell confirms when he writes that the *corridos* take us into a "primarily masculine world.... Most composers and performers of *corridos* in the Costa Chica are male, and the main audience for *corrido* performance is male as well."[13] This echoes Keith Nurse's assertion that often "masculinism, as the hegemonic ideational construct, achieves a logocentric posture" and thus becomes "a pervasive, familiar and powerful narrative by which we organize our understanding of social reality."[14]

Arguably, the relationship between hegemonic and subordinate masculinities may be paradoxical, for even subordinate masculinity can be compliant with patriarchy and sexism. The subjectification of the "other" through difference, stigmatization, and stereotyping has proven to be fundamental to the constitution of hegemonic masculinity. Kimmell and Messner cogently capture how subordinate masculinities may, at times, assume hegemonic qualities. They claim that "most masculinities are compliant in patriarchy" and that the marginalization of subordinate masculinities is an essential component to the myth of male power.[15] Nurse builds on this idea, writing that "most men are not as powerful as they are made out to be. The problem is that they are socialized to see male power and privilege as an entitlement, if not even endowment; this is the essential contradiction in the dominant construction of masculinity."[16]

In the Afro-Mexican *corridos*, all images of freedom, agency, subjectivity, resistance, defiance of figures of oppression, and injustice are embodied in the Afro-Mexican male protagonists. Consequently, even though theirs may be regarded as a subordinated masculinity because they constitute a marginalized group in Mexico, the absence of any association of females with power implies a kind of collusion with hegemonic masculinity, which marginalizes females and projects them as having no roles to play in the Afro-Mexican community or in maintaining a particular image of Afro-Mexican society. As Nurse observes: "The poetics and politics of representation are such that victims can be co-opted by strategies of resistance just as victors display their anxieties and repressed fantasies through the projection of power. This appreciation of the working of power and powerlessness provides a useful framework for analyzing the relationship between hegemonic and subordinated masculinities."[17]

This particular construction of masculinity simultaneously suggests that only black men can claim to have roles in the Afro-Mexican community or in the nation building process. This implied parallel between men and nation and community building, on the one hand, and self-assertion, on the other, is problematic and recalls Homi Bhabha's claim that "nation building is about public identification. The 'other,' the foreigner, is feminized."[18] In other words, this gendering of Afro-Mexican's achievements, affairs, and participation in protecting an Afro-Mexican context may be an unconscious or unintended reassertion of dominant masculinity, albeit in a marginalized context. The result is the deliberate or instinctive alliance between sexism and racism as they relate to Afro-Mexican females. Connell warns of how difficult it is not to aid this agenda in societies that move toward equality for women and subordinated groups.[19]

One of the most powerful *corridos* unapologetically establishes the Afro-Mexican's spirit of autonomy and resistance to striking opponents, achieving this through a very generic masculinism. The fearless hero figure of "La mula bronca" emphatically declares the creed that governs his life of toughness and his rejection of the dominant system of authority: "pa' morir nacen los hombres / no van a estar de esclavitud" (Men were born to die / they will not be slaves). The use of the term *los hombres* presumes an all-embracing belief that man or male is universal. Moreover, following Roland Barthes, it betrays an acceptance of one of the contentions of feminists that "masculinism is a totalizing philosophical value system in the gender framework."[20] It further underpins the claim proposed by Nurse that "men rarely see themselves as a gender, and society generally treats masculine characteristics as the prototype of human behavior, irrespective of time and space."[21] The irony of this lies, undoubtedly, in the understanding and acceptance that the subversive intent of the *corridos* is for the benefit of a society comprising men and women. While this is true, it simultaneously strengthens certain myths that men are brave protectors of weak women. Herein lies the tension between two agendas—the one to project masculinity as necessary in resisting hegemonic rule and contesting the subversion of a community's identity and importance to nation building in Mexico and the other to suggest that it is the responsibility of men or males to fight for the freedom of the community, or even that they have a right to freedom. As a result, writes McClintock, "Nationalism becomes . . . radically constitutive of people's identities through social contexts that are frequently violent and always gendered."[22]

In a previous study, I argued that the collusion between the subordinate masculinity of Afro-Mexicans and the hegemonic masculinity of the status quo is revealed in the extent to which, in the *corridos*, "self-glorification facilitates the restoration of masculine identity. From one *corrido* to the next, an unmistakable correlation between *machismo* and self-praise is established."[23] Undoubtedly, the display and the praise of toughness, as well as the self-consciousness based on confidence in fighting ability, are evident in the hero and become means of "channeling undetermined manhood into rhetorical aggression and defiance."[24] So, while in the work of the *corridos* there is an important quest for self-validation and vindication in a system in which the Afro-Mexican community's understanding of self-worth as a marginalized group is undermined, the agenda is also about masculine validation: establishing manliness as a means of recovering and affirming subjectivity. This sense of synonymity between subjectivity, manliness, and masculinity is further confirmed by the negative images of females in some *corridos*. In these cases, women are often portrayed in stereotypical images as weeping mothers, disloyal partners who are not deserving of the men's trust, or young and self-absorbed girls who are terrified that they will lose their men (who are often in battle).

In *Feminism Is for Everybody*, bell hooks calls for a visionary masculinity or a feminist masculinity that is typified by "political solidarity" and shared sympathy for common suffering. This visionary masculinity is a reconstruction of that masculinity that is opposed to patriarchy and that "encourages men to be pathologically narcissistic, infantile, and psychologically dependent on the privileges (however relative) that they receive simply for having been born male."[25] Indeed, I underline the absence of *corridos* that explicitly highlight an interest in "mutual advancement," in recognition of the shared context of inequality. For if we must and should regard consciousness-ness raising as the subject of the *corrido*, then there is a need for women to be depicted in them as central to a revolutionary movement and as having an awareness of their centrality to a process that is beneficial to men and women alike. Perhaps some new *corridos* will meaningfully show Afro-Mexican women as integral parts of the process of changing directions in Mexico as they affect Afro-Mexicans in general.

This call may seem contradictory given my previous claims that the *corridos* have been preserved by the community in general. Against the fact that they give voice mainly to men's expressions, the implication, from a feminist position, is that they leave no space for marginalized women to assert their own subjectivity. It can be concluded, then, that the *corridos* allow redefinition of self for men and result in empowerment for men, who rewrite their textual selves as they give expression through powerful language to a masculinity that is often compliant with sexism and even racism.

NOTES

1. Robin Lakoff, "Language and Woman's Place," *Language and Society* 2 (1973): 79.
2. Sally Johnson and Ulrike Hanna Meinhof, eds., *Language and Masculinity* (Oxford: Blackwell, 1997), 22.
3. Ibid., 23.
4. Shari Kendall and Deborah Tannen, "Gender and Language in the Workplace," in *Gender and Discourse*, ed. Ruth Wodak (London: Sage Publications, 1997), 91.
5. Jameelah S. Muhammad, *No Longer Invisible: Afro-Latin Americans Today* (London: Minority Rights Publications, 1995).
6. Kenneth Ramchand, "Calling All Dragons: The Crumbling of Caribbean Masculinity," in *Interrogating Caribbean Masculinities: Theoretical and Empirical Analyses*, ed. Rhoda Reddock (Kingston, Jamaica: University of the West Indies Press, 2004), 313.
7. Gordon Rohlehr, "I Lawa: The Construction of Masculinity in Trinidad and Tobago," in *Interrogating Caribbean Masculinities: Theoretical and Empirical Analysis*, ed. Rhoda Reddock (Kingston: University of the West Indies Press, 2004), 336.
8. R. W. Connell, *Masculinities*, 2nd ed. (Berkeley: University of California Press, 1995), 21–27.
9. Johnson and Hanna Meinhof, *Language and Masculinity*, 9.
10. Davis Graber, "Political Language," in *Handbook of Political Communication*, ed. Dan Nimmo and Keith Sanders (Los Angeles: Sage, 1981), 195.
11. Penelope Eckert and Sally McConnell-Ginet, *Language and Gender* (Cambridge: Cambridge University Press, 2007), 93.
12. Norman Fairclough, *Language and Power* (London: Routledge, 2013), 2.
13. John McDowell, *Poetry and Violence: The Ballad Tradition of Mexico's Costa Chica* (Chicago: University of Illinois Press, 2000), 7.
14. Keith Nurse, "Masculinities in Transition: Gender and the Global Problematique," in

Interrogating Caribbean Masculinities: Theoretical and Empirical Analysis, ed. Rhoda Reddock (Kingston: University of the West Indies Press, 2004), 5.
15. Michael Kimmel and Michael Messner, *Men's Lives* (New York: Allyn and Bacon, 1995), 19.
16. Nurse, "Masculinities in Transition," 13.
17. Ibid., 8.
18. Homi Bhabha, *The Location of Culture* (London: Routledge, 2012).
19. Connell, *Masculinities*, 13.
20. Roland Barthes, *Elements of Semiology*, trans. Annette Lavers and Colin Smith (New York: Hill and Wang, 1968).
21. Nurse, "Masculinities in Transition," 5.
22. Anne McClintock, *Imperial Leather: Race, Gender and Sexuality in the Colonial Context* (New York: Routledge, 1995), 353.
23. Paulette Ramsay, "History, Violence and Self-Glorification in Afro-Mexican *corridos* from Costa Chica de Guerrero," *Publication of the Afro-Latin/American Research Association (PALARA)* 7 (2003): 74.
24. Christian Habekost, *Verbal Riddim: The Politics and Aesthetics of African-Caribbean Dub Poetry* (Amsterdam: Rodopi, 1993), 121.
25. bell hooks, *Feminism Is for Everybody: Passionate Politics* (Cambridge, MA: South End, 2000), 70.

WORKS CITED

Barthes, Roland. *Elements of Semiology*. Translated by Annette Lavers and Colin Smith. New York: Hill and Wang, 1968.
Bhabha, Homi. *The Location of Culture*. London: Routledge, 2012.
Connell, R. W. *Masculinities*. 2nd ed. Berkeley: University of California Press, 1995.
Eckert, Penelope, and Sally McConnell-Ginet. *Language and Gender*. Cambridge: Cambridge University Press, 2007.
Fairclough, Norman. *Language and Power*. London: Routledge, 2013.
Graber, Davis. "Political Language." In *Handbook of Political Communication*, edited by Dan Nimmo and Keith Sanders. Los Angeles: Sage, 1981.
Habekost, Christian. *Verbal Riddim: The Politics and Aesthetics of African-Caribbean Dub Poetry*. Amsterdam: Rodopi, 1993.
hooks, bell. *Feminism Is for Everybody: Passionate Politics*. Cambridge, MA: South End, 2000.
Johnson, Sally, and Ulrike Hanna Meinhof, eds. *Language and Masculinity*. Oxford: Blackwell, 1997.
Kendall, Shari, and Deborah Tannen. "Gender and Language in the Workplace." In *Gender and Discourse*, edited by Ruth Wodak, 81–92. London: Sage Publications, 1997.
Kimmel, Michael, and Michael Messner. *Men's Lives*. New York: Allyn and Bacon, 1995.

Lakoff, Robin. "Language and Woman's Place." *Language and Society* 2 (1973): 45–80.
McClintock, Anne. *Imperial Leather: Race, Gender and Sexuality in the Colonial Context.* New York: Routledge, 1995.
McDowell, John. *Poetry and Violence: The Ballad Tradition of Mexico's Costa Chica.* Chicago: University of Illinois Press, 2000.
Muhammad, Jameelah S. *No Longer Invisible: Afro-Latin Americans Today.* London: Minority Rights Publications, 1995.
Nurse, Keith. "Masculinities in Transition: Gender and the Global Problematique." In *Interrogating Caribbean Masculinities: Theoretical and Empirical Analysis*, edited by Rhoda Reddock, 3–33. Kingston: University of the West Indies Press, 2004.
Ramchand, Kenneth. "Calling All Dragons: The Crumbling of Caribbean Masculinity." In *Interrogating Caribbean Masculinities: Theoretical and Empirical Analyses*, edited by Rhoda Reddock, 309–325. Kingston, Jamaica: University of the West Indies Press, 2004.
Ramsay, Paulette. "History, Violence and Self-Glorification in Afro-Mexican *corridos* from Costa Chica de Guerrero." *Publication of the Afro-Latin/American Research Association (PALARA)* 7 (2003): 62–78.
Rohlehr, Gordon. "I Lawa: The Construction of Masculinity in Trinidad and Tobago." In *Interrogating Caribbean Masculinities: Theoretical and Empirical Analysis*, edited by Rhoda Reddock, 326–403. Kingston: University of the West Indies Press, 2004.

CORRIDOS

"Chicharrón." In *Poetry and Violence: The Ballad Tradition of Mexico's Costa Chica.* Compiled by John McDowell, 221–23. Chicago: University of Illinois Press, 2000.
"Fan (Juan) Chanito." *Traigo una flor hermoso y mortal: Los Cimatrones Band.* 1975. Sound recording.
"La Gallinita." In *¡Corrido!: The Living Ballad of Mexico's Western Coast.* Collected, transcribed, arranged, and annotated by John Holmes McDowell, 48–52. Albuquerque: University of New Mexico Press, 2000.
"La Mula Bronca." *Traigo una flor hermoso y mortal: Los Cimatrones Band.* 1975. Sound recording.
"Pedro el Chicharrón." In *Poetry and Violence: The Ballad Tradition of Mexico's Costa Chica.* Compiled by John McDowell, 227–31. Champaign: University of Illinois Press, 2000.

◆ CHAPTER 2

A Post-Ethnic/Racial Futurescape in Wingston González's *cafeína MC*

Juan Guillermo Sánchez Martínez

I first encountered Wingston González's work while searching for contemporary Indigenous authors in Guatemala. I was looking for "Mayan authors," and his poetry and performances forced me to question my own expectations about "Indigenous" literatures. Born in Livingston (Izabal, Guatemala) and raised speaking Garífuna among his Afro/Black-Indigenous community, González left the Caribbean coast in his teenage years to live in the highlands of Guatemala and to write poetry, mostly in Spanish. González has published *Los magos del crepúsculo (y blues otra vez)* (2005), *cafeína MC (segunda parte, la fiesta y sus habitantes)* (2010), *cafeína MC: primera parte, la anunciación de la fiesta* (2011), *san juan: la esperanza* (2013, 2015), *Miss muñecas vudu* (2013), *Espuma sobre las piedras* (2014), *¡Hola Gravedad!* (2016), and *Nuevo manual para una educación sentimental* (2017). Gonzalez's literature does not engage explicitly with his Black and Indigenous heritages. On the contrary, like several authors from the "Guatemalan postwar generation" who were published after the 1996 Peace Accords, González has built an urban, intimate, and experimental poetic universe that unsettles fixed definitions of Blackness, Indigeneity, and nationality. My goal in this chapter is to reflect on this "absent presence of race" and ethnicity in González's work and to celebrate his fractured poetic aesthetics as a powerful strategy for disrupting internalized colonial classifications (Black, white, Indigenous, *mestizo/ladino*).[1]

Here, I briefly contextualize Garínagu history and their diaspora in terms of the current tensions between the United States's racial categories and Latin America's conceptualizations of multiculturalism and *mestizaje*. Then, I interpret *cafeína MC*'s dislocated Spanish and cartography as a creative Garínagu resistance. I argue that González's poetic aesthetics (irony, fragmentation, urban realism) align with the literary postwar generation, who chose an experimental subjectivity as a way of establishing freedom in a context where writers had been obligated to write exclusively on damage, civil conflict, and ethnic tensions. González's dislocated poetic aesthetics is not intended to erase strategic groupness, as in the case of the OFRANEH, or the New Yorker and Honduran Garífuna communities' self-representation in the censuses of their respective nation states, but to stand for a more fluid self-identification as a migrant and artist.[2] Instead of feeling comfortable with fixed institutional categories, as in the case of the census or official forms (race, ethnicity, *poblaciones*), this poetry invites the reader to unselect and question those boxes and reclaim a cross-cultural creativity in a post-ethnic/racial futurescape.

In the context of hyper-racialized societies and systems, such as those found in the United States, I echo Petra R. Rivera-Rideau, Jennifer A. Jones, and Tianna S. Paschel when they ask in the introduction of *Afro-Latin@s in Movement*: "how do ideas about blackness move across the Americas, not only from the United States to Latin America but also from Latin America to the United States? How do people's ideas about blackness shift (or not) when they encounter new forms of politics or cultural representations from elsewhere?"[3] At the crossroads of the politics on identity in the United States and Latin American nation states, I find González's poetry liberating. Furthermore, Peter Wade's reflection on how the domain of twentieth-century anthropology was Indigeneity, while twentieth-century sociologists and historians were concerned with Blackness, brings me to consider the role of literary studies then and now.[4] This essay thus also reflects on questions such as: is literary creativity a place where groupness and racial and ethnic classifications are currently being contested? Furthermore, how do literary critics "study" Garífuna expressions that are suspicious about academic discourses on Blackness and Indigeneity?

cafeína MC's Beat (*Toda la ceniza de las palabras no conoce el dolor*)

The Garífuna nation (the Garínagu)—like González's poetry—crosses historical and imagined boundaries between nations, races, ethnicities, and cultures. Paul Joseph López Oro summarizes their history as follows:

The Garínagu or Garífuna, as they are popularly known, are black indigenous people born out of the mixture of shipwrecked West African slaves and Carib Arawak indigenous people on the island of St. Vincent in 1635. The account of Garífuna as descendants of shipwrecked slaves is widely accepted in the collective memory among Garínagu as an experience rooted in marronage and resistance to enslavement. This ethnogenesis account divorces them from the transatlantic slave trade and plantation life in the Americas, as well as shapes and influences their relationships with African-Americans. This marronage occurred in the midst of wars of colonial domination between the Spanish, the British, and the French. Garífuna were exiled from St. Vincent to the Caribbean coast of Central America in 1797 by British colonial rule.[5]

Around five thousand Garífunas were displaced by the English to the island of Roatán in 1797, and henceforth their language, worldview, and belief system spread throughout the coasts of Honduras, Belize, Guatemala, and Nicaragua, generating more trans-Indigenous exchanges, particularly with the Maya communities.[6] According to ONEGUA (a Black Guatemalan Organization), the first Garífuna community arrived in Guatemala around 1802, prior to Guatemala's independence in 1821, and there are currently seventeen thousand people who identify as Garífuna in the Central American country.[7] Today, the Garínagu also include the migrant experience of subjects and communities in cities such as Tegucigalpa, Trujillo, El Progreso, Livingston, Guatemala City, as well as New York, Miami, Houston, and Los Angeles.[8]

As López Oro reports, "New York City is home to the largest Garífuna communities outside of Central America with an estimated 290,000 living in all five boroughs, specifically in the working-class, immigrant neighborhoods of Eastern Brooklyn and the South Bronx."[9] Several scholars have explored this transnational and multiethnic experience of the Black-Indigenous identity, which has been affected by multiple colonial histories and national strategies to control Indigeneity, Blackness, and homogeneity.[10] The racial and ethnic categories (e.g., Black, Latino/a, Native American, White, Pacific Islander) employed in the United States, for example, do not align with Guatemalan *poblaciones* (*ladino*/mixed-race, Maya, Xinca, and Garífuna).

Internalized colonization via *mestizaje* and liberal multiculturalism has subtracted both Blackness and Indigeneity from mixed-race individuals and elites, both in the United States and Latin America, promoting whitening and race-denial. Even so, the growing field of Afro-Latin American Studies has paid close attention to this north/south crossroads:

This persistent narrative of Latinos centering their ethnic diversity rather than racial identity maintains the fallacy that Latinos are magically so racially mixed that they transcend racial discourse and the US black and white binary. Fetishizing US Latinos as a multiracial and multicultural subject not only reinscribes Latin American mestizaje in the United States, a delusional myth that racial mixture creates racial sameness and racial democracy but also dismisses centuries of black and indigenous political mobilization against racial injustices and inequalities in Latin America and the Caribbean.[12]

Though González's poetry does not embrace *mestizaje* narratives, I am interested in analyzing the "absent presence of race" and ethnicity in *cafeína MC*'s dislocated poetic aesthetics. On the last page of *cafeína MC*, there is a picture of González's identification card, from which the reader learns that he was born in Livingston, Izabal, in 1986. Without this piece of information, there is a possibility that the reader would not consider the writer's origin or his race/ethnicity. Guatemalan critic Aída Toledo, however, has shown a possible reader's itinerary toward ethnicity. Beyond group membership, collective worldview, or explicit self-classification as a Garífuna, González dislocates Spanish syntax (via Garífuna idiolect and slang), as well as the "traditional" typography for verses, titles, capital letters, and parentheses. In this interpretation, which I prefer to call the "reader's itinerary," González questions literary expectations as well as literacy inequality. I choose the word "itinerary" as a way of underlining the subjective nature of any given interpretation. The reader's itinerary becomes a "journey" in which the choices made reveal the reader's own expectations on identity. The possibilities for itineraries surpass the writer's own intentions.

cafeína MC (segunda parte, la fiesta y sus habitantes) is sixty-one pages of César Vallejo's style, Oliverio Girondo's fatigue in the *másmedula*, surrealist imagery, literary references (Heany, Rulfo, Dalton, Proust, Whitman, Dante), and a crossover playlist (Celia Cruz, The Fania All Stars, El Gran Combo, Andrés Caicedo), including some *chucu-chucu* (Jossie Esteban y la patrulla 15, El Grupo Niche, Jamiroquai). In this volume, a dance troupe of masked characters goes from motel to motel and from beach to beach, stopping by "cellophane-wrapped bars." Mirroring the title of the book itself, each verse begins with lower cases (except for names) and most of them seem unrelated. At the end of each poem, in the lower right-hand corner of the page, there is always a parenthetical aside, as if it were a stage direction of a play: "*(what Gabriela said to Juan Rulfo about a song by Celia Cruz),*" "*(hangover all star),*" "*(the return of the space cowboy).*" The "stage direction" is also common in all of his titles: *Los magos del crepúsculo (y blues otra vez), cafeína MC (primera parte: la anunciación de la fiesta), san juan: la esperanza (apéndice de un mundo encontrado/jardín y representaciones atonales)*. The parentheses and stage directions are signs for the reader who endeavors to break González's code. In the introduction of González's *san juan: la esperanza (apéndice de un mundo encontrado/jardín y representaciones atonales)* (2013), critic Manuel de J. Jiménez describes the poet's way of dislocating and fragmenting language as micro-poetic scenes that omit purposely the world to which they belong, as well as habitable and transmissible pieces of a world, which Jiménez calls a "garden."[13] In both cases, the intimacy of the vignettes burns the reader, who does not know how to interpret this poetry. Perhaps one key that could be used to access "González's garden" is the synecdoche, or the part that stands in for the whole.

cafeína MC (segunda parte, la fiesta y sus habitantes) is divided into two parts. First, "maestros de ceremonia" (masters of ceremony) introduces the "inhabitants" or characters: Roxana, Josselin, Elena, Natalí, Marlene, Glendy, Sonia, Beatriz (or Beatrix), Judith, and Mamá Morelia. Second, "vista desde la catedral metropolitana" draws a post-national and post-ethnic cartography in which the poetic subject—both the female inhabitants and the poet—constantly speaks against the "patriarchy of language" and the need to find a key for a new aesthetics. In line with this linguistic disposition, capitalization, italics, and bold font are recurrent features of the verses:

brutalmente iluminado; sientes destrozarte en el movimiento
la dura resistencia que por un lapso sostuvo la mano del otro
que es como talar y sentir las fuerzas dulcificarse de repente

y así pensamos que nace el milagro, la espuma en la boca

qué animal de espuma ni qué ocho cuartos, *reventamos*
estamos que reventamos, estrellita puta de papel
en cierto cielo de cumpleaños
de misericordia en casa de niños
hartos de otra memoria de mierda
            qué va
                      na

memorial de plantas, ponme en el cielo, que me
anclaré a unas hermosas palabras para que caigan a
la tierra como lluvia de peñones. cinematográficos

y sorprendentes. rayando una altura más densa
que el centro de las palabras, BRUTALMENTE
ILUMINADO, que qué recuerdo yo de los anteriores.
qué vamos a recordar si lo que aquí se intenta es
desaparecer, huir, diciendo *primero yo y luego
nosotros*. Salsatown y el patriarcado del lenguaje
(Glendy predice la resurrección de la Fania en el baile de año nuevo)[14]

brutally illuminated; you feel you break in the movement / the strong resistance that for an instance held the other's hand / which is like cutting trees down and feeling the forces soften suddenly / and so we think this is how the miracle is born, foam in the mouth // foam animal, my foot! reventamos / estamos que reventamos, little paper whore / in a random birthday sky / of mercy in children's house / tired of another fucking memory / no way / nada // memorial of plants, put me in the sky, I will / anchor myself to some beautiful words so they fall into / the earth like a rain of cliffs. cinematographic / and surprising. streaking a denser height than the core of words, BRUTALLY / ILLUMINATED, you ask me what I remember of the previous ones. / but what are we going to remember if what we are trying to do here is / disappear, run away, saying first I and then / we. Salsatown and the patriarchy of language / **Glendy predicts the resurrection of Fania at the New Year's ballroom***)*[15]

In the context of Afrodescendant writers in Latin America, Doris Sommer has explained that "a line of literary experimentation can upset the hierarchy of history with new unauthorized authority."[16] Memories cross the poem as "miracles," as lightning, but we witness how these images fade while we follow the verses, until finally memories become "shit, *nothing*," disappearance, and escape. How does the reader face this constant blurring and linguistic failure? "The patriarchy of language"—semantic cohesion, syntax, the full context of what is being said, univocal meaning, monolingualism, and formal Spanish without idioms, sayings, and vernacular—becomes oppressive. The poet says "espuma en la boca" (foam in the mouth), echoing the poem "Intensidad y altura" by César Vallejo: "Quiero escribir, pero me sale espuma" (I want to write, but all that comes out is foam). Images and rhythm interrupt each other in González's poem while a salsa song by Grupo Niche plays in the background: *"reventamos, estamos que reventamos."*

In searching for a hermeneutic path, I return to a verse or chorus of *cafeína MC*: "Toda la ceniza de las palabras no conoce el dolor / de las cuentas del mundo / visitando estos dedos // Toda la ceniza de las palabras no conoce el dolor / ni los spotlights que anuncian las nuevas versiones de Dante" (All the ashes of words do not know the pain / of the world accounts / visiting these fingers // All the ashes of words do not know the pain / nor the spotlights that announce the new versions of Dante).[17] *cafeína MC*'s aesthetics struggle with the inadequacy of cohesive speech to express its own archipelago of dislocated images and references. As a creative response, each poem looks like an agglutination of scenes from different movies. Javier Payeras names this aesthetic approach "radical baroque."[18] Uroyoán Noel and José García Escobar, the translators of González's work in English, describe this playfulness of González's poetry as irreverent, ambivalent, and hostile toward Spanish through its Black vernacular and vertiginous and messy verses.[19] In disrupting cohesion, González chooses to juxtapose (non)related details, perhaps as "exophoric devices"—references that have not been introduced to the reader—such as the epic day-to-day traveling from an infernal disco to paradise and then back to any bar in San Salvador with a condom dispenser in the washroom, as in the poem "Helen ve aproximarse el difuso final del mediodía" (Helen Sees the Diffused End Approaching at Noon). Fingers, spotlights, and condom dispensers are pieces of a dislocated imaginary that can be reconstructed through synecdoche. What images does the reader see?

cafeína MC's rhythm and intermittency reflects the unease of a transnational generation in between global and local aesthetics, whose crossover anthem is comfortable with mixing merengue, jazz, metal, and *labugana* (a Garínagu genre). As explained by López Oro, cross-cultural identities speak to many Garífuna subjectivities in the diaspora:

> Garínagu people are members of three diasporas: the African diaspora, the Garífuna diaspora, and the Central American diaspora. They are simultaneously black, indigenous, and Latino; they can be Honduran, Belizean, Guatemalan, Nicaraguan, and American; they are part of Central America and part of the Caribbean. As an ethnic group they share a common language and culture, as well as histories of colonialism, displacement, and transnational migration that unite them across nation-state borders. Garífuna subjectivity is rooted in dispossession and resistance to colonialism and nation-states. As such, Garífuna communities are fundamentally transnational with multiple homes of dislocation.[20]

Does González's poetry mirror this historical dislocation? Are his dislocated poetic aesthetics a strategy to disrupt Guatemalan literary history? In an interview for *Asymptote* by José García Escobar, González confirms that his resistance is manifested through his rebellion against literacy and the internalized colonization imposed by the Guatemalan education system after centuries of epistemicide:

WG: I grew up speaking Garífuna. I used Garífuna until I got into school. My grandmother, who spoke Garífuna and Spanish, used to say things like, "You're going to school now, and you have to speak Spanish, otherwise you'll fail your classes." So, I dropped the Garífuna. It was a type of linguistic weaning. People taught me that Spanish was the *average* language and the one that will allow me to make the best out of education. From then on, I spoke in Spanish. And then I found out about a different kind of Spanish—a Spanish I found in books that was different from the one I heard in school or out in the streets, or out of the mouths of the characters I told you about. And I took that new kind of Spanish and used it to color my speech. Right now, I'm trying to recover Garífuna. I find beauty in it. Currently, people are teaching in Garífuna and Q'eqchi' in Livingston, though Spanish is still the predominant language. And speaking of languages, English was also an essential part of my upbringing.[21]

Following the invitation to shift the question from "if" to "how" race matters in Latin America, it is important to emphasize that, in the last five hundred years, racism and heteropatriarchy have weaponized literacy and literary prestige in Latin America.[22] This has contributed to the oppression of Black and Indigenous peoples and diminished their expressions, following the observations of Gloria Chacón, Joanne Rappaport and Tom Cummins, and Gordon Brotherston.[23]

Fortunately, González's poetry—like most contemporary Indigenous expressions—challenges this internalized logocentric-colonial system by code-switching, blurring Western literary genres, and unsettling expectations of *literature*.[24] Jennifer Carolina Gómez Menjívar has analyzed González's code-switching as a way of being in three dimensions at once, arguing that his poetry bridges the Garínagu language and spirituality with the linguistic diversity and cross-cultural context references of twenty-first-century Livingston: "The poetic voice conjures up the spirit world in order to highlight the fine distinction between the voices of the spirits and those of the living, reality and television, as well as the presence of those who remain in Livingston and those who are away, either in Belize or the United States."[25] As González has mentioned in interviews, he has recently reclaimed his Garífuna language while undertaking deeper research into the Caribbean archive.[26]

Dislocation is not just happening in *cafeína MC*'s language but also in the places visited by its "inhabitants": San Salvador, Guatemala City, San Marcos, and the Caribbean. All places look abandoned: "milagrosa y metamórfica, ciudad medieval / se borran las visiones / y entre la niebla que despierta abandonada / la mañana será un bosque de ruinas" (miraculous and metamorphic, medieval city / visions are erased / and within the abandoned fog that wakes up / the morning will be a forest of ruins).²⁷ Here, places belong to nations and flags that are "dirty and cursed."²⁸ Furthermore, if the social contracts and constitutions of nation states have been written and imposed with the same "patriarchy of language," then their cartographies and borderlines must be disrupted. The character of "the mother," for example, who constantly speaks with the dead, reveals the coordinates to understand this dislocation:

> mamá, acá se muerde el frío con toda la memoria.
> lenguaje no hay; es un arma en la ciudad de los
> muertos. acá los recuerdos, si se descuidan, crecen
> tanto hasta hacerse piedras que uno carga desde el
> fondo del Caribe. se van secando las piedras y los
> mares   (**nota para Hazel Reyes el día de mi muerte**)²⁹

mom, here we bite the cold with all our memories. / there is no language; it's a weapon in the city of / dead. here memories, if you don't take care of them, they grow / so much that become stones that one carries from the / bottom of the Caribbean. stones and seas start drying up (**note to Hazel Reyes on the day of my death**)

In González's poetry, verbal language is not something to trust; it is literally a weapon. The tension between *here* and *there* intensifies, while memory persists as a diasporic watermark. *Here* is the present of the poet, while *there* is a place from where the memories that "grow heavy" come. The dead and the *there* dialogue with each other; beyond words, the presence of both fill the horizon.

The Garífuna Itinerary (*espuma de Yurumein*)

If the reader follows the "Garífuna itinerary" within *cafeina MC*, she will soon find the dead. According to Aida Toledo, González's poetry separates itself from the conversational poetry of the previous generation (*Soledad brother* by Javier Payeras is a renowned example) by focusing on the use of the subconscious as a poetic strategy and practice.³⁰ Beyond the incoherent word games of an anachronic avant-garde, González inserts other elements that refer us back to the intimate and original world of the poet.³¹ In Toledo's interpretation, the matrilineal tradition and the celebration of the dead are Garífuna signatures. Yet, when reading González's poetry, the Garífuna itinerary is only one possible path to follow.

Researchers such as Nancie L. Solien González, Mario Gallardo, and Francesca Gargallo have described the Garífuna belief system, its practices, and its protagonists, including the ancestors (gúbida), the different levels of the spirit (the soul or iuani, the vital force or anigi, and the astral double in between or áfurugu), the cugú and the dugú ceremonies (payments to the gúbida), the "sorcerer" (gariahati), the healer (surusie), and the medium (buyei).[32] Gallardo, for example, observes that for, the Garífuna, the dead represent another stage in the path of reuniting with the gúbida. They are sad, but they also dance and sing and drink.[33] If the reader dives deep into the Garífuna worldview, practices involving the dead will likely be unintelligible. Nevertheless, this ontological effort could eventually help the reader to interpret González's dislocated poetic aesthetics and cartography as a subjective Garífuna means of paying homage to the dead.[34] In the poem "(gorriones amados para Sonia)," Gonzalez uses italics to speak with Mama Morelia:

(cuida mamá Morelia a tus muertos,
si sólo bailas con ellos
cuando en abril abran la puerta bailarán también
en esos jardines tres páginas al hocico del sueño
cuida mamá Morelia a tus muertos
de verdad que los hongos tocan la luz de adentro al límite
ajá
ojalá el límite sea una mariposa sorprendente brotando
de una flauta por lo menos
de un gesto crítico o alguna isla
como mínimo)

soy un arcángel
y esto es una morgue
o un frasco de veneno
o esta moda de temblar si en cien puertas
la soledad colectiva se ve más pequeña

como una tarde de alambres eléctricos
o un eslabón perdido en la angustia[35]

(take care of your dead Mama Morelia, / if you only dance with them / when the door is open in April they will dance too / in those gardens three pages to the snout of dream / take care of your dead Mama Morelia / It is true that mushrooms touch light within the limit / really / I hope the limit is an amazing butterfly sprouting / from a flute at least / from a critical gesture or some island / at least) / I am an archangel / and this

52   AMÉFRICA IN LETTERS

is a morgue / or a bottle of poison / or this fashion of trembling if collective / loneliness seems smaller // like an afternoon of electric wires / or a missing link in anguish

By putting together nouns and microcosms via synecdoche in this dialogue with Mama Morelia—dead, dance, morgue, limit, flute, island—the poem projects an image: a ceremony and a good relationship with the gúbida (ancestors), who are present even though the poetic voice is far away from the coast, in downtown Guatemala City. Despite physical migration, dispossession, and diaspora, the poem "(gorriones amados para Sonia)" preserves a bridge with the Garínagu. In the poem "(Celofán)," Mama Morelia is again the protagonist. In this piece, she is concerned about the disdain directed toward her. Disdain from whom? Who is Mama Morelia?

naciste esperando mar
más orilla al otro lado
mamá Morelia
americana pura
¿quieres bailar, andarme de un lado al otro, niño?
oh niño mío ¿por qué
he merecido este desdén que menos hiere
que el olvido?

juego a tener la verdad en la cabeza[36]

you were born waiting the sea / more shore on the other side / Mama Morelia / pure american / Do you want to dance, walk me from one side to the other, boy? / oh my boy, why / have I deserved this / disdain that hurts lesser / than oblivion? // I imagine having the truth in my head

In "(gorriones amados para Sonia)," we read that Mama Morelia takes care of her dead while dancing with them. In "(Celofán)," we learn that she was born waiting for the sea and she is "pure American." As one of the "masters of ceremony," her constant presence stands out in this urban and diasporic poetic imaginary. She belongs to a *there* that flickers throughout *cafeína MC*, a *there* that is reminiscent of Livingston but not exactly Livingston, a *there* that the poet calls a cursed town but which he cannot help but love:

fosforesce el día. qué va, aún falta mucho
la luz temprana es sueño de estrella negra,

sueño, en que la oscura espuma de Yurumein
juega a ser la arañita que me despierta de la vigilia
mientras vacila viendo el reloj de catedral metropolitana

alguien enciende la tarde, alguien intenta
esconder la sombra de los otros
mientras Dios vuelve a pronunciar pirotecnia

"*es mi vida y adiós a la gloria*"

pero yo soy memoria autómata, algo inútil
frente al potrero y frente a las ovejas evocadas
cadáver de eras que alientan a llegar
al pueblo maldito, a decir *I love you labugana psyco
donde todo se ilumina con lo improbable, con el exterminio*
I FUCKIN' LOVE YOU[37]

phosphoresce the day, no way, there's still a long way to go / early light is a dream of a black star, / dream, in which the dark foam of Yurumein / play to be the little spider that wakes me up from vigil / as she hesitates looking at the metropolitan cathedral clock // someone lights up the afternoon, someone tries / to hide others' shadow / while God pronounces pyrotechnics once more // "this is my life and goodbye to glory" // but I am automaton memory, something useless / in front of the pasture and in front of the evoked sheep / corpse of eras that encourage to arrive / to the cursed town, and say I love you labugana psyco / where everything is illuminated with the improbable, with extermination / I FUCKIN' LOVE YOU

In the heart of Guatemala City, the poet's vigil is crossed by Yurumein, the island of St. Vincent, in the shape of a little spider. Far from the Caribbean, memory brings rhythms of *labugana* while the poet feels like a corpse. In my own reader's itinerary, all the loose ends of *cafeína MC* are tied in the last poem, "(tower)," where the uncertainty between *here* and *there* creates further room for interpretation:

hermoso es fragmentar la vida propia y caerse en pedazos sobre el papel. Livingston alumbra el mar y qué bonita se mira irse. mamá lo pide todo bajo el cielo de lujo y por la tarde suele mirar su telenovela. la ventanilla del barco parecía una t.v a full color encadenada a un reality show maldito. la mejor venganza es dejar al pueblo chico cada vez más lejos. si ardiera seguiría mi rumbo con calma en la cabeza de las olas. si ardiera mi cabeza sería una canción de Miles Davis. Si ardiera sería un cómic de Grant Morrison que dure para siempre. floto. no me despido de nadie ni lloro por nadie. sólo floto.[38]

> *how beautiful it is to fragment your own life and falling into pieces on a page. Livingston lights the sea and how beautiful it is looking how the town goes away. mom asks for everything under the fancy sky and she usually watches her soap opera in the afternoon. The ship's window looked like a full-color TV chained to a damn reality show. the best revenge is to leave the small town further and further away. if it burned I would calmly follow my path in the waves' head. if my head burned it would be a Miles Davis song. If it burned it would be a Grant Morrison's comic that lasts forever. I float. I don't say goodbye to anyone nor cry for anyone. I just float.*

The ancestors, native language, the mother's voice, and Guatemala's disdain toward the Garífuna Caribbean coast are all fragments rocked by the waves from the poet's *here* to the distant *there*. If there is a "Garífuna itinerary" to take when reading *cafeína MC*, it does not lead toward a utopian past or a romanticized ceremony but toward an ancestral futurescape that is constantly changing and transforming. As evidenced in the examples above, González's Garínagu way is both ancient and postmodern, and Yurumein's breeze is present both in the Caribbean and Guatemala City's metropolitan cathedral.

The Postwar Generation Itinerary (*no se preocupe, man, everything is gonna be all right*)

Based on current debates regarding the classifications or expectations used to group literatures written in Indigenous languages, translated or otherwise, *cafeína MC*'s "Garífuna itinerary" can be challenging. Mixe linguist Yasnaya Aguilar has questioned the use of ethnic labels and the Indigenous/non-Indigenous binarism, responding to the fact that most contemporary Indigenous writers are bridging cross-cultural audiences and ascribing their work into "Western" literary production through the traditional venues of books, authors, readers, poetry, and performance. Furthermore, if the ethnic label is problematic when a poem is written in a native language, it is even more questionable when it is written only in Spanish by a transnational Black-Indigenous author. Finding themselves at a crossroads, the reader's choice reveals the reader's own understandings of race, ethnicity, and literature. Why do we want to divide? What is the purpose? At the same time, González mentions Yurumein and includes fragments from his memories of twenty-first-century Livingston, and his poetry distrusts ethnic/racial classifications and generalizations. We can read in the poem "(hangover all star)":

> los demonios de la cloaca vecina dicen que no
> que no, *que no; que no se preocupe compadre, todo está arreglado*
> *tiene su ictiosauros de cartón en su biblioteca ¿qué más quiere?*
> *vive lejos del basural y es un negrito respetado ¿no ve?*
> *no se preocupe, man, everything is gonna be all right*
> por eso mismo estoy que me doblo de la alegría
> por eso[39]

> *the neighboring sewer's demons say no / no, no; don't worry buddy, everything is settled / you have your cardboard ichthyosaurs in your library. What else do you want? / you live far / from the garbage dump and are a respected little black man, don't you see? / don't worry, man, / everything is gonna be all right / that's why I am jumping for joy // that's why*

According to the voice in italics, the "literate poet" has been able to challenge racial stereotypes because he is currently a "respected little black man" who now belongs to a "better" class, "far away from the garbage dump." A voice asks the poet: "What else do you want?" The poet's sarcastic comment, "that's why I am jumping for joy," suggests questions such as: How is my situation positive if my people are still struggling? What is the price of literary prestige in a classist and racist Guatemalan or Latin American society? The person who is chatting with the poet reinforces the coloniality of power, a matrix that comes from the colonial violence and remains today the foundation of inequality among races, ethnicities, classes, and gender. The sarcastic laughter becomes resistance, and González's empowerment through poetry is a counterweapon. It reveals logocentrism's responsibility and literary prestige's debt to inequality—in the shape of a bookcase. In another poem, "(el fin de la fiesta)," we read:

> el bestiario iluminado consta de putas que parecen ladridos de perros y travestis que comienzan su danza de tristeza. de niñas andrógenas y clones subiendo las gradas del Palacio Nacional de la Cultura.

> saltan a las ventanas para ver traspasar las paredes, ronronear, volar en pedazos el gran registro de identidad y hacer el amor como hippies melancólicos. enfermos de toda esa mierda étnica.[40]

the illuminated bestiary consists of whores that look like dog barks and transvestites that begin their sad dance. androgenic girls and clones climbing the steps of the National Palace of Culture. // they jump to the windows to see and go through the walls, purr, blow the great identity record apart and make love like melancholic hippies. sick of all that ethnic shit.

While poverty and illiteracy feed racist stereotypes, culturalism and romanticism coopt Indigeneity. Those melancholic hippies by the National Palace of Culture are also perpetuating the coloniality of power when they appropriate the "ethnic shit." Reflecting on the reader's expectations of "ethnic authenticity," Gómez Menjívar captures the complexity:

If the reader wishes the poetic voice to conform, to settle, to remain chained to one way of rhythm, the poetic voice has effectively problematized that expectation. He is at once a different configuration of tempos converging, and yet as equally complex an arrangement as the interlocutor. A central premise of this work, then, is that black indigeneity is beyond the outsider's ken so long as the wish is to freeze that experience in a single status and state without allowing for movement, transformation and renewal.[41]

cafeína MC questions univocal identities, homogeneous subjectivities, and group labels that build walls between oneness and otherness. As Claire Smith and Grame K. Ward explain in *Indigenous Cultures in an Interconnected World*, stereotypes can be broken by making cultural crossroads explicit and public and allowing actors themselves to take control of definitions and classifications.[42] In going from *here* to *there*, *cafeína MC*'s cadence confronts the reader's "Garífuna itinerary" with its constant dislocations.

In the 1995 *Agreements on Guatemalan Indigenous Peoples and Identities*, twenty-one Mayan nations, as well as the Garífuna and the Xinca, were recognized for the first time by the nation states as part of its multiethnic and multilingual history and present.[43] After three decades of genocide and human rights violations against Indigenous peoples and campesinos, in December 1996, representatives from the Alvaro Arzú presidential administration and the Guatemalan National Revolutionary Unity (UNGR) signed the *Guatemalan Peace Accords*, in which they acknowledged Indigenous identities as necessary for peace and unity.[44]

The 2012 literary anthology *El futuro empezó ayer* brought together more than fifty contemporary Guatemalan authors and critics of different ages who published after these two major events in the political history of the Central American country. Despite the political context, all the voices compiled in *El futuro empezó ayer* align with a postwar literary generation who turned away from themes of ethnic struggle and civil war to a more intimate, sarcastic, and chaotic urban realism. Beyond ethnicities and origins, a priority for this trans-national experimental aesthetics was to blur boundaries between genres like poetry, video, and performance. Festivals, bookstore shelves, websites and blogs, and anthologies grew to become cross-cultural stages. For the Guatemalan postwar generation, a volcano appeared more meaningful than a flag or a nationality.[45] The forced silence during the most violent years of the Mayan genocide created a historical trauma in the collective body, which resisted being represented through literature. Instead, the new aesthetics intentionally mixed dislocation, eroticism, mass-media, and marginality.

Anabella Acevedo Leal emphasizes that this subjective experimentation may seem non-political; however, its marginality is extremely political because, for this generation of writers, politics was a word linked to violence, the nation states, and political parties. These authors preferred to be outside of the establishment.[46] Acevedo lists multiple names and genealogies that were adopted by the postwar generation in Guatemala City: la Casa Bizarra, Tortilla y Coca-Cola, Generación X. At the time, dislocation mirrors the decentralization of literary production and the canon. Groups such as Metáfora (Quetzaltenango) and writers such as Humberto Ak'abal, Maya Cú, Rosa Chávez, Pablo García, Daniel Caño, Esteban Sabino, Manuel Tzoc, and Wingston González were producing superb literature both outside and inside Guatemala City. For the first time in Guatemalan literary history, Indigenous writers from Quiché, Sololá, Quetzaltenango, Huehuetenango, and Livingston were being included in "national" anthologies, such as the aforementioned anthology and the subsequent edited volume, *Aldeas mis ojos: 10 poetas guatemaltecos después de la posguerra*. At the same time, ethnic and racial labels were not always explicit in the authors' works and biographies in these literary collections. Some of the authors were actually suspicious of these ethnic labels because of their cooptation by scholars and critics, particularly from institutions in the United States, who consistently asked about origins, filiations, and differences. This is Maya Cú's experience:

> En 1996, llegó a Guatemala una académica norteamericana, Gail Ament, interesada en mi literatura y en la de Gaspar Pedro González. Fue la primera vez que fui calificada de "poeta maya" o "poeta indígena." Pero fue hasta después del año 2000 que me empezaron a nombrar de ese modo. A mí nunca se me había ocurrido colocar a la par de la identidad de poeta mi identidad étnica. En ciertos momentos, esto me hacía sentir incómoda, puesto que me parecía que se utilizaba la identidad con fines de notoriedad.[47]

> *In 1996, an American scholar, Gail Ament, came to Guatemala, interested in Gaspar Pedro González's literature and mine. It was the first time that I was described as a "Mayan poet" or as an "Indigenous poet." But it was not until the year 2000 that they began to label me that way. It never occurred to me to place my ethnic identity beside my identity as a poet. At times, this made me feel uncomfortable, since it seemed to me that my ethnic identity was being used for the purpose of notoriety.*

Despite the good intentions of scholars who want to make visible an underrepresented literary corpus, Cú's essay raises unresolved questions about "ethnic labels" and "ethnic renaissance celebrations": How does this cultural validation make an impact on social and political inequality? How am I—as a critic, author, or reader—positioning myself in a conversation where privilege is decisive? In the postwar generation, Afrodescendant, Indigenous, and *mestizo/ladino* poets became critical about their own internalized colonization. In his renowned work, *Poemas sensibles*, Guatemalan poet Alan Mills writes:

> el indio empuja con su fuerza de siglos,
> emerge ardoroso y se le sale,
> con lo guardado,
> con lo que dura doliendo.
> No, no es otro,
> El indio soy yo, a ver, repita conmigo[48]

> *the Indian pushes with his force of centuries, / emerges burning and comes out, / with what is kept, / with what lasts hurting. / No, it is not the other, / The Indian is me, repeat with me, ready?*

Honesty, intimacy, and experimentation bind together diverse voices from the literary Guatemalan postwar generation. In questioning narratives on ethnicity, race, and otherness created by settler colonialism and *ladino/mestizo* nation states, writers of this generation, such as González, Cú, and Mills, demand equity and self-reflection.

The Absent Presence of Race (*hay una equis sobre nuestro origen*)

In the history of the Garífuna's self-representation as a collective, different organizations have strategically emphasized Indigeneity, African ancestry, or both:

OFRANEH (Afro-Indigeneity), ODECO (Blackness and anti-racism), and ONEGUA (Blackness/*negritud*).[49] In the context of Latin American multiculturalism, "from the 1980s, Garífuna activists adopted a model of Indigenous rights and actively allied with Indigenous activism."[50] Therefore, racial- or ethnicity-based models could generate "discursive power," depending on a given nation states's politics on identity.[51] As Gómez Menjívar explains, "Blackness and black indigeneity have had a place in Belizean national discourse, but these concepts have been largely omitted in the racial discourses of Guatemala."[52] This ambiguity surrounding race and ethnicity has a long history of tensions and distortions among three non-fixed, ever-changing nodes and forces: Blackness, whiteness, and Indigeneity.[53] In the history of North America—as explained by Eve Tuck and K. Wayne Yang—Indigenous peoples and Afrodescendants have been racialized in opposing ways that nonetheless support settler-colonial logic: "Through the one-drop rule, blackness in settler colonial contexts is *expansive*, ensuring that a slave/criminal status will be *inherited* by an expanding number of 'Black' descendants. Yet, Indigenous peoples have been racialized in a profoundly different way. Native Americanness is *subtractive*: Native Americans are constructed to become fewer in number and less Native, but never exactly white, over time."[54]

The same conclusion is not transferable to the Garínagu and Central American contexts because internalized colonization via *mestizaje* and liberal multiculturalism has subtracted both Blackness and Indigeneity from mixed-race individuals and elites, promoting race whitening and race-denial. There is an advantage, however, in juxtaposing hemispheric politics on race, as Juliet Hooker states: "For thinkers in both traditions mythologies of race were formed in relation to an American other."[55] Though Hooker analyzes nineteenth and twentieth-century thinkers from the United States and Latin America—Frederick Douglass, Augusto Sarmiento, W. E. B. Du Bois, and José Vasconcelos—her study reminds us that nation states' politics on race in both contexts interpret the same racist scientific archive (American ethnology, social Darwinism, and eugenics) to support their own economic and political agendas:

> For Latin Americans, meanwhile, racist science posed "a difficult intellectual dilemma." On the one hand, many of the region's most influential thinkers embraced scientific racism because it provided a convenient explanation for the region's post-independence turmoil (which could be attributed to Latin American racial deficiencies), and because it justified the dominance of a white Europeanized elite over a large nonwhite or mixed-race population. Yet, on the other hand, the idea of Anglo-Saxon superiority was also problematic for Latin Americans as it

served as a justification for U.S. imperial expansion to the region. Scientific racism was thus deployed in service of both promoting and resisting US expansionism to Latin America at different points in time.[56]

The understanding of whiteness by mixed-race populations in both the United States and Latin America is crucial to visualizing the complexity of "the dilemma": How does a Guatemalan *ladino* or a Colombian *mestizo* imagine their multiracial identity? How do they perceive themselves as mixed-race people within a racist society? Are they embracing "whiteness" when they celebrate being multiracial? Do they imagine their whiteness differently if they live in the United States or in Latin America? In this hemispheric juxtaposition of politics on race, transhemispheric Black Indigeneity unsettles the projects of *ladino/mestizo* nation states, as well as *ladino/mestizo* identities (as in Mill's poem above).[57] Between expansive and subtractive forces, Garífuna social movements and literatures reveal settler and *ladino/mestizo* tactics of segregation and genocide in both the United States and Latin America—laws to criminalize, labels to classify, and narratives to misinform—so that communities and individuals can be divided and broken.

"The absent presence of race" is an expression borrowed from Wade's research on genomics in Latin American nations.[58] I borrow it here to name a paradox of the heteropatriarchal, colonial, and economic matrix in Latin America: race and ethnicity are social constructs, and yet they are used both to dominate and to liberate communities and individuals, depending on who is identifying or self-identifying. In the context of literary studies and González's poetry, more questions arise: What do I imagine, for example, when I say "Yurumein"? What does González mean when he says it? *Who* is speaking and *how* do they reveal their intentions and "discursive power"? Context matters in reading literatures written by individuals who identify as Indigenous or Afrodescendant.[59]

I started this chapter wondering about the role of literature and literary studies in the conversation of race and ethnicity. Following Doris Sommer, I believe that González's dislocated poetic aesthetics highlights freedom and agency:

> Afrodescendant writing in Latin America displays a strategic attention to formal literary decisions as opportunities to exercising authority, no matter how inevitable the content or the theme of the writing may be. This appreciation for artistic decision-making as a vehicle for freedom makes the study of literature significant beyond the historical or sociological information that creative writing offers. Even before they start writing, creative authors consider questions about how to strategize representations of themes they may not have freely chosen. The freedom is in the how, not the what.[60]

González's treatment of semantic cohesion and synecdoche, as well as Central American geography, is part of his "strategic representation." Both itineraries—the Garífuna and the postwar generation—are possible pathways for readers of González's *cafeína MC*. One itinerary makes race and ethnicity visible, while the other makes them "absent presences." González's "literary decisions" suggest a post-ethnic/racial futurescape in which his agglutinant and cross-cultural aesthetics exercise authority over a violent heteropatriarchal and colonial manipulation of identity. This literary project has nothing to do with the *mestizo*/multicultural Latin American project of erasing race; on the contrary, this work creates space for change and transformation among individuals who identify as Indigenous, Black, and mixed-race. González's poetry invites the reader to unselect colonial and institutional boxes to reclaim a cross-cultural creativity in an ever-changing world. The alphabetic writing system is still a protagonist in such "images at war."[61] While disrupting the formal speech and semantic cohesion of Spanish, González questions literary expectations and unequal access to literacy.

NOTES

1. Peter Wade et al., "Nation and the Absent Presence of Race in Latin American Genomics," *Current Anthropology* 55, no. 5 (2014): 497–522.
2. Paul Joseph López Oro, " '*Ni de aquí ni de allá*': Garífuna Subjectivities and the Politics of Diasporic Belonging," in *Afro-Latin@s in Movement: Critical Approaches to Blackness and Transnationalism in the Americas*, eds. Petra R. Rivera-Rideau, Jennifer A. Jones, and Tianna S. Paschel, 61–83 (New York: Palgrave Macmillan, 2016).
3. Petra R. Rivera-Rideau, Jennifer A. Jones, and Tianna S. Paschel, "Introduction: Theorizing Afrolatinidades," in *Afro-Latin@s in Movement: Critical Approaches to Blackness and Transnationalism in the Americas*, eds. Petra R. Rivera-Rideau, Jennifer A. Jones, and Tianna S. Paschel (New York: Palgrave Macmillan, 2016), 12.
4. Peter Wade, "Afro-Indigenous Interactions, Relations and Comparisons," in *Afro-Latin American Studies: An Introduction*, eds. Alejandro de la Fuente and George Reid Andrews (Cambridge: Cambridge University Press, 2018), 92.
5. López Oro, " '*Ni de aquí ni de allá*,' " 62.
6. Wade, "Afro-Indigenous Interactions," 98.
7. Dony Stewart and Eduardo González, "Pueblo Garífuna: 215 años de existencia y aún lucha por desarrollo e inclusión," *Prensa Libre*, November 25, 2017, accessed May 2020, https://www.prensalibre.com/ciudades/izabal/pueblo-garifuna-215-aos-de-existencia-y-aun-luchan-por-desarrollo-e-inclusion/.
8. For a detailed history of the Garínagu in relationship with Wingston González's poetry, see Jennifer Carolina Gómez Menjívar, "Straight Outta Livingston: Black Indigeneity,

Wordsmithing and Code-Switching in Wingston González's Poetry," *TRANSMODERNITY: Journal of Peripheral Cultural Production of the Luso-Hispanic World* 7, no. 1 (2017): 124–145.

9. López Oro, " '*Ni de aquí ni de allá*,' " 63.
10. See Wade, "Afro-Indigenous Interactions"; Francesca Gargallo, *Garífuna, Garínagu, Caribe: Historia de una nación libertaria* (Buenos Aires: siglo XXI editores, 2002); and Jennifer Carolina Gómez Menjívar and William Noel Salmon, *Tropical Tongues: Language Ideologies, Endangerment, and Minority Languages in Belize* (Chapel Hill: University of North Carolina Press, 2018).
12. López Oro, " '*Ni de aquí ni de allá*,' " 62.
13. Manuel de J. Jiménez, "Introduction," in s*an juan: la esperanza (apéndice de un mundo encontrado/jardín y representaciones atonales)*, Wingston González (México: Literal, 2013), 6.
14. Wingston González, *cafeína MC (segunda parte, la fiesta y sus habitantes)* (Guatemala: Catafixia, 2010), 29.
15. *cafeína MC* has not been translated into English yet. All translations here are personal attempts. It is important to remember that González's experimentation and code-switching challenges any translation.
16. Doris Sommer, "Literary Liberties: The Authority of Afrodescendant Authors," in *Afro-Latin American Studies: An Introduction*, eds. Alejandro de la Fuente and George Reid Andrews (Cambridge: Cambridge University Press, 2018), 326. Perhaps the most experimental book so far published by González is *Miss Muñecas Vudu* (2013), translated as *No Budu Please* (2018) by Urayoán Noel and Ugly Duckling Press. See Juliana Clark, "Review: No Budu Please," *Columbia Journal*, December 14, 2018, accessed May 20, 2020, http://columbiajournal.org/review-no-budu-please-by-wingston-gonzalez/.
17. González, *cafeína MC*, 19–20.
18. Javier Payeras, "Apuntas para ensamblar Frankensteins," *El futuro empezó ayer*, ed. Luis Méndez Salinas and Carmen Lucía Alvarado (Guatemala: Catafixia, 2012), 215.
19. José García Escobar, "Two Failed Rappers Translating a Garífuna Wordsmith: An Interview with Uroyoán Noel," *Asympote*, March 4, 2019, accessed May 2020, https://www.asymptotejournal.com/blog/2019/03/04/two-failed-rappers-translating-a-garifuna-wordsmith-an-interview-with-urayoan-noel/.
20. López Oro, " '*Ni de aquí ni de allá*,' " 63.
21. José García Escobar, "From the Headbanger, the Metalhead, All the Way to the Failed Hip-Hopper: An Interview with Wingston González," *Asymptote*, August 6, 2018, accessed May 2020, https://www.asymptotejournal.com/blog/2018/08/06/in-conversation-wingston-gonzalez/.
22. Rivera-Rideau, Jones, and Paschel, "Introduction," 6.
23. See Gloria E. Chacón, *Indigenous Cosmolectics: Kab'awil and the Making of Maya Zapotec Literatures* (Chapel Hill: University of North Carolina Press, 2019); Joanne Rappaport and Tom Cummins, *Beyond the Lettered City* (Durham: Duke University Press, 2012); and Gordon Brotherston, *Book of the Fourth World: Reading the Native Americas*

Through Their Literature (Cambridge: Cambridge University Press, 1992).
24. See Paul M. Worley and Rita M. Palacios, *Unwriting Maya Literature: Ts'íib as Recorded Knowledge* (Tucson: University of Arizona Press, 2019); and Miguel Rocha, *Mingas de la palabra: Textualidades oralitegráficas y visiones de cabeza en las oralituras y literaturas indígenas contemporáneas* (Cuba: Casa de las Américas, 2016).
25. Gómez Menjívar, "Straight Outta Livingston," 127.
26. Currently, González is researching the colonial Caribbean archive and books such as William Young's *Account of the Black Charaibs in the Island of St. Vincent* (1773). Phone conversation on May 10, 2020.
27. González, *cafeína MC*, 46.
28. Ibid., 32.
29. Ibid., 40.
30. Aida Toledo, "La escritura joven guatemalteca. A propósito de la poesía de Wingston González," *Centroamericana* 15 (2009): 90.
31. Ibid., 91.
32. See Nancie L. Solien González, *Sojourners of the Caribbean: Ethnogenesis and Ethnohistory on the Garífuna* (Chicago: University of Illinois Press, 1988); Mario Gallardo, "La persistencia de la memoria: Tradición oral de los garífunas de la costa atlántica de Honduras," *Espéculo* 35 (2007), accessed May 20, 2020, https://webs.ucm.es/info/especulo/numero35/garifun.html; and Gargallo, *Garífuna, Garínagu, Caribe*.
33. Gallardo, "La persistencia de la memoria."
34. See Alí Allié's 1999 film *El espíritu de mi mama*, where the dead, the mother, and the diaspora are clearly interconnected: elespiritudemimama.com/ver/.
35. González, *cafeína MC*, 15.
36. Ibid., 22.
37. Ibid., 50.
38. Ibid., 59.
39. Ibid., 48.
40. Ibid., 55.
41. Gómez Menjívar, "Straight Outta Livingston," 129.
42. Claire Smith and Grame K. Ward, eds. *Indigenous Cultures in an Interconnected World* (Vancouver: University of British Columbia Press, 2000), 3.
43. See the full text of *Acuerdo sobre Identidad y Derechos de los Pueblos Indígenas*, available online.
44. Several documents were published around the same date. See full list and original documents available through the United States Institute for Peace website (https://www.usip.org/publications/1998/11/peace-agreements-guatemala).
45. Diego Azurdia, "Escribir para merecer volcanes," in *El futuro empezó ayer*, eds. Luis Méndez Salinas and Carmen Lucía Alvarado (Guatemala: Catafixia, 2012), 24.
46. Anabella Acevedo Leal, "Notas para la elaboración de una cartografía de la literatura contemporánea en Guatemala," in *El futuro empezó ayer*, eds. Luis Méndez Salinas and Carmen Lucía Alvarado (Guatemala: Catafixia, 2012), 35.

47. Maya Cú, "Poetas y escritoras mayas de Guatemala: Del silencio a la palabra," *Diálogo* 19, no. 1 (2016): 81–82.
48. Quoted in Luis Méndez Salinas and Carmen Lucía Alvarado, eds., *El futuro empezó ayer* (Guatemala: Catafixia, 2012), 106.
49. One example of contemporary collaborative Afro-Indigenous activism and resistance is the work by the COPINH and the OFRANEH in Honduras. See the film "Berta Cáceres Vive!"
50. Wade, "Afro-Indigenous Interactions," 114.
51. Martin Lienhard, "Voces marginadas y poder discursivo en América Latina," *Revista Iberoamericana* 193 (2000): 785.
52. Gómez Menjívar, "Straight Outta Livingston," 131.
53. Wade, "Afro-Indigenous Interactions," 121.
54. Eve Tuck and K. Wayne Yang, "Decolonization Is Not a Metaphor," *Decolonization: Indigeneity, Education and Society* 1 (2012): 12.
55. Juliet Hooker, *Theorizing Race in the Americas: Douglass, Sarmiento, Du Bois, and Vasconcelos* (Oxford: Oxford University Press, 2017), 3.
56. Ibid., 8.
57. As the world witnessed in the Rios Montt 2013 trial (see Pamela Yates's documentary *500 years*), the *ladino* elite responsible for the Maya genocide in Guatemala were supported by the Ronald Reagan administration and believed in the extermination of a race/ethnicity for the sake of exploiting their land.
58. "It is important that race is usually not explicitly mentioned in this Latin American genetic science and in some cases is vehemently denied as a biological reality. It is thus an absent presence. This is both because race is a contested concept in genomics generally and because the particular instances of genomics science we are exploring here are located in Latin American nations, where race has long been an absent presence in society." Wade et al., "Nation and the Absent Presence of Race in Latin American Genomics," 498.
59. More literary criticism needs to be done on the rest of González's books, as well as on other Garífuna writers, such as Nora Murillo, and Afro-Indigenous authors, such as Estercilia Simanca Pushaina (Wayuu/Colombia).
60. Sommer, "Literary Liberties," 320.
61. See Serge Gruzinski, *Images at War: Mexico from Columbus to Blade Runner (1492-2019)* (Durham: Duke University Press, 2001).

WORKS CITED

Acevedo Leal, Anabella. "Notas para la elaboración de una cartografía de la literatura contemporánea en Guatemala." *El futuro empezó ayer*, edited by Luis Méndez Salinas and Carmen Lucía Alvarado, 30–39. Guatemala: Catafixia, 2012.

Aguilar, Yasnaya. "(Is There) An Indigenous Literature?" *Diálogo* 19, no. 1 (2016): 157–59.
Azurdia, Diego. "Escribir para merecer volcanes." In *El futuro empezó ayer*, edited by Luis Méndez Salinas and Carmen Lucía Alvarado, 24–29. Guatemala: Catafixia, 2012.
Brotherston, Gordon. *Book of the Fourth World: Reading the Native Americas Through Their Literature*. Cambridge: Cambridge University Press, 1992.
Chacón, Gloria E. *Indigenous Cosmolectics: Kab'awil and the Making of Maya Zapotec Literatures*. Chapel Hill: University of North Carolina Press, 2019.
Clark, Juliana. "Review: No Budu Please." *Columbia Journal*. December 14, 2018. Accessed May 20, 2020. http://columbiajournal.org/review-no-budu-please-by-wingston-gonzalez/.
Cú, Maya. "Poetas y escritoras mayas de Guatemala: Del silencio a la palabra." *Diálogo* 19, no. 1 (2016): 81–88.
De Sousa Santos, Boaventura. *Descolonizar el saber, reinventar el poder*. Chile: Trilce, 2013.
Gallardo, Mario. "La persistencia de la memoria: Tradición oral de los garífunas de la costa atlántica de Honduras." *Espéculo* 35 (2007). Accessed May 20, 2020. https://webs.ucm.es/info/especulo/numero35/garifun.html.
García Escobar, José. "From the Headbanger, the Metalhead, All the Way to the Failed Hip-Hopper: An Interview with Wingston González." *Asymptote*. August 6, 2018. Accessed May 2020. https://www.asymptotejournal.com/blog/2018/08/06/in-conversation-wingston-gonzalez/.
———. "Two Failed Rappers Translating a Garífuna Wordsmith: An Interview with Uroyoán Noel." *Asympote*. March 4, 2019. Accessed May 2020. https://www.asymptotejournal.com/blog/2019/03/04/two-failed-rappers-translating-a-garifuna-wordsmith-an-interview-with-urayoan-noel/.
Gargallo, Francesca. *Garífuna, Garínagu, Caribe: Historia de una nación libertaria*. Buenos Aires: siglo XXI editores, 2002.
Gómez Menjívar, Jennifer Carolina. "Straight Outta Livingston: Black Indigeneity, Wordsmithing and Code-Switching in Wingston González's Poetry." *TRANSMODERNITY: Journal of Peripheral Cultural Production of the Luso-Hispanic World* 7, no. 1 (2017): 124–145.
Gómez Menjívar, Jennifer Carolina, and William Noel Salmon. *Tropical Tongues: Language Ideologies, Endangerment, and Minority Languages in Belize*. Chapel Hill: University of North Carolina Press, 2018.
González, Nancie L. Solien. *Sojourners of the Caribbean: Ethnogenesis and Ethnohistory on the Garífuna*. Chicago: University of Illinois Press, 1988.
González, Wingston. *cafeína MC (primera parte: la anunciación de la fiesta)*. Buenos Aires: Folía editores, 2011.
———. *cafeína MC (segunda parte, La fiesta y sus habitantes)*. Guatemala: Catafixia, 2010.
———. *Los magos del crepúsculo (y blues otra vez)*. Guatemala: Editorial Cultura, 2005.
———. *Remembranzas del recuerdo*. Guatemala: San marquitos editores, 2008.
———. *san juan: la esperanza (apéndice de un mundo encontrado / jardín y representaciones atonales)*. México: Literal, 2013.
Gruzinski, Serge. *Images at War: Mexico from Columbus to Blade Runner (1492-2019)*. Durham:

Duke University Press, 2001.

Hooker, Juliet. *Theorizing Race in the Americas: Douglass, Sarmiento, Du Bois, and Vasconcelos*. Oxford: Oxford University Press, 2017.

Lienhard, Martin. "Voces marginadas y poder discursivo en América Latina." *Revista Iberoamericana* 193 (2000): 785–798.

López Oro, Paul Joseph. " '*Ni de aquí ni de allá*': Garífuna Subjectivities and the Politics of Diasporic Belonging." In *Afro-Latin@s in Movement: Critical Approaches to Blackness and Transnationalism in the Americas*, edited by Petra R. Rivera-Rideau, Jennifer A. Jones, and Tianna S. Paschel, 61–83. New York: Palgrave Macmillan, 2016.

Méndez Salinas, Luis, and Carmen Lucía Alvarado, eds. *El futuro empezó ayer*. Guatemala: Catafixia, 2012.

Payeras, Javier. "Apuntas para ensamblar Frankensteins." *El futuro empezó ayer*, edited by Luis Méndez Salinas and Carmen Lucía Alvarado, 212–216. Guatemala: Catafixia, 2012.

Rappaport, Joanne, and Tom Cummins. *Beyond the Lettered City*. Durham: Duke University Press, 2012.

Rivera-Rideau, Petra R., Jennifer A. Jones, and Tianna S. Paschel, eds. *Afro-Latin@s in Movement: Critical Approaches to Blackness and Transnationalism in the Americas*. New York: Palgrave Macmillan, 2016.

Rocha, Miguel. *Mingas de la palabra: Textualidades oralitegráficas y visiones de cabeza en las oralituras y literaturas indígenas contemporáneas*. Cuba: Casa de las Américas, 2016.

Smith, Claire, and Grame K. Ward, eds. *Indigenous Cultures in an Interconnected World*. Vancouver-Toronto: UBC, 2000.

Sommer, Doris. "Literary Liberties: The Authority of Afrodescendant Authors." In *Afro-Latin American Studies: An Introduction*, edited by Alejandro de la Fuente and George Reid Andrews, 319–347. Cambridge: Cambridge University Press, 2018.

Stewart, Dony, and Eduardo González. "Pueblo Garífuna: 215 años de existencia y aún lucha por desarrollo e inclusión." *Prensa Libre*. November 25, 2017. Accessed May 2020. https://www.prensalibre.com/ciudades/izabal/pueblo-garifuna-215-aos-de-existencia-y-aun-luchan-por-desarrollo-e-inclusion/.

Toledo, Aida. "La escritura joven guatemalteca. A propósito de la poesía de Wingston González." *Centroamericana* 15 (2009): 87–96.

Tuck, Eve, and Yang, K. Wayne. "Decolonization Is Not a Metaphor." *Decolonization: Indigeneity, Education and Society* 1 (2012): 1–40.

United States Insitute for Peace. "Peace Agreements: Guatemala." *Peace Agreements Digital Collection*. November 1998. Accessed May 2020. https://www.usip.org/publications/1998/11/peace-agreements-guatemala.

Wade, Peter. "Afro-Indigenous Interactions, Relations and Comparisons." In *Afro-Latin American Studies: An Introduction*, edited by Alejandro de la Fuente and George Reid Andrews, 92–129. Cambridge: Cambridge University Press, 2018.

Wade, Peter, Vivette García Deister, Michael Kent, and María Fernanda Olarte Sierra, and Adriana Díaz del Castillo Hernández. "Nation and the Absent Presence of Race in Latin American Genomics." *Current Anthropology* 55, no. 5 (2014): 497–522.

Worley, Paul M., and Rita M. Palacios. *Unwriting Maya Literature: Ts'síib as Recorded Knowledge*. Tucson: University of Arizona Press, 2019.

◆ CHAPTER 3

Antonio Preciado
Ecuador's Afrocentric Poet

Michael Handelsman

> Un siglo despues, otras manos fuertes y callosas baten los mismos tambores, ya olvidados de sus dioses africanos. Pero en ello hay algo más que simples evocaciones: la persistencia del propio pueblo negro.
> —MANUEL ZAPATA OLIVELLA, ¡LEVÁNTATE MULATO!

> *A century later, other strong hands with callouses beat the same drums, now forgotten by their African gods. But here there is something more than mere evocations: the persistence of black people themselves.*

In an interview in May 2010, Antonio Preciado Bedoya (b. Esmeraldas, Ecuador, 1941) expressed categorically his disagreement with all efforts to categorize him as a Black or Afro poet.[1] Furthermore, he rejected the value of anthologies dedicated strictly to Afro writers, stating that such projects only contributed to marginalizing those writers from the literary canon, whether national or Latin American. In fact, Preciado repeated several times that he is a poet without categories who writes literature for everyone. Curiously, however, during that same conversation, he was equally adamant about acknowledging his identity and heritage as an Afrodescendant, a product of Barrio Caliente in Esmeraldas.[2]

More than a contradiction of terms, this double positioning as both a poet without specific descriptors and as an Afrodescendant marks a long history of the African diaspora in the Americas. Indeed, a source of tension common to many Black writers, for example, continues to be their struggle to affirm and legitimize their intellectual and artistic relevance to all readers within the so-called Lettered City without minimizing or whitening their racial heritage as a vital source of everyone's humanity.

Understandably, identity constitutes a slippery slope for Blacks (as well as for most marginalized communities), particularly in light of Abuelo Zenón's call for Blacks to reclaim their humanity in places where they have traditionally been dehumanized ("volver a ser donde no habíamos sido").[3] Abuelo Zenón and his teachings clearly embody the fundamental principles that constitute a decolonial response and challenge to the coloniality/modernity matrix of power that, in its most general sense, refers to those social relations of power predicated upon racism, sexism, homophobia, and classism, first introduced by the European conquerors and settlers who arrived in the Americas beginning in the sixteenth century.

Coloniality, with its logic of domination and its rhetoric of modernity (i.e., civilization as opposed to barbarianism, progress as opposed to primitiveness, development as opposed to backwardness) was used to justify Europe's superiority and its "natural right" to "civilize" such "heathens" as the Indians and to enslave African Blacks. Clearly, the coloniality/modernity matrix of power has taken on many iterations through the centuries and continues today to undermine the construction of societies characterized by social justice and equal opportunities. It is precisely this matrix of power that helps contextualize the significance of Abuelo Zenón's ancestral teachings and the social and artistic relevance of Antonio Preciado's poetry.

Undoubtedly, Preciado understands the noxious implications of being categorized as Black by others, the majority of whom are not Black. The racist history that constitutes one of the principal pillars of coloniality as a hegemonic system has constructed dehumanizing images of Afrodescendants, and, thus, Preciado has assumed the responsibility of deconstructing longstanding stereotypes by affirming his own totality as a human being. Not coincidentally, Frantz Fanon has also stated: "Mi piel negra no es depositaria de valores específicos" (My black skin is not a depository of specific values).[4] It is precisely this same essentialism against which Preciado, along with other Esmeraldans, fights to overcome and defeat. According to Papá Roncón, a musician and mentor to Esmeraldan youth: "Son muchos los activistas del pueblo Afroecuatoriano que se resisten a ser identificados solo con la música y el baile de la marimba y con mucha razón insisten en que los negros de Esmeraldas no somos solo música de marimba, somos mucho más que eso. Somos un pueblo culturalmente diferente, con todo lo que eso significa" (There are many activists in the Afro Ecuadorian communities who resist being identified only by music and marimba dances, and they correctly insist that

Esmeraldan Blacks are not only marimba music, we are much more than that. We are a people culturally different along with all that that implies).⁵

Blackness and the Recovery of History

The poet Antonio Preciado has not been immune to this struggle against racism, in general, nor to the racism that he himself has had to endure. When contemplating a pre-Columbian archeological artifact, "la cabeza 'tolita' de un negro indiscutible" (the Tolita skull of a person undeniably Black), Preciado experienced a reencounter with his roots. He writes that:

> desde ese instante ya éramos
> casi toda la tribu
> en pie de guerra contra los historiadores,
> > contra su historia,
> > contra su silencio.⁶

> *from that instant we were now / almost the entire tribe / at war against the historians / against their history / against their silence*

This war against official histories that runs through the national imaginaries of the entire American continent highlights a process of resignification and re-appropriation of the multiple identities of Afro descendants, many of whom have been silenced and forgotten by both external and internal forces. Regarding the role that poetry ought to play in that process, it is instructive to identify representation as a site of struggle. Stuart Hall has pointed out that the practices of representation "always implicate the positions from which we speak or write—the positions of *enunciation*. [That is] who speaks, and the subject who is spoken of, are never identical, never exactly in the same place. Identity is not as transparent or unproblematic as we think. [Thus] we should think ... of identity as a 'production,' which is never complete, always in process, and always constituted within, not outside, representation." As part of the same reflection, Hall also emphasizes, "We all write and speak from a particular place and time, from a history and a culture which is specific. What we say is always 'in context,' *positioned*."⁷

Afro literature as process is rooted in a profoundly conflicted history in which much of aesthetic representation continues to be debated from colonial differences, both from those imposed and those appropriated.⁸ Basically, all thought about Blackness throughout the diaspora inevitably begins with enslavement as the origin of innumerable social and cultural discontinuities. In reference to Ecuador and the Pacific Basin, for example, Abuelo Zenón has pointed out that "no podemos olvidar que el camino que nos trajo a estas tierras no es el camino de andar y apropiar el mundo por nuestra voluntad de colonizar y conquistar. Llegamos aquí siguiendo el camino de la injusticia, de la dispersion obligada que para los pueblos de origen africano significó la esclavitud en esta region y en otras de América" (we cannot forget that the road which brought us to these lands is not the road we chose to travel in order to appropriate the world based on our desire to colonize and conquer. We arrived here following the road of injustice, of forced dispersion which for Afrodescendants meant enslavement in this region and throughout the Americas).[9]

In his poem "Sincretismo," Preciado reveals the extent to which his identity as a person and as a poet comes from his efforts to position himself vis-à-vis his Afrodescendant heritage and his subjectivity as a modern Western man. According to the poem:

Si Exú le corresponde a San Antonio
(o viceversa)
sin ser un arribista
o cualquier otra cosa
. . . .
yo vengo a ser, entonces,
la indiscutible parte que me toca
de una divinidad
Soy mi lado de acá,
mi nombre en carne propia,
una de las dos sombras de hace tiempo
moviéndose en la sombra más sombra
del siglo,
el otro subrepticio del encuentro;
soy pues, ahora con toda claridad
y de tú a tú,
medio tocayo con un ser de luz,
o sea que tengo
parte en algún fulgor del firmamento.[10]

If Exú corresponds to Saint Anthony / (or vice versa), / without being a social climber / or anything else / . . . / I come to be, then, / the indisputable part given to me / by a divinity. / I am my place here, / my name in the flesh, / one of the shadows of long ago / moving about in the darkest shadow of the century, / the surreptitious other of the encounter; / I am, then, in all clarity / and between us, / half namesake with someone aglow / that is I have / a part of me in some brilliant place in the heavens.

Although Preciado highlights a cultural syncretism that could be read as a happy medium between the past and the present, and therefore a successful overcoming of the tensions and conflicts, being Afro and assuming that condition as a process eternally open to representations does not resolve the contradictions of coloniality. Even though the modern Antonio identifies as the child of a double religious heritage expressed in terms of Exú and Saint Anthony, and he considers himself "the indisputable part . . . / of a divinity," the supposed fusion crumbles in "Desolación," another poem from the same poetry collection entitled *Jututo* (1996). What is most interesting here is absence: "mis más altos parientes consanguíneos / . . . / hace mucho no están" (my most sacred blood relatives / have been long gone). Later, the poetic voice confesses his pain and suffering:

> ellos no me hablan,
> tampoco yo los llamo
> y nos vamos sintiendo cada día más lejos
> Es estricta justicia,
> deberían ser dos culpas
> porque son dos olvidos;
> pero tan solo a mí
> me toca el peso enorme de sentir
> todo el remordimiento.[11]

they do not speak to me, / nor do I call on them / and we go about feeling each day more distant / It is clear justice, / both ought to be guilty / because they both forget / but only I / feel the enormous weight of feeling / all the remorse.

Reading these two poems together is essential to grasp fully the tension that permeates Preciado's oeuvre. By identifying with the orisha Exú and his Catholic counterpart Saint Anthony, as expressed in "Sincretismo," the poet appears to assume their roles as intermediaries between the living and the dead.[12] Referring to Exú—one of several names given to Elegba—the Afro-Colombian writer Manuel Zapata Olivella explains: "Es imprescindible su invocación y presencia para que desciendan las demás deidades. Sin su ayuda ningún difunto encuentra el camino que conduce hacia la Morada de los Ancestros" (Invoking him and his presence is essential for other deities to descend. Without his assistance, the dead cannot find the roads that lead to their ancestors).[13]

Thus, despite what first appears to be a harmonious encounter of the past with the present, a split emerges in "Desolación" ("they do not speak to me / nor do I call upon them") that signals the impossibility of achieving a state of existential completeness ("and go about feeling each day more distant"). Because this state of incompleteness evokes a long history of silencing and making invisible the collective memory of Afrodescendants throughout the diaspora, one can understand the remorse and sense of loss that Preciado laments in his poem. Consequently, for the poet, being named Antonio is not incidental. Rather, he embraces the notion of his name as a kind of divine sign that carries with it the responsibility of ensuring the continuity of Afro ancestral traditions, the same ones that, according to Zapata Olivella, serve as testimony to "the persistence of black people themselves."

For any critic inclined to classify this estrangement from one's ancestors as an abstract topic or as some kind of poetic conceit, one need only look to Juan García Salazar's compilation of Esmeraldan *décimas*, *Los guardianes de la tradición* (*The Guardians of Tradition*). In this collection, Juan García situates historically the problematics of ancestral knowledge and memory for the Afro communities of Esmeraldas. According to García Salazar: "*Los guardianes de la tradición* es una obra clave en un momento crítico para las comunidades afro esmeraldeñas; es un momento en que el gran capital agro industrial y minero avanza de manera sostenida en el territorio ancestral de las comunidades del norte de Esmeraldas; es el momento del 'peligro de desarraigo, es el momento de la tentación del embeleco del desarrollo que en su nombre sacrifica todo lo que está a su paso incluyendo culturas e identidades' " (*Los guardianes de la tradición* is a key text at a critical moment for Afro-Esmeraldan communities; it is a moment when powerful sources of capital from agro-industrial and mining interests steadily advance in the ancestral territories of Esmeraldas' northern communities; it is the moment of the 'danger from deterritorialization, it is the moment of the temptation from a phony development strategy which on its behalf sacrifices everything that lies in its wake, including cultures and identities').[14] Later in the same text, García Salazar explains more precisely the significance of cultural deterritorialization: "Las historias de vida de los guardianes de la tradición decimera son sin duda la afirmación de que los pueblos de origen africano que viven en la gran comarca del Pacífico son dueños de una amplia tradición cultural que pocos conocen en su real dimensión y que hoy está en peligro de perderse de manera definitiva, como consecuencia de la pérdida sistemática de sus territorios ancestrales" (The life histories of the guardians of *décima*-tradition undoubtedly affirm that the Afrodescendant communities that live along the Afro-Pacific Basin possess a broad cultural tradition which few people know about or understand fully and which today is in danger of being lost definitively as a result of the systematic dispossession of their ancestral lands).[15]

It is imperative to bear in mind that Juan García's reference to cultural tradition is deeply rooted in those territories where Blacks, through the centuries, have (re)created and (re)signified the meaning of what constitutes being descendants of Africa in the Americas. Thus, territory is history. It is the place where Afrodescendants have reclaimed their humanity despite official policies of negation central to the coloniality/modernity matrix of power. To displace Blacks from their territories where communities have nurtured and reinvented their ancestral roots is tantamount to erasing those histories. In effect, deterritorialization in no small measure is always an attack against cultural identity precisely because ancestral territories are "construcciones filosóficas propias, con profundos contenidos culturales, sociales, políticos, espirituales y religiosos" (original philosophical constructions, with deep cultural, social, political, spiritual, and religious content) and therefore are "vitales para permanecer como pueblo, para crecer como comunidad . . . para recrearnos como familias" (vital to live on as a people, to grow as a community . . . to recreate ourselves as families).[16] Antonio Preciado has indeed embraced poetry as his means of reminding readers that deterritorialization is yet another colonial strategy to dehumanize Black communities and impose one absolute overarching understanding of reality and truth.

Critic Richard L. Jackson comments that the act of reading Afro-Hispanic literature "forces readers to open their minds to multiple interpretations of or perspectives on reality."[17] Moreover, according to Jackson, "Black literature in Latin America is definitely Afro-centered but it is also Latin American. . . . The black experience is one of the most universal experiences the world has ever known 'because it includes all the pain, sorrow, hardships and frustrations that are fundamental to man.'"[18] What Jackson proposes, then, acquires its true meaning when one ponders blackness from coloniality, a system of power that ought to be understood as a body of economic, social, cultural, and political continuities responsible—since the sixteenth century—for institutionalized acts for excluding, making invisible, and silencing. Thus, Preciado's reencounter with his Afro ancestral roots, along with his poetry, points to a reconstruction and resignification of all modern Western history. Preciado's reencounter with his ancestral roots marks the beginning of his transformation as opposed to some final destiny. That is, blackness as history and memory that demands total decolonization must not only be an issue related to Afrodescendants precisely because everyone is a product—although from diverse histories—of the same coloniality of power, knowledge, being, and Nature.

A Black Poet on Coloniality

In Ecuadorian literary circles, Preciado appears in all the principal anthologies and critical histories of national literature. Hernán Rodríguez Castelo, for example, has commented: "Hace ya bastante tiempo que Preciado es la gran voz de la negritud en el Ecuador. Con lenguaje recio y tierno, sustantivo; original y vigoroso en el juego imaginativo; rítmico y musical. Y con una poética enraizada en lo negro—de donde le vienen antiguas sabidurías y resonancias mágicas—, pero abierta, generosamente abierta, a lo contemporáneo" (Preciado has for a long time been the grand voice of blackness in Ecuador. With a tender and robust language, substantive; original and vigorous with the imagination; rhythmic and musical. And with a poetics rooted in blackness—from whence come ancient knowledge and magical resonances—but open, generously open, to what is contemporary).[19] This openness to contemporary matters supposedly marks Preciado's high degree of development and evolution in his poetic repertoire and approach to writing. Marvin Lewis, a critic from the United States, offers the same troubling appraisal: "Preciado begins his poetic trajectory by interpreting his most immediate experiences—the lives of black people in his community in Ecuador. But, as with most concerned artists, Preciado seeks to transcend his immediate local circumstances and enter into the poetic mainstream of his culture."[20]

Of course, one must weigh these two apparently positive critiques in the specific context of diaspora poetry and its intrinsic transcendence within the history of the coloniality of power, recognizing that any reference to a "poetic mainstream" is problematic, especially in countries rooted in the coloniality/modernity matrix of power, like Ecuador. In these contexts, the rhetoric of "national" projects has customarily favored literary whiteness and intellectual imports from the well-known metropolitan centers of power, both of which have been adopted as the ultimate manifestation of progress and modernity. Although a detailed analysis of this colonial legacy and its toxic effects on the ancestral populations throughout the Americas goes beyond the immediate objectives of my study, I want to emphasize the danger of confusing the positive intent of the above-mentioned critics and the colonial ways of reading "mainstream" and "contemporary" as the antithesis of non-Western traditions and knowledges.

According to Manuel Zapata Olivella, "Latin America's contemporary literati, at least the most submissive to intellectual colonialism, declare themselves as European and bourgeois. For them, mestizaje, the recreation of imposed values, oral traditions, and ancestral memory does not exist."[21] Dominican poet Blas Jiménez highlights the origin of the same submissiveness deplored by Zapata: "The alienation that we live as American Blacks is due to the forces of European culture that have tried to erase the images of the African past in order to give us an empty existence in which we cannot recognize our status as Blacks (with the exception of small movements of self-recognition in Haiti, the USA, Cuba, and Brazil), we find ourselves totally dispossessed of all contact with an intellectual or political movement capable of helping us recognize our own identity."[22]

Much has been written recently about the relation between coloniality and modernity, and critics have put forth the argument that colonial structures are the dark side of modernity because they complement one another, often in violent ways.[23] Indeed, since the sixteenth century, all concepts of the "other" (i.e., civilization versus barbarianism, writ large) have served to justify domination in the Americas. Paradoxically, one might ask who has actually been more modern (i.e., civilized, developed), the enslaved or the enslavers? In other words, in the context of the colonial structures of power, Blackness has always been "contemporary" and "mainstream." One should not forget that the systems of enslavement and forced labor (of Blacks and Indians) have constituted the very center of much of the natural resources (and workers) responsible for the industrialization and modernization of the metropolitan economies. Certainly, the hierarchy of the social relations of power between the colonized and the colonizers has consciously blurred and denied what Javier Sanjinés has coined "la contemporaneidad de lo no contemporáneo" (the contemporaneous of the non-contemporary).[24] Whether they be life experiences or knowledge, these colonial differences have been the foundation of subaltern identities, which have always coexisted with their "civilized" counterparts from the North and, thus, need to be identified as constitutive of modernity.

As for Preciado's poetry, there has certainly been a process of maturation and growth over the years, but he should always be understood in linguistic terms and based on his creative talents as a poet. Consequently, Blackness as his formative foundation, which is so evident in his early work, has not been transcended nor has it become "contemporary" through the years—it has always been transcendent and contemporary despite being subjected to countless forms of exclusion in literary and intellectual circles. What really characterizes Preciado's poetry, then, is its transformation from a descriptive perspective of Afrodescendance to one that is more complex. That is, instead of a preponderance of onomatopoeias, made-up words, and other poetic tropes that are typical of writers like the Puerto Rican Palés Matos or Cuba's Nicolás Guillén, as well as Preciado's own

Jolgorio (1961), Preciado's later poetry involves more complex metaphors and a challenging ambiguity of images, which make multiple readings and interpretations of Blackness possible.

Consequently, Blackness is never far from his poetic gaze or imagination. In fact, his best Afro poetry is that which puts aside hackneyed stereotypes and embraces that previously mentioned archaeological artifact, whose mouth "no habla y, sin embargo, / visiblemente a gritos / dice a los cuatro vientos lo que calla" (doesn't speak and, yet, / visibly at the top of his voice / says to the four winds what he keeps silent).[25] Preciado transforms Afrodescendants, then, from objects of an outsider's gaze to subjects who think from their difference and who, in the face of official paradigms of the coloniality of power, reinvent themselves from history's silences. For that reason, one can clearly understand Preciado's uneasiness upon hearing that he is "Ecuador's major poet of Blackness."

Regrettably, for the majority of white *mestizos*, the qualifier of blackness is still exclusionary. Based on concepts inherited from coloniality, blackness exists outside the so-called centers constructed arbitrarily by those who have written our collective official history. With the hope of contributing in some modest way to the decolonization of the epistemic structures of power, I have chosen to insist upon the centrality of Blackness that Preciado highlights masterfully in his later poetry and which many mainstream readers prefer and praise. The paradox, however, is that much of that praise rings hollow because it continues to be nurtured by a colonial aesthetic whose "cosmopolitan" values cannot yet embrace fully Preciado's blackness as transcendent and paramount to everyone's humanity.

NOTES

1. The translation of the epigraph as well as all translations that follow are mine.
2. This interview was conducted by Rebecca Howes in Managua, Nicaragua, at Preciado's residence during his tenure in the country as Ecuador's ambassador. Howes completed her PhD dissertation in Modern Foreign Languages at the University of Tennessee in 2013. Her dissertation was titled "Antonio Preciado and the Afro Presence in Ecuadorian Literature."
3. El Abuelo Zenón is considered in Ecuador and parts of Colombia's Pacific Coast to be one of the principal guardians of collective memory and ancestral knowledge in the Black community. References to Abuelo Zenón throughout this essay are cited from Juan García Salazar and Catherine Walsh, *Pensar sembrando/sembrar pensando con el Abuelo Zenón* (Quito: Universidad Andina Simón Bolívar, Sede Quito, and Abya-Yala, 2017).
4. Frantz Fanon, *Piel negra, mascaras blancas* (La Habana: Instituto del Libro, 1968), 293.

5. For more biographical information about Papá Roncón, whose birth name is Guillermo Ayoví Erazo, see Juan García Salazar, ed., *Papá Roncón (Historia de vida)* (Quito: Universidad Andina Simón Bolívar, 2003). Also noteworthy is that Papá Roncón received the Eugenio Espejo Prize for his cultural contributions in August 2011. This Prize is the most prestigious one awarded by the Ecuadorian government to those Ecuadorians who have made significant contributions in the arts and other areas of cultural production.
6. Antonio Preciado, "poema para ser analizado con carbono 14," in *Antonio Preciado: Antología personal* (Quito: Editorial Casa de la Cultura Ecuatoriana, 2006). The Tolita culture was located at a pre-Columbian site in what is today the Esmeraldas province and dates back to 500–700 AD. According to archaeological research, the Tolita culture is distinguished for being a center of ceramics and metallurgy. Although the origins of the site continue to be an enigma, what is known is that the entire Pacific coast of the Americas absorbed continuous migratory contacts from diverse peoples who arrived from distant lands. The reference to the "Tolita skull of a person undeniably Black" cited above stands as an intriguing expression of that history of cultural encounters and dis-encounters.
7. Stuart Hall, *Cultural Identity and Diaspora: Identity, Community, Culture, Difference*, ed. Jonathan Rutherford (London: Lawrence and Wisehart, 1990), 222.
8. Pertinent to this discussion is Wolfgang Iser's reception theory that can be used to create a reading and interpretation strategy relevant to Afro-diaspora literatures. Bearing in mind Hall's notion that representation is a permanent process, one can understand more fully Iser's call to critics to approach the text as process rather than as a definitive product. Consequently, according to Iser, the objective of the interpreter should be "not to explain a work, but to reveal the conditions that bring about its various possible effects. If he clarifies the *potential* of a text, he will no longer fall into the fatal trap of trying to impose one meaning on his reader, as if that were the right, or at least the best, interpretation." Wolfgang Iser, *The Act of Reading: A Theory of Aesthetic Response* (Baltimore: Johns Hopkins University Press, 1978), 18.
9. García Salazar and Walsh, *Pensar sembrando*, 349.
10. Preciado, *Antonio Preciado*, 197.
11. Ibid., 195–96.
12. According to African traditions, Saint Anthony was adopted as the Catholic version of Elegba and other orishas charged with opening roads and doors to the devotees, children, and their followers.
13. Manuel Zapata Olivella, *Changó el gran putas* (Bogotá: Editorial La Oveja Negra, 2010), 517.
14. Juan García Salazar, *Los guardianes de la tradición (compositores y decimeros)* (Esmeraldas: PRODEPINE, 2003), 8.
15. Ibid., 13.
16. García Salazar and Walsh, *Pensar sembrando*, 53.

17. Richard L. Jackson, *Black Writers and the Hispanic Canon* (New York: Twayne Publishers, 197), 1.
18. Richard L. Jackson, *Black Literature and Humanism in Latin America* (Athens: University of Georgia Press, 1988), xv.
19. Hernán Rodríguez Castelo, ed., *Lírica ecuatoriana contemporánea* (Quito: Círculo de Lectores, 1979), 583.
20. Marvin Lewis, *Afro-Hispanic Poetry (1940–1980): From Slavery to "Negritude" in South American Verse* (Columbia: University of Missouri Press, 1983), 120.
21. Manuel Zapata Olivella, *La rebelión de los genes (El mestizaje americano en la sociedad futura)* (Bogotá: Altamir Ediciones, 1997), 16–17.
22. Blas R. Jiménez, "Negritud y trabajo agrícola," *Hoy*, December 25, 1984, 5.
23. For a more detailed explanation of the coloniality/modernity matrix of power, see Catherine Walsh, "Las geopolíticas de conocimiento and colonialidad del poder: Entrevista a Walter Mignolo," *Polis* 4 (2003), https://journals.openedition.org/polis/7138.
24. See Javier Sanjinés, *Rescoldos del pasado: Conflictos culturales en sociedades postcoloniales* (LaPaz: PIEB, 2009).
25. Preciado, *Antonio Preciado*, 244–47.

WORKS CITED

Fanon, Frantz. *Piel negra, mascaras blancas*. La Habana: Instituto del Libro, 1968.
García Salazar, Juan, ed. *Los guardianes de la tradición (compositores y decimeros)*. Esmeraldas: PRODEPINE, 2003.
———, ed. *Papá Rincón (Historia de vida)*. Quito: Universidad Andina Simón Bolívar, 2003.
García Salazar, Juan, and Catherine Walsh. *Pensar sembrando/sembrar pensando con el Abuelo Zenón*. Quito: Universidad Andina Simón Bolívar, Sede Quito and Abya-Yala, 2017.
Hall, Stuart. *Cultural Identity and Diaspora: Identity, Community, Culture, Difference*. Edited by Jonathan Rutherford. London: Lawrence and Wisehart, 1990.
Iser, Wolfgang. *The Act of Reading: A Theory of Aesthetic Response*. Baltimore: Johns Hopkins University Press, 1978.
Jackson, Richard L. *Black Literature and Humanism in Latin America*. Athens: University of Georgia Press, 1988.
———. *Black Writers and the Hispanic Canon*. New York: Twayne Publishers, 1997.
Jiménez, Blas R. "Negritud y trabajo agrícola." *Hoy*. December 25, 1984.
Lewis, Marvin. *Afro-Hispanic Poetry (1940–1980): From Slavery to "Negritude" in South American Verse*. Columbia: University of Missouri Press, 1983.
Preciado, Antonio. *Antonio Preciado: Antología personal*. Quito: Editorial Casa de la Cultura Ecuatoriana, 2006.
Sanjinés, Javier. *Rescoldos del pasado: Conflictos culturales en sociedades postcoloniales*. LaPaz: PIEB, 2009.

Walsh, Catherine. "Las geopolíticas de conocimiento and colonialidad del poder: Entrevista a Walter Mignolo." *Polis* 4 (2003). https://journals.openedition.org/polis/7138.

Zapata Olivella, Manuel. *Changó el gran putas*. Bogotá: Editorial La Oveja Negra, 2010.

———. *La rebelión de los genes (El mestizaje americano en la sociedad futura)*. Bogotá: Altamir Ediciones, 1997.

Part II: Lettered Outliers

◆ CHAPTER 4

Transatlantic Routing and Rooting in Quince Duncan's *Kimbo*

Gloria Elizabeth Chacón

The enduring historical, political, and cultural exclusion of Afro-Costa Ricans from national belonging ironically fuels fervent counternarratives that resolutely highlight their place in the nation, particularly for members of the third generation who embrace Costa Rica as their own homeland. Quince Duncan emerges as the first Afro-Costa Rican author who sheds light on this exceptional experience. He represents one of the most versatile intellectuals, who, in addition to being a novelist, is also a noted historian and literary critic. Duncan's work engages with the firmly rooted racial and institutional discrimination in Costa Rica, while recording and reconciling the multiple aspects of African, Jamaican, and Costa Rican identity, all of which constitute contemporary Afro-Costa Rican subjectivity. Duncan's oeuvre transforms Limón, a town on the Caribbean coast of the country, from an alienated space within the nation state known for its West Indian or *antillano* population, into a trans-Atlantic place with roots and routes within and beyond Costa Rica, to the Antilles and ultimately to Africa. Nonetheless, while Duncan's opus couples Costa Rica with the Antilles and the African continent, the novel *Kimbo*, as I demonstrate, indigenizes the *antillano* to the nation and cultivates an Afro-Costa Rican subjectivity. Although a discussion of settler colonialism and the question of land and labor is beyond the scope of this paper, it is important to note that, while traditional views, like that of Patrick Wolf, perceive Indigenous peoples as colonized for their lands and blacks for their labor, Robin D. G. Kelley had argued that this erroneously presupposes no Indigenous cultures existed in Africa.[1] While the *antillanos* were brought to Costa Rica to labor and thus may be placed in the position of colonial settlers, particularly as they maintained linguistic and religious ties to the British, Duncan's novel offers us a different way of thinking about Afro-Costa Ricans.

Costa Rica's White Myth

Of all the countries in the isthmus, Costa Rica is distinctive for its desire to appear European, democratic, and middle class.[2] The aim of the political elite is to whiten the nation's body and continue to erase its rich cultural tapestry, much to the detriment of the multiple racial ethnicities that have constituted Costa Rica since its inception. Furthermore, until the 1950s, Costa Rica traditionally defined and imagined its Antillean-descended population as alien to its national discourse. Nevertheless, the African presence in Costa Rica can be traced back to the very beginning of Spanish settlers.[3] As Franklin Perry and Kathleen Sawyers Royal point out, this population grew over the next two hundred and fifty years, as a "sizeable numbers of people of African origin came from the Caribbean islands to settle on the Eastern Atlantic Coast."[4] The 1927 Costa Rican census reported 19,136 black inhabitants, of whom 17,245 were listed as Jamaican foreigners.[5] It was only after the civil war, when a new constitution was drawn in 1949, that Afro-Costa Ricans were given full citizenship.[6] In fact, Afro-Costa Ricans were "restricted to the Atlantic Coast by law until 1949."[7] The forced segregation of the *antillanos* also exacerbated their absence in the national body politic.[8] As Dorothy Mosby holds, Afrodescendant writer Quince Duncan experienced this alienation firsthand, as his original birth certificate stated he was born in Jamaica despite having been born in Costa Rica. After the 1949 amendment to the constitution, however, Duncan's reissued birth certificate accurately reflected his birth in Limón.[9] Nonetheless, his racialized experiences inspired the themes treated in his fiction, essays, and criticism.

This chapter underscores that Duncan's *Kimbo* (1989), his fifth published novel, unravels the official version of Costa Rica as mainly of European descent, bucolic, and peaceful. In this undoing of the national myth, Duncan makes the novel's protagonist and his unjust public lynching and execution an opportunity for the country's collective self-examination on its prejudiced attitudes toward blackness.

In collating and documenting the evidence, the narrative underlines state-sponsored violence, demonstrates the immorality of the Catholic church, and unfolds the racial stratification of society. Former Costa Rican president Oscar Arias received the Nobel Peace Prize for his efforts to broker peace in the Isthmus, internationalizing the nation's status as edenic. *Kimbo*, then, unmasks the national and international myth that Costa Rica represents an exception when compared to other Central American countries. Instead, it shows readers the racism operating in its treatment of its Afrodescendant population. In effect, as Liz Harvey-Kattou demonstrates in her discussion of the novel, Duncan positions the nation at the "scene of the crime."[10]

In addition, Duncan underpins a theory of Afro-realism in the text by weaving the Anancy folktales and by evoking the power of the *samamfo*, or ancestors—a paradigm that further demythologizes Costa Rica's imagined singularity in the region as the little Switzerland of Central America and indigenizes the oral culture and the spiritual traditions that the community has inherited from their African ancestors via the Antilles to Costa Rica's Atlantic Coast and beyond. According to Duncan, "Afro-realism carries within it the world of the ancestors, all of those events that happened a long time ago and continue to affect us. These things that are passed from mouth to mouth and form our tradition give us identity that legitimizes our survival. Through these handed-down stories we know that we form part of a fragmented cultural collective."[11] This intertextuality allows Duncan to establish trans-Atlantic routes and roots from Africa to Central America and the Antilles, as well as between the latter, but also to indigenize these routes and roots to Costa Rica. His Afro-realism theory is grounded in the immediate, geo-political work needed to remedy the social conditions Afro-Costa Ricans face. In this sense, the text is not concerned with tidalectics á la Kamau Brathwaite or my theoretical paradigm of "Indigenous cosmolectics" in the Maya and Zapotec context, which are dominated by a vertical and horizontal conversation between history and the cosmos. In effect, Duncan's paradigm is a politically grounded intervention in the everyday. As he writes, "Afro-realism draws upon the Africanizing subversion of the language, recurring references to previously unknown traditions or at least until now marginal such as Muntu, *samamfo*, Ebe yiye, the vindication of Yemayá, and the incorporation of Atlantic Coast English Creole."[12] Said differently, these spiritual forces are not in the realm of the supernatural or abstract but manifest in the quotidian life in defense of the difficult social reality faced by Afro-Costa Ricans. In the next sections, I turn to the text and the narrative's affirmation of Afro-realism through two of its main constitutive elements: *samamfo* and the Anancy tales.

Kimbo in Brief

Kimbo is the name of the novel and its protagonist. The novel narrativizes Kimbo's biased criminalization by various sectors of society for being Black. Structurally, the text is divided into four parts—each of which is written in multiple voices that condemn or absolve the central character who has been wrongly accused of kidnapping a local businessman. Witnesses to the crime claim to have seen a Black man and "rationally" decided it must have been Kimbo—even though he was not near the site of the crime. A key eyewitness comes forward and swears under oath that he saw Kimbo carry out the abduction after being paid to lie. Considering this testimony, a colonel subjects Kimbo to physical and psychological torture to extract a confession. The different voices in the text represent community members, police, religious figures, friends, and present and past lovers. Meanwhile, readers learn that the actual kidnappers have a political affiliation with an extremist group of the political right. A member of this group (presumably Black) feels guilty for Kimbo's imprisonment and suggests to his accomplices a foolproof plan to extricate themselves from any suspicion while also freeing Kimbo. This is an important detail, as it points to an understanding of racism beyond left or right political alignments. The group's scheme is to demand the government release Kimbo in another country in exchange for the kidnapped businessman. In this manner, the perpetrators reason, Kimbo will be set free, and their request will strengthen his involvement in the kidnapping. The government's acceptance of the terms resonates with the older tendency to see West Indians as belonging to somewhere else and not to Costa Rica. Though the exigencies are met—the businessman is freed unscathed and Kimbo is released to another country—the narrative reaches its denouement with the exile's return to Costa Rica. Neither the kidnappers nor the rest of civil society could have foreseen Kimbo's insistence on returning to the country to clear his name. Kimbo's return symbolizes how the Afro-Costa Rican community—despite how the government may easily see them as belonging somewhere else—is indeed already home. The story also suggests that Kimbo's insistence on clearing his name is related to the encouragement of the ancestors, particularly Miss Robinson and his mother. Moreover, the story proposes that these ancestors are in Costa Rica and not in Jamaica or Africa. As I have already pointed out, these ancestors are then given roots in Central America.

Throughout the narrative, the reader never hears Kimbo's voice. Dramatically, just as he is about to speak in front of the press, the Colonel (who had previously tortured him) fears that Kimbo has returned for retribution and fires a fatal shot. The people who witness the Colonel fire at Kimbo are in denial, while the official story is that the shot came from the crowd outside and that its point of origin is impossible to determine. This is another significant detail in the novel because it speaks to a collective desire to believe in Costa Rica as exceptional in the region. As a twist to the end of the novel, a letter that Kimbo writes describing the entire experience, and especially his torture, surfaces posthumously. Seventy copies of the document are circulated around the country. The cab driver who had picked up Kimbo during the kidnapping—and who was his only alibi—was not initially found, but he finally appears and authenticates Kimbo's whereabouts at the time of the crime. The document proves his innocence posthumously. Importantly, the unexpected document serves as a source of pride for the community, because it represents the dignity and upright moral upbringing of their "native son." In turn, Kimbo's expiation is an allegory of freedom for other marginalized Afro-Costa Rican subjects in the tradition of martyrdom, one that sets out to challenge the perception of blackness as criminal. In doing so, Duncan deconstructs the idyllic perception of Costa Rica as democratic and peaceful before carefully bringing to bear the role of the *samamfo* and oral folktales and their pivotal role in Afro-Costa Rican survival.

Deconstructing "La pequeña Suiza"

The unveiling of state-sponsored violence against black bodies remains an important lodestar of the novel. Few hear of the human rights abuses in Costa Rica, and most Costa Ricans revel in the political fantasy that, unlike the rest of the isthmus, their government does not reproduce state violence. While readers do not get a strong sense of Kimbo's own purchase of the national exception, I would argue that any modicum of an illusion he may hold quickly and utterly disintegrates during his interrogation. The voice of the Colonel who tortures and ultimately murders Kimbo represents the wielding of power by the state and political elites who want to uphold a white national ideal. His hatred against Kimbo is part of the systemic alienation that Afrodescendant citizens in Costa Ricans face. Readers hear the state's systematized racism of Afrodescendants ventriloquized by the Colonel:

> Era bien sencillo lo que me dijeron que averiguara y él lo único que tenía que hacer es decírmelo . . . pero el tipo estaba hecho un pedante. Eso sí que no lo perdono, y mucho menos en un condenado negro. Porque es bien negro el mulo este. Por eso me enojé con él y lo tuve despierto treinta horas. Y cada vez que se iba quedando dormido lo chuzaba. Así lo tuve y paré porque se me quedó en blanco en

una de tantas. Yo creí que estaba muriendo y me asusté porque tampoco tenia que matarlo. En el país no hay torturas ni esas cosas y si se me hubiera quedado iba a ser torta.[13]

It was very simple what they asked me to find out and he just had to tell me . . . but the guy was pretentious. That I do not forgive, much less coming from someone black. Because that mule is so black. That's why I got mad at him and kept him awake for thirty hours. And every time he had fallen asleep, I would poke him. I had to keep at it, but I stopped because he fainted. I thought he was dying, and I got scared because I didn't have to kill him either. In the country there are no tortures or such things and if he had not revived, I would be toast.

The absurdity of state repression is highlighted through the intimate thoughts of the Colonel, where blackness remains incompatible with human rights, thus betraying the fantasy of Costa Rica as a bastion of peace that symbolically rejects violence by its disarticulation of a national army. This is a moment of dissonance for the reader as she is challenged to stop or reconsider the impervious myth that Costa Rica is a site of idyllic democracy. The physical torture of the black body in this scene echoes the injurious physical and emotional treatment of slaves on plantations in other parts of the Americas.[14] This scene is also reminiscent of other violent episodes, such as Juan Francisco Manzano's *Autobiografía de un esclavo* (*Aubiography of a Slave*, 1835), in which he shares how he was once accused of stealing a chicken and beaten by the master to extract the truth of his crime. In both cases, a white subject in the position of master believes truth can only be extracted out of the black body by brute force, and Duncan implicitly draws on these continental connections.

Duncan's deft use of irony in the text transforms such lofty ideals as "liberty" and "justice" into their opposite by exposing what is concealed under their veneer. The highly decorated and overzealous Colonel understands his mission's aims and plays his role with a perfect pitch: "Defendemos esta vaina contra los extremistas: contra derechas y contra izquierdas. Nosotros garantizamos, nosotros sí (ninguno de estos perros hacen nada por el país), excepto, claro poner la nalga para que la gente pueda seguir siendo libre" (We defend this place against extremists: against right and against left. We guarantee [democracy], yes, us [none of these dogs do anything for the country], except, of course, get screwed so that people can remain free).[15] Through the Colonel's discourse, Duncan demonstrates how rape and murder are rationalized and employed to uphold democracy in the nation.

In the previous excerpt, the Colonel states that the police would do everything to uphold democracy except get "fucked." This passage is contrasted with the threat of rape on the black body to re-establish social order. The Colonel reasons:

> Ahora me lo traen de nuevo. Esta vez lo voy a agarrar por el lado moral y lo vamos a hacer molida. Allá él. Para que no digan, desde temprano le voy a advertir que si no canta nos vamos a pasear en su mujer. La de la finca. Nos la vamos a comer allí mismo, enfrente del carajo, todos los seis, uno por uno. Y va a tener que cantar o inventar un cuento si es que la muchacha le importa. Son cosas del oficio. Es un trabajo feo, lo acepto, pero no me da pena decir que alguien tiene que hacer la parte fea.[16]

> *Now they bring him back to me. This time I will appeal to his moral side and we will grind him. It will be up to him. So that no one can criticize, early on I will announce to him that if he does not sing, we are going to walk all over his wife. The one from the farm. We are going to eat her right then and there, and fuck her, all six of us, one by one. He's going to have to sing or invent a story if he cares for the girl. These are things of the trade. It's an ugly job, I accept it, but I'm not sorry to say that someone has to do the ugly part.*

Physical violence and rape subtend white nationalist masculinity in the Americas, with the ultimate goal of the degradation of the black body—practices that inevitably resonate with Hartman's analysis of "scenes of subjection" in the practice of the trans-Atlantic slave trade and the establishment of plantation, where the "erotics of terror" contain the sexual violence of blacks.

Samamfo, Catholicism, and the Ancestors

Like the institution of democracy, the all-mighty Catholic Church is another locus of power that Duncan indicts for its racial discrimination. Counterposed in the text to *samamfo*, or the power of the ancestors, the church's representative serves as another primary prosecution witness of the kidnapping, who unrepentantly claims to have indeed seen Kimbo perpetuate the crime. While the representative of God falsely accuses Kimbo, the text charges him with a greater crime: racism. It is not until after the priest hears a poor peasant confess that he did not witness Kimbo partake in the kidnapping but was paid to lie that the priest begins to doubt himself. This situation alerts the reader that the individual who is most guilty of stereotyping blacks is the priest, which illustrates the hypocrisy in the phrase, "all god's children are equal." Duncan here deconstructs the sanctity of the cloth and simultaneously mocks the stereotype of people of color as an undifferentiated mass stripped of their individuality. This priest is not redeemed in the narrative. He never seizes the opportunity to corroborate Kimbo's testimony because all blacks look alike to him, and he staunchly insists that he saw Kimbo. The state's political, judicial, and religious institutions are thus equally responsible for sustaining and perpetuating racial prejudice embedded in Costa Rican society.

The everyday coexistence of the ancestors counters the Catholic trope throughout the narrative and serves as the second most important mechanism to disrupt yet another trait of cultural normativity. Duncan defines *samamfo* as "la memoria colectiva de la raza-cultura que pasa de generación a generación y que se actualiza en los ritos religioso-seculares del pueblo, en sus luchas, en sus experiencias. Los ancestros nunca han abandonado a sus herederos" (the collective memory of race-culture that passes from generation to generation and that is updated in the religious-secular rites of the people, in their struggles, in their experiences. The ancestors have never abandoned their heirs).[17] In a 1998 interview, Duncan states, "everything that comes out is going in the direction of a search for this *Samamfo*."[18] A collective belief in Samamfo affirms and inscribes an African Indigeneity onto Costa Rica's national body. It is in this manner that Kimbo, as stated by one of the voices of a Miss Robinson who taught him about the oral tradition, embodies the *samamfo*: "cuando nuestra hermana la madre del muchacho dijo que ese era su hijo amado, yo pienso que él es nuestro hijo amado, yo pienso que él es hijo de Samamfo, y que la mejor manera de definirlo es decir que él es nuestro hijo amado" (When our sister, the boy's *mother* said that this was her beloved son, I think that he is our beloved son, I think that he is *samamfo's* son, and that the best way to define him is to say that he is our beloved son).[19] The ancestors claim Kimbo; he belongs the collectivity.

The active role of the ancestors in Kimbo's life defies the expectations that he would be content in exile without going back to rectify the injustice. The community's kin ties Kimbo to his mother, and the governing of *samamfo* allows people to realize that his dead mother influenced his decision to return to Costa Rica and to claim his innocence and set the record straight. The narrative voices of the community never falter in their belief of his innocence. They understand the Manichean maneuvers directed against blacks in Costa Rican society, as one of the community voices reaffirms: "Nosotros en el pueblo no creemos que fue él.

Nunca lo vimos andando de gresca en gresca. Ese muchacho que ha viajado alrededor del mundo y donde quiera que va dice que es de aquí. Y uno se pregunta, Qué tiene de especial este sitio? Pero nosotros los viejos mientras quede un solo de nosotros vivos, vamos a ser eso para él: sus raíces. Y es que ese muchacho está ya en la cumbre y eso les molesta" (Those of us in the town, we do not believe it was him. We never saw him going from problem to problem. That boy who has traveled around the world and wherever he goes he says he is from here. And one wonders, what is special about this site? But we, the elders, while only one of us remains alive, we will be that for him: his roots. That boy is already at the top and that bothers them).[20] That voice embodies the generational differences in their relationship to Costa Rica. The elders, the *samamfo*, root Kimbo to the site. A collective belief in *samamfo* affirms and inscribes color onto the national body.

The Limonese community's sense of unity is evident throughout the novel. In fact, when Kimbo returns to Costa Rica, everyone from the community seems to be waiting at the airport, including his mother and Miss Robinson, who speak in the narrative as if they were indeed alive (as I mentioned before the ancestors are present in everyday reality). Miss Robinson remembers him as her own progeny and comments: "Era de la misma generación y del mismo tiempo que la madre. Lo había conocido desde niño, y yo ayudé a criarlo. Nuestros hijos entonces eran hijos de la comunidad. Diga pues nuestro hijo. Siempre he sabido y he dicho que estaban mintiendo" (I was from the same generation and the same time as the mother. I had known him since he was a child, and I helped raise him. Our children were then children of the community. Our child, then. I've always known and said they were lying).[21] These spirits assist Kimbo and witness his defense. The role of the ancestors in the townspeople's daily practices becomes a source of cultural strength. This narrative thread focused on the community reveals the diaspora's connection to African culture and identity that asserts itself above the official narrative. These ancestors are indigenized, as they have passed away in Costa Rica. It is Miss Robinson and his mother who represent the *samamfo* and guide him. Moreover, the Anancy tales instruct Kimbo on how to deal with a more powerful adversary.

Anancy as Oral Tradition

In addition to the *samamfo*, Duncan draws parallels between Kimbo's story and the Anancy folktales to disrupt the cultural homogeneity of Costa Rica and to indigenize them to Limón. The Anancy stories are attributed to the oral tradition and are deployed by Miss Robinson to teach Kimbo about brother tiger and brother spider. The weaving of the Anancy folktales in the novel forge cultural ties to Africa, and these are discursively ascribed over Costa Rica's imaginary body. Kimbo's situation is analogous to Anancy the spider, who is wronged by envy. As Ramsey points out with reference to *Kimbo*, "the folk hero Anancy is one of the cultural survivals of the infamous middle passage from west Africa to the Caribbean, Anancy plays a pivotal role in the pantheon of many west African peoples, notably the Akan, the group having historical and cultural precedence in the early slave settlement of Jamaica."[22] These tales, as Ramsey states, serve as the "undeniable links of the Afro-Costa Ricans West Indian descent to the Caribbean. For in the case of Costa Rica, Anancy has been doubly transplanted, first from Africa to the islands of the Caribbean and then from these islands by the people who went to build the railroad in Costa Rica."[23] Through this double transplantation, the Anancy stories serve the Limonese community as tools for understanding their survival. Seen in this light, *Kimbo* can be understood as a counternarrative to the Europeanized and Catholic hegemony in Costa Rica, one that rests on the affirmation of a belief system that takes us back to Africa and the Antilles, with new roots in Costa Rica. The folktales are not simply part of the past but are relevant in the present, as they are adapted to Limón and become a pedagogical tool about power and survival.

Both *Kimbo* and the Anancy tales remind their readers (or listeners) that, when an individual faces a more powerful nemesis, they must use their wits and cunning to defeat them. Ramsey pointedly claims: "The folktales are interlocked into the structure of the work either as a metaphor for the survival of the Afro-Costa Rican and by extension of all human beings, or to analogize some aspect of the work itself. Anancy, therefore, represents a very complex metaphor and archetype for the post-colonial Afro-Caribbean experience as it elucidates the plight of Kimbo, a victimized Afro-Costa Rican in a dominant Latino society."[24] Anancy must learn to rely on her patience and smarts to outdo the tiger, who has not worked hard for the attributes he is admired for in the jungle. Indeed, Kimbo's own silence parallels Anancy the spider's waiting to take on Brother Tiger, a more powerful creature. Kimbo mimics Anancy and outsmarts those who condemned him: "Kimbo. Kimbo el silencioso. Kimbo con los kilómetros de historia cargando sobre él como leyenda" (Kimbo. Kimbo the silent one. Kimbo with kilometers of history weight on him like a legend).[25] Kimbo represents the entire Limonse community, who has been found guilty of a crime it did not perpetrate and whose name will be cleared with Kimbo's foresight to send and write a document proving his innocence.

Connecting Diasporas

The novel's insistence on a unique set of literary, cultural, and spiritual connections rests in its invocation of other Afrodescendant writers in Latin America. Duncan recreates this literary, cultural, and spiritual link through textual excerpts from the Cuban Carmen Naranjo, the Colombian Manuel Zapata Olivella, and the Panamanian Gerardo Maloney, as well as others who write about the African experience in the Americas. Reproduced as epigraphs between chapters, these excerpts accentuate Afro-centric literary routes and roots, suggesting that the criminalization of blackness and the common struggle to undo this unfair, historical scapegoating is a shared Afro-Hispanic experience in the Americas. Kimbo's very name represents a signifier of Jamaican vernacular expression, connecting the Antilles to Central America. Defined by Duncan as a word that "deriva de la expression *kimbo off on me.* Expresión antillana que describe una situación de desafío, cabeza levantada, manos a la cintura" (derives from the expression *kimbo off on me* . . . an Antillean expression that describes a situation of defiance, head high, hands on waist).[26] While Kimbo remains silent in the narrative, the document penned and circulated before he arrives to the airport contests and proves wrong all of the eyewitness testimonies against him and represents his last defiant move. As a hero, he knows he will be murdered, but, like the spider Anancy, he outwits his opponent in the conclusion of the narrative.

The murder of Kimbo, the novel's protagonist, can be interpreted as pessimistic. His innocence, unjust treatment, and murder do not make for a traditional closure. However, in order to fully understand the redeeming aspect of this otherwise unhappy ending, we must understand how *samamfo* and the Anancy folktales structure and affect the text. The protagonist's crucifixion and eventual murder embody a long history of scapegoating the Afrodescendant population in the Americas; however, in the end, the power of the ancestors and the wisdom of the Anancy folktales redeem Kimbo, and by extension all of the Limonese community, in the face of an unjust system. In Duncan's narrative, Afro-Costa Rican expression points to a different spiritual and oral literary tradition for the nation. As McKinney explains regarding Eulalia Bernard, an Afro-Costa Rican author of Duncan's generation, Bernard "demystifies a favorite national fiction: despite its first-world trappings and rhetoric of development, Costa Rica is not Switzerland. Its problems and possibilities, contradictions, and aspirations, languages and peoples are those of a developing country with multicultural resources not yet fully brought to national consciousness."[27] This observation can also be made with respect to the ideological work of Duncan's text.

In Closing

Afro-Costa Rican literature has slowly gained some national and international visibility. As Quince Duncan discloses in a 1998 interview: "I feel now that the candle is lit and the torches will be carried on into the next generation."[28] The Afro-Costa Rican literary heritage has been carefully woven parallel to Anancy's oral tradition. Duncan and other writers, like Delia McDonald and Shirley Campbell, who have written about the "plight of the Negro" in Costa Rica, have become foundational in their contributions to Latin American literature.[29] This literary canon unmasks Costa Rica's myth as homogenous, Catholic, and democratic. It forces the nation to face its institutional violence against its Afrodescendant population and to move beyond the myth of exception, while also indigenizing them to the nation. It is no longer about simply being *antillanos* in Costa Rica but about being Afro-Costa Ricans. Duncan accomplishes this re-semantization by demonstrating the rich cultural relevance of the oral storytelling tradition, incorporating the antihero of Anancy, establishing the permanence of African spirituality embodied by *samamfo* in Limón that harks back to the Middle Passage and the transplantation of black bodies from Africa to the Antilles, and, ultimately, indigenizing them to Central America. *Kimbo* embodies "an African-centered literary criticism [because it] embraces a communal doctrine that has its roots in the interconnectedness and well-being of all blacks in Africa and the diaspora."[30] Blackness in Costa Rica should not be seen as the opposite of Indigeneity but its counterpart.

NOTES

1. Robin D. G. Kelley, "The Rest of Us: Rethinking Settler and Native," *American Quarterly* 69, no. 2 (2017): 3.
2. Kitzie McKinney, "Costa Rica's Black Body: The Politics of Difference in Eulalia Bernard's Poetry," *Afro-Hispanic Review* 15, no. 2 (1996): 11.
3. Franklin Perry and Kathleen Sawyers Royal, "Costa Rica," in *No Longer Invisible: Afro–Latin Americans Today* (London: Minority Rights Group, 1995), 215.
4. Ibid., 215.
5. McKinney, "Costa Rica's Black Body," 11.
6. Perry and Royal, "Costa Rica," 218.
7. McKinney, "Costa Rica's Black Body," 11.
8. I use the term *antillano* because it is the more common use in Spanish. Ian Smart uses West Indian to describe the community that migrated from the lesser Antilles to Central

America in the nineteenth century to work in the Canal and banana plantations, but, in Spanish, West Indian is not in common usage. See Ian Smart, *Central American Writers of West Indian Origin* (Washington, DC: Three Continents Press: 1984). However, it is important to note that people from the Antilles may not have seen themselves as part of the nation until the third generation. See Dorothy E. Mosby, *Quince Duncan: Writing Afro-Costa Rican and Caribbean Identity* (Tuscaloosa: University of Alabama, Press, 2014), 3. In terms of debates around Indigeneity and the Caribbean, Shona N. Jackson takes a different stance. She examines how enslaved Africans and indentured Indians in Guyana became Creoles whose descendants fashioned themselves as Indigenous, thus displacing Indigenous peoples through their adopted colonial outlooks and procedures. See Shona N. Jackson, *Creole Indigeneity: Between Myth and Nation in the Caribbean* (Minneapolis: University of Minnesota Press, 2012).

9. Mosby, *Quince Duncan*, 5–6.
10. Liz Harvey-Kattou, "Collective Culpability in Costa Rica: The Case of Quince Duncan's *Kimbo*," in *Crime Scenes: Latin American Crime Fiction From the 1960s to the 2010s*, ed. Charlotte Lange and Ailsa Peate (Oxford: Peter Lang, 2019), 90.
11. Quoted in Mosby, *Quince Duncan*, 13.
12. Ibid., 7.
13. Quince Duncan, *Kimbo* (San José: Editorial Costa Rica, 1989), 27–28. All translations are mine.
14. See Saidiya V. Hartman, *Scenes of Subjection: Terror, Slavery, and Self-making in Nineteenth Century America* (Oxford: Oxford University Press, 1997).
15. Duncan, *Kimbo*, 29–30.
16. Ibid., 30.
17. Ibid., 153.
18. Tomás Wayne Edison, "An Interview with Afro-Costa Rican Writer Quince Duncan," *Afro-Hispanic Review* 18, no. 1 (Spring 1999): 30.
19. Duncan, *Kimbo*, 122.
20. Ibid., 49.
21. Ibid., 99.
22. Paulette Ramsay, "Representations of Anancy in Selected Works of the Afro-Costa Rican Writer Quince Duncan," *Afro-Hispanic Review* 18, no. 2 (1999): 32.
23. Ibid., 3.
24. Ibid., 35–36.
25. Duncan, *Kimbo*, 13.
26. Ibid., 153.
27. McKinney, "Costa Rica's Black Body," 18.
28. Edison, "Interview," 31.
29. Ibid., 32.
30. Dellita Martin-Ogunsola, *The Eve/Hagar Paradigm in the Fiction of Quince Duncan* (Minneapolis: University of Missouri Press, 2004), 167.

WORKS CITED

Duncan, Quince. *Kimbo*. San José: Editorial Costa Rica, 1989.
———. "Visión panorámica de la narrative costarricense." *Revista Iberoamericana* 53, no. 139 (1987): 79–94.
Edison, Tomás Wayne. "An Interview with Afro-Costa Rican Writer Quince Duncan." *Afro-Hispanic Review* 18, no. 1 (1999): 29–33.
Hartman, Saidiya V. *Scenes of Subjection: Terror, Slavery, and Self-making in Nineteenth Century America*. Oxford: Oxford University Press, 1997.
Harvey-Kattou, Liz. "Collective Culpability in Costa Rica: The Case of Quince Duncan's *Kimbo*." In *Crime Scenes: Latin American Crime Fiction From the 1960s to the 2010s*, edited by Charlotte Lange and Ailsa Peate, 89–109. Oxford: Peter Lang, 2019.
Jackson, Shona N. *Creole Indigeneity: Between Myth and Nation in the Caribbean*. Minneapolis: University of Minnesota Press, 2012.
Kelley, Robin D. G. "The Rest of Us: Rethinking Settler and Native." *American Quarterly* 69, no. 2 (2017): 267–276.
Martin-Ogunsola, Dellita. *The Eve/Hagar Paradigm in the Fiction of Quince Duncan*. Minneapolis: University of Missouri Press, 2004.
McKinney, Kitzie. "Costa Rica's Black Body: The Politics of Difference in Eulalia Bernard's Poetry." *Afro-Hispanic Review* 15, no. 2 (1996): 11–20.
Mosby, Dorothy E. *Quince Duncan: Writing Afro-Costa Rican and Caribbean Identity*. Tuscaloosa: University of Alabama, Press, 2014.
Perry, Franklin, and Kathleen Sawyers Royal. "Costa Rica." In *No Longer Invisible: Afro-Latin Americans Today*, 215–24. London: Minority Rights Group, 1995.
Ramsay, Paulette. "Representations of Anancy in Selected Works of the Afro-Costa Rican Writer Quince Duncan." *Afro-Hispanic Review* 18, no. 2 (1999): 32–35.
Smart, Ian. *Central American Writers of West Indian Origin*. Washington, DC: Three Continents Press: 1984.

◆ CHAPTER 5

The Palimpsestic Afro-Panamanian Woman in Melanie Taylor Herrera's *Camino a Mariato*

Ángela Castro

> I am an urban woman, daughter of the achievements of twentieth-century feminism, black and aware of it, but I do not restrict my writing to black themes or themes of social criticism or even exclusively Panamanian topics.
> —MELANIE TAYLOR HERRERA, "EXPANDING DEFINITIONS"

In 2009, Melanie Taylor Herrera wrote *Camino a Mariato*, in which she narrates the histories and experiences of Panamanian women. That same year, the book received the Central American Rafaela Contreras prize for women writing short fiction. Literary critic Sonja Stephenson Watson has argued that this novel surpasses the notion of "race" and focuses instead on the idea of "becoming," as the female protagonists struggle with "contemporary themes that plague the twenty-first century: identity, suicide, silence, and solitude."[1] Departing from this assertion, I propose that, despite Taylor Herrera's depiction of a *palimpsestic* Afro-Panamanian woman who is not defined only by race, her female protagonists cannot escape being demarcated by it. In the first part of this essay, I work with Watson's argument that the identities of Taylor Herrera's female protagonists resist racial interrogation. In the second part of the essay, I describe how this involuted, palimpsestic portrayal of Panamanian women establishes the impossibilities of writing beyond blackness and race in *Camino a Mariato*. I use the notion of the palimpsest as described by Sara Dillon in *The Palimpsest: Literature, Criticism, Theory*; she describes the palimpsest as an involuted phenomenon involving otherwise unrelated texts that are entangled and interwoven, interrupting and inhabiting each other. I argue that this palimpsestic description becomes a metaphor of identity in *Camino a Mariato* not only to represent a complex definition of the Afro-Caribbean woman but also to examine how these women inhabit each other, thus illustrating how race is constructed and how convoluted the notion of race was in Panama in the twentieth century. I also examine Taylor Herrera's work using Mercy Ezeala and Almantas Samalavičius's idea of the palimpsest in postcolonial African novels. According to Ezeala and Samalavičius, the palimpsest becomes a self-reflective "metaphor for understanding the effects of colonialism, the complicities of Africa in the colonial enterprise and the need to forge a future that transcends the colonial experiences," as well as the remembrances and assessments of the past.[2] What they imply is that the palimpsest helps us to understand the present in the marks of the past, providing an understanding of our current history in past events.

In "La identidad afropanameña," Watson argues that Panama has had interethnic tensions since 1789. In colonial times, slaves and free slaves made up to 63 percent of the population of Panama, and this was reinforced by the arrival of Afro-Antilleans during the construction of the Panama Canal (1904–1914). Writers such as José Dolores Urriola (1834–1883), Gaspar Octavio Hernández (1893-1918), Carlos "Cubena" Guillermo Wilson (1941), and Melva Lowe de Goodin (1945) have portrayed these tensions. In *De/From Barbados a/to Panama* (1999), for example, Lowe de Goodin reclaims Afro-Antillean identity and memory. However, there is a new approach to race that deals with similar tensions, seen not only in Taylor Herrera's writing but also in the works of other contemporary female writers, such as Lucy Cristina Chau, Isabel Herrera de Taylor, and the diasporic Afro-Panamanian writers Veronica Chambers and Yvette Modestin. Afro-Panamanians intend to write to surpass race, and the Afro-diasporic writers continue to expose the Afrodescendant experience in their work. Watson argues in *The Politics of Race in Panama* that Taylor Herrera portrays women who are marginalized and oppressed, emphasizing how the writer wants to build a universe where women can be perceived only through their social and internal struggles. Although surpassing race is what Taylor Herrera intends to do, I demonstrate that this is not what *Camino a Mariato* ultimately does. Even though most of Taylor Herrera's stories omit explicit racial description, the women in her stories are constructed as palimpsests in which the racial component cannot be avoided. These stories are connected through objects and a historical shared identity. According to Sarah Dillon, the use of objects is central to the involuted process of the palimpsest: "our deepest thoughts and feelings pass to us through perplexed combination of *concrete* objects ... in compound experiences incapable of being disentangled."[3] These inextricably entangled experiences are featured in Taylor Herrera's stories; they are connected, one to another, and should be read as a response to Panama's colonial past. At the same time, the shared historical identity is experienced and seen in every female's story in *Camino a Mariato*, each of which is associated with the other short stories as texts. The women inhabit one another, until some of them cannot resist being characterized by their racial identities. This connectivity lets us perceive the complexity of the Panamanian black woman and her colonial experience.

Palimpsestic Involutedness: Concrete Objects in *Camino a Mariato*

Taylor Herrera has written *Tiempos acuáticos* (2000), *Amables predicciones* (2005), *Microcosmos* (2008), *Camino a Mariato* (2009), and *Atrapasueños* (2010), but it is in *Camino a Mariato* that she offers the deceptive illusion of an unknown location and unspecified racial identity. Nevertheless, in most of the short stories, the author offers some hints that let us trace these spaces and identities. For instance, we can find landmarks of Panama, such as Mariato, Atalaya, Pacora, Natá, and the island of Taboga, to mention a few. What interests me in her writing is how her stories build the identities of these female characters, entwining them with space, location, and objects that, ultimately, as I will explain later, exhibit their racial identity. As Watson suggests, these women are portrayed from a space of loneliness, abandonment, and oppression. Her protagonists are women who work in bars and as prostitutes. In one case, a woman is a thief, in another a witch; one has a rare condition where she was born already old, and another endlessly seeks for a maternal figure. Apparently, these characters share a social condition, but their description slowly builds a palimpsest that not only depicts their struggles but also recreates them in relationship with objects. This palimpsestic construction helps us to interpret Taylor Herrera's writing and to visualize her characters through several social and physical lenses of knowledge where their textuality builds new stories that are intertwined with the use of objects.

To understand the use of objects in Taylor Herrera's writing, we have to see the strategy in relationship with the palimpsest as an involuted phenomenon. If we follow Dillon's argument on the involutedness of the palimpsest and its sense of a "perplexed combination of *concrete* objects ... in compound experiences incapable of being disentangled," the same process is visible in every single story by Taylor Herrera. For instance, in her opening short story, "Dance with Death," the writer establishes her aesthetics, tone and, essentially, articulates her vision of "surpassing of race." Taylor Herrera tells the story of two men who enter a bar twice in one night, their brief interaction with two nameless women (a redhead and a blonde), and the aftermath of the encounter. Taylor Herrera writes that the first time the men leave the bar, they drive their dark blue 4x4 truck "with tinted windows and stolen plates ... to a high-rise building called Roca Vieja" to check on a man who arrives home in his red Audi A4.[4] They look at him from a distance and perceive how the man smokes a cigarette before he enters his building. The second time the men enter the bar, they decide to dance cheek to cheek with the two women. The redhead feels a tickling in her stomach while dancing with one of them. After the spontaneous dance, the two men leave the bar again, and Taylor Herrera writes how, at 11:15 pm the following day, the man in the red Audi A4 is shot. After describing the encounter, the writer enters the women's intimate spaces to narrate their personal lives by portraying their interactions with the objects that delineate their daily ways of living. The reader can only see the two women surrounded by objects. What we read is how, at 11:30 pm on the same night, the redhead leaves the fast-food restaurant where she works as a clerk, puts on her high heels, and takes a sip of her coffee before catching the bus home. With coffee in hand, she remembers the night before. The blonde woman, on the other hand, at 11: 45pm, "Wakes up to the sound of her youngest son, just six months old, screaming and crying. With sleep nagging her and an unbearable heat that the fan can't disperse, she turns on the television. As she's fixing a bottle, she hears the midnight news announce that assassins have just killed an important businessman in his car outside the Roca Vieja building."[5] The narrative focuses on objects (e.g., a cup of coffee, high heels, a bottle) to facilitate our appreciation of the identities of these women, and these objects allow us to experience aspects of their lives that are not portrayed or understood in the urban space.

While the story narrates the experiences of these nameless women, the perplexed objects move by themselves. Following Dillon and her reference to a "perplexed combination of concrete objects," as well as to those experiences that are incapable of being disentangled, we can say that Taylor Herrera depicts these women as connected to objects that help them express their nostalgia and sense of abandonment in a society in which they are liminal. Thus, the following stories revolve around the lives of women who try to survive and who are abused by people in power. Many of these women have double identities, but, once again, we can read them through the objects they possess, use, and transform. Objects allow the writer to expose their solitary subjectivities and bodies, their dreams, and their parallel lives. The stories and lives of these women not only display their inner struggles but also a palimpsest construction that is intersected by an object. In Taylor Herrera's anthology, these "concrete objects" act as a metaphor that turns the gaze away from the racial theme; however, the writer obfuscates her own writing by using objects to expose her characters bodies and explore their deepest thoughts and feelings. To explore this sense of involutedness and its implied succession of deep thoughts and feelings through concrete objects, I will analyze Taylor Herrera's third story "Piel." In "Piel," or "Skin," a woman described as M.S or Laos is a fugitive from justice, and she remembers the events that made her a fugitive and put her into forced confinement. The story is told through her memories and how she relates to words and objects. At the beginning of the story, Laos says, "With the persistence with which the waves break on the rocks, every day, day after day, I narrate these memories. I take them as rare objects from an archaeological site and say this is the end, or look here is a piece that must belong to the knot . . . The end was an event that transcended the public thanks to a note."[6] The story unfolds as a palimpsest and connects Laos's memories with the present, where she reveals how she changed her identity to participate in an online fraud proposed by a coworker, Mr. Thiers. She describes how, at night, she looks at her tattoos and bodily traces to fall asleep: a rose on her ankles and a word on one of her buttocks. Laos compares these physical marks with her everyday metaphorical tattoos: her fake glasses, her serene face, her dresses that make her look like a respectable lady, and her tied back hair.[7] (18). This narration resonates with Stephenson Watson's argument of "becoming" because Laos's bodily traces reveal other margins of her individuality and self-image. It is important to note that the description of Laos's skin is not associated with race. For instance, Mr. Thiers insists that Laos should not change her skin, ought not to transform it, but she chooses to cover her body and narrate her own story. Her skin becomes the object that enables her to be part of a scheme, but it is also what allows her to leave it.

In Taylor Herrera's fourth story, "Camino a Mariato," the author describes a palimpsestic journey where several, apparently unrelated stories reveal the main story. Taylor Herrera centers her narration on María, a nameless narrator, and her drive with a friend to Atalaya to find "la cosa" (the thing). When they get closer to Atalaya, and after describing other sub-stories, María tells her friend that what she is looking for is a lilac platinum ring that she stole from her. Here, the "concrete object" is what connects the stories and the characters while revealing the collective agony of the characters. This use of palimpsestic concrete objects is also present in "La Sombra," where Taylor Herrera describes the life of Maria del Pilar, a young woman who sees a shadow of herself in the past. What Maria del Pilar sees is a simple body, which she perceives as having some imperfections: long nose, small breasts, and humble clothes. In the present, she touches herself and feels her implants and a small, pointy nose. Her implants are the objects that she sees in the mirror. She had transformed her body to build a new identity, but her shadow reminds her that she cannot escape her original self. For Elezala and Samalavičius, these examples of identity seen through a layer of material objects can be explained from a palimpsestic reading as "a means of remembering the past, a remembrance to help the people create a niche for progress based on the assessment of the past."[8] In the titular story, the characters travel to the past to understand their present and to find meaning in their existence, demonstrating that their lives have different, palimpsestic, compound experiences that are incapable of being separated from their identities. Stephenson Watson adds that avoiding the topic of race dates to the sixteenth century. Writers like the Spanish Juan Latino, Afro-Peruvian José Manuel Valdés, and Panamanian poet Gaspar Octavio Hernandez chose a "national affiliation by avoiding racial identification in their writings," and, similarly, Taylor Herrera does not have a nationalistic affiliation.[9] Nevertheless, the hidden discourse of the stories in *Camino a Mariato* conveys the detriment of national racial and social identity. The female characters often finish their journeys discouraged, but this begins a process of internal transformations. All the short stories up to this point consist of unfulfilled situations, which creates a sense of stagnation.

The Voyage and the Impossibility of Writing "Beyond Blackness"

In her study of Taylor Herrera and Panama, Stephenson Watson notes that writers such as Nancy Morejón, Georgina, and Excilia Saldaña try to respond to the question, "What does it mean to be a negra or mestiza or mulata in a country that defends and validates European colonization and acculturation?" For Stephenson Watson, writers born after 1970, such as Taylor, distance themselves "from an exclusively racialized discourse."[10] Taylor Herrera can accomplish this distance, to a certain extent, by avoiding allusions or references to racial aspects of colonized women's spaces and identities. But the past reappears in every single story, reminding readers how these women react as a result of their histories. In Taylor Herrera's eleventh story, one perceives a sense of female emancipation in their journeys and not a stagnation as we experience in her other short stories. In "The Voyage," the author depicts the colonial Panamanian past as a concrete palimpsestic object, where the main layer in the narrative is an object that ends the condition of slavery. Even though the author tells two simultaneous stories, one about colonial Panama and the other about the survival of a female slave, the former is a façade while the latter is more fully developed. Thus, she validates the struggle and resilience of the female slave, while the canonical Panamanian history gradually vanishes until it becomes a fictionalized story in which the notion of truth is interrogated. I propose that, by writing this story, in which the colonial reminiscences of Panama—even when depicted as less important than the resilience of the character—cannot be ignored, Taylor Herrera demonstrates that it is impossible to write beyond Blackness, or to surpass race.

The short story "El Viaje," or "The Voyage," changes the dynamic of writing in her other stories, where racial aspects of the women goes undescribed or is simply obliterated.[11] Unexpectedly, in her eleventh short story, Taylor Herrera introduces the words "slave," "Black," and "free woman." By using these words in "The Voyage," the writer deploys the strategies of postcolonial literature, which "step[s] in to overwrite the various layers of identities ascribed to Africa by calling up the previous writings with the intent of charting a path for Africa built on a solid foundation of knowledge. Like the palimpsest, these writings are a conglomeration of pre-colonial, colonial and postcolonial writings on Africa. The writings call Africa to accept its belonging to what Chakrabarty calls 'a negative universal history.'"[12] It is this negative, universal history that Taylor claims in "The Voyage." Despite the palimpsestic use of concrete objects in the rest of her stories, she now presents a palimpsestic postcolonial story that seeks the roots of Panama in the women who were part of that history.

It is essential to deconstruct this story, in which Taylor Herrera recreates different mechanisms of resistance and survival for six black female servants during the arrival of the English in seventeenth century Panama, while it was still under the jurisdiction of Spain. The author opens the story with the memories of a slave woman and her arrival to the Convent of the Concepción in Panama. Her memories are described in the third person and go from the remembrance of the Middle Passage to a procession in town. The narrator starts with the description of the journey and how the slave women suffers the most terrible pain, as well as the smell that surrounds their bodies. Taylor Herrera writes how "some of the oldest women would describe the voyage in all its details: the nauseating smell of feces, urine, blood and spoiled food; the heartrending cries of those who died suffering the most terrible pains while tied to their shackles; the cry of infants and children, sometimes still trying to suck from the breast of a mother already dead; the conversations shouted from one end of the boat to the other among the few who could understand each other."[13] Suddenly, the narratives switch from these memories of the Middle Passage to a description of a religious procession. To develop the lives of the six women, Taylor Herrera describes how the procession is organized by social class and status: the governor leads and behind him are important religious dignitaries, gentlemen from the wealthiest families, some monks, priests, and a few nuns. Behind them are the Spanish families and their domestic servants, and further behind are the less affluent families, the free black men and women, and the Indians. The narrative ends abruptly and then re-centers on the life of an initially nameless slave woman who, having arrived at an early age, rarely leaves the Convent of the Conception.

Taylor Herrera goes inside the servants' kitchen and depicts the fear they sense regarding the rumors of English pirates arriving in Panama. The reader is taken back to colonial Panama in 1671, when the buccaneer Henry Morgan invaded the country. In the story, the new slave, named Mercedes by the rest of the servants, is ridiculed because she does not speak Castilian. She learns how to take care of the orchard and the kitchen, and, finally, she learns how to interact and get along with the other maids. The story then returns to the events that lead to the arrival of Morgan, layering it with descriptions of the Mercedes's reminiscence of how she landed in Panama. When we think that we have an idea of who Mercedes is, Taylor Herrera then introduces other women who work in the convent: Skinny María, Fat María, a free black woman known as One-Eye, María Pieta, the cook Teresa, Caimana, and the two Soledades (a pair of young twins who look after children from prominent families). In the kitchen, these women learn that the nuns plan to leave Panama before the arrival of the pirates. They plan to take with them the Soledades because they were "born slaves on Spanish soil. And since the nuns raised them, they're docile and speak Castilian well."[14] Taylor Herrera uses palimpsestic writing to delineate the lives of each slave woman in dialogue with Panamanian history, recreating what Gavin Lucas in *Archeology of Time* describes as the past becoming inseparable from the present.[15] Taylor Herrera first narrates the fear of these women; for example, she describes how Caimana, after listening to how they will be forgotten by the nuns, considers joining the *Cimarrons*.[16] After demonstrating their anxiety, the author explains how their desperation reflects the history of Panama, as if it were part of these women's subjectivity.

The key point in Taylor Herrera's palimpsestic writing is how dread and anxiety are not the only emotions the slaves experience. She describes how some enslaved women are resistant to pain and to the arrival of Morgan. Thus, in the middle of their cavillations, the author shows their desire for resilience. Caimana leaves for the Atlantic, searching for a *palenque*, where the Africans were "their own masters and lords."[17] She does not fear the jungle, the Spanish, or any deities. María Piera leaves with Juan, a muleteer who she meets at the chapel of Santa Ana. Mercedes, who is listening to the slaves, does not want to go anywhere: "She didn't want to escape, or find the runaways, or cross through to Malambo with a few of the boatmen or water carriers; she didn't want to be made to serve elsewhere either. Perhaps she could somehow hide in the convent and the English wouldn't find her."[18] Only Teresa, Skinny, and Mercedes remain in the convent. The three of them are then described in the interior of the convent, sitting on a table and enjoying the wine that had been taken away from the nuns. They invite another servant named Perea to share their feast, and, at this moment, Taylor Herrera concentrates on the slave women and their authority after the nuns leave. The space of subordination is transformed, and we see another palimpsestic layer, where their bodies are now the center of the story. The author then mentions the arrival of the English on January 18, 1671, describing how the city was consumed by flames despite how it was the most beautiful day in the city. Taylor Herrera then centers her description in the convent, mentioning that Teresa and Skinny lose consciousness. They never learn that Caimana made it to an unknown *palenque*, where people greet her with their arms open. Meanwhile, in the convent, "A man entered the enclosure and unexpectedly grabbed Mercedes by the waist. She couldn't break free; she couldn't see the face of the man who pulled her forcefully. Without thinking she began to feel for the saber secured to the man's belt and then pulled. With her own hands and with all of the strength she could muster, she buried the saber in her body. The man finally let go, let her fall. As her life left her, she could see the pirate's face, his astonishment. Then darkness."[19] Mercedes's suicide is essential to Taylor Herrera's idea of emancipation.

This scene is so powerful that the account of what happened to the pirates reads like fiction. What matters is Mercedes's body on the floor. It does not matter that Morgan's men stayed in the city for three weeks, and it is not important that the Spanish hid their money and managed to escape. It is also unimportant that the pirates searched the city and gained so little that Morgan abandoned his crew before they rebel. Even though, in her other short stories, Taylor Herrera describes how most women are unable to survive their destiny and are stuck in a society that punishes them for their personal choices, in this story, she complicates the vision of the black slave women. She does not describe Mercedes's origins because they are lost in the description of her initial voyage to Panama and in the smell of the boat. Her identity is unknown, and the reader does not discern who she really is. However, how she dies becomes a fragile but dominant layer that makes us realize that Mercedes prefers to take her own life than to live only according to the will of another.

"The Voyage" contradicts the discourse on writing beyond blackness for several reasons. Because the story is conveyed through an enslaved female's gaze, it positions black bodies as subject to white control and re-tells colonial Panama's past, linking these to memories and to the present. The story is written through palimpsestic layers that let us hear and read the voices and thoughts of different enslaved women in the interiority of a kitchen. Only progressively does the story start to move to the exterior of the convent where they are confined. The fact that Taylor Herrera uses this short story to construct a connection between the initial stories and its female characters, each of whom inhabits the others, creates an involuted palimpsestic narrative. Dillon describes this aspect of the involution as "the relationship between the texts that inhabit the palimpsest as a result of its palimpsesting and subsequent textual reappearance. The palimpsest is thus an involuted phenomenon where otherwise unrelated texts are involved and entangled, intricately interwoven, interrupting and inhabiting each other."[20] These stories appear to be unrelated, but they are embedded in the destinies the characters face. "The Voyage" becomes essential to examining and understanding *Camino a Mariato* because it rejects the designation of writing beyond blackness and writing as only becoming. The decision to include it among a depiction of contemporary female narratives reasserts the role of black enslaved women in Panama's history and in its present without writing a story about the black Panamanian women of today. The complexity in Taylor Herrera's writing is contained by how she disallows homogeneity, which is the essence of palimpsestic writing and reading.[21] Her palimpsestic writing distorts the continuity of the definition of Panamanian women to create a more multifaceted understanding of Panamanian women and history.

NOTES

1. Sonja Stephenson Watson, *The Politics of Race in Panama: Afro-Hispanic and West Indian Literary Discourses of Contention* (Gainesville: University Press of Florida, 2014), 131.
2. Mercy Ezeala and Almantas Samalavičius, "Palimpsest in Postcolonial African Novels," *European Journal of Literature, Language and Linguistics Studies* 2, no. 1 (2018): 84.
3. Sarah Dillon, *The Palimpsest: Literature, Criticism, Theory* (London: Bloomsbury Academic, 2014), 4.
4. Taylor Herrera's story, "Baile con la muerte" (Dance with Death) was translated for the magazine *Words Without Borders* in 2018 by Christina Vega-Westhoff. I will be using this translation when referring to this story. Melanie Taylor Herrera, "Dance with Death," trans. Christina Vega-Westhoff, *Words Without Borders*, August 2018, accessed July 2020, https://www.wordswithoutborders.org/article/august-2018-panama-dance-with-death-melanie-taylor-herrera-christina-vega.
5. Ibid.

6. Melanie Taylor Herrera, *Camino a Mariato* (Managua, Nicaragua: Editorial Amerrisque, 2009), 17. These translations are mine.
7. Ibid., 18.
8. Ezeala and Samalavičius, "Palimpsest in Postcolonial African Novels," 93.
9. Sonja Stephenson Watson, "Expanding Definitions of Caribbean Identity Through Contemporary Panamanian Fiction by Melanie Herrera," *Cincinnati Romance Review* 40 (2016): 203.
10. Watson, *The Politics of Race in Panama*, 201–2.
11. Taylor Herrera's story "El Viaje" was translated for the magazine *Asymptote* in 2013 by Christina Vega-Westhoff. I will be using this translation when referring to this story. Melanie Taylor Herrera, "The Voyage," trans. Christina Vega-Westhoff, *Asymptote*, March 2019, accessed July 2020, https://www.asymptotejournal.com/fiction/melanie-taylor-herrera-the-voyage/.
12. Ezeala and Samalavičius, "Palimpsest in Postcolonial African Novels," 96.
13. Taylor Herrera, "The Voyage," 2.
14. Ibid., 4.
15. Quoted in Ezeala and Samalavičius, "Palimpsest in Postcolonial African Novels," 86.
16. Taylor Herrera, "The Voyage," 4.
17. Ibid., 10.
18. Ibid., 5.
19. Ibid., 9.
20. Dillon, *The Palimpsest*, 4.
21. Ezeala and Samalavičius, "Palimpsest in Postcolonial African Novels," 86.

WORKS CITED

Dillon, Sarah. *The Palimpsest: Literature, Criticism, Theory*. London: Bloomsbury Academic, 2014.
Ezeala, Mercy, and Almantas Samalavičius. "Palimpsest in Postcolonial African Novels." *European Journal of Literature, Language and Linguistics Studies* 2, no. 1 (2018): 84–100.
Lucas, Gavin. *The Archaeology of Time*. New York: Routledge, 2005.
Taylor Herrera, Melanie. *Camino a Mariato*. Managua, Nicaragua: Editorial Amerrisque, 2009.
———. "Dance with Death." Translated by Christina Vega-Westhoff. *Words Without Borders*. August 2018. Accessed July 2020. https://www.wordswithoutborders.org/article/august-2018-panama-dance-with-death-melanie-taylor-herrera-christina-vega.
———. "The Voyage." Translated by Christina Vega-Westhoff. *Asymptote*. March 2019. Accessed July 2020. https://www.asymptotejournal.com/fiction/melanie-taylor-herrera-the-voyage/.
Watson, Sonja Stephenson. "Expanding Definitions of Caribbean Identity Through

Contemporary Panamanian Fiction by Melanie Herrera." *Cincinnati Romance Review* 40 (2016): 201–214.

———. "La Identidad Afropanameña en la literatura desde el siglo XX hasta el nuevo milenio." *LiminaR. Estudios Sociales y Huamanistivos* 13 (2015): 27–37.

———. *The Politics of Race in Panama: Afro-Hispanic and West Indian Literary Discourses of Contention*. Gainesville: University Press of Florida, 2014.

◆ CHAPTER 6

Black Lives Matter in Brazil
Cidinha da Silva's *#Parem de nos matar*

Eliseo Jacob

#Parem de nos matar (#Stop Killing Us), the focus of study for this chapter, is an anthology of 72 *crônicas* (chronicles) by the Afro-Brazilian writer, intellectual, and activist Cidinha da Silva.[1] Many of the *crônicas* were previously published online, including at the *Portal Geledés*, with other online publications, and on her own blog.[2] The book, published in 2016, is dedicated to the Black social movement Reaja ou será morta (React or Die), founded in 2005 by Hamilton Borges in Salvador, Bahia, which organizes marches against police violence, has a school to educate and empower Black youth, and engages in advocacy work both in Brazil and abroad. One *crônica* from the anthology, "Quanto mais negro, mais alvo!" (The blacker you are, the likelier you are to be a target!), encapsulates the overall theme of the book by capturing the crisis of state violence against Black communities in Brazil. In the *crônica*, Cidinha da Silva references the Afro-Brazilian contemporary poet Ricardo Aleixo's poem, "rondó da ronda noturna" (night patrol rondo):

q	uanto +		h	owever +
p	obre +		p	oor +
n	egro		b	lack
q	uanto +		h	owever +

q	uanto +		h	owever +
n	egro +		b	lack +
a	lvo		a	target
q	uanto +		h	owever +
a	lvo +		a	target +
m	orto		d	ead
q	uanto +		h	owever +
m	orto +		d	ead
u	m		o	ne +[3]

The poem, written with white letters against a black background, incorporates characteristics of a rondo, or a poem structured around a fixed pattern of repetition. It merges those characteristics with the aesthetics of Brazilian concrete poetry, which focuses on visual structures, or word-objects, such as the use of the plus symbol in place of the Portuguese word *mais* (more)—the word used in Portuguese in arithmetic equations. This allows the poet to use the classical structure of the rondo of four three-line stanzas, combined with the visuals of a math equation, to critique the logic of the Brazilian state apparatus that uses law enforcement to dehumanize Afro-Brazilians by targeting Black bodies. The poem ends with the simple, yet impactful phrase, "*mais um*" (one more), which tells us that the victim of violence will become one more number in the statistics compiled each year of the number of Black Brazilians killed by state violence. Aleixo's powerful words hearken back to the sobering statistics. According to the Instituto de Pesquisa Econômica Aplicada, in their study *Atlas da Violência 2017*, of every four people murdered in Brazil, three are Black.[4] While the overall homicide rate that same year was 43.1 per 100,000, for non-Blacks it was 16 per 100,000, again illustrating what Ricardo Aleixo has observed: if you are Black, you are more likely to become a target of some form of violence and added as one more number in this sobering statistic.

Returning to Cidinha da Silva's *crônica*, she echoes Aleixo's words: "Engana-se quem pensa que somos vítimas de racismo, somos alvo do racism ... Quanto mais negro, mais alvo, só seria dito assim por um poeta" (You are mistaken if you think we are victims of racism, we are targets of racism ... However more Black, more a target. It could only be said in such a way by a poet).[5] The author's argument that Blacks in Brazil are the target of racism, and not merely victims, challenges the state's narrative that race is irrelevant to why certain citizens are frequently detained, harassed, or killed.[6] The author's comments also clearly indicate that political policies have been enacted and certain social norms have developed that directly impact Black Brazilians in targeted and harmful ways.

The political work involved in discussing the value of Black life in *#Parem de nos matar* is evident throughout Cidinha da Silva's career as an activist and writer. In the preface of the book, Sueli Carneiro, one of the most important contemporary Afro-Brazilian woman intellectuals, asserts that da Silva's career as a writer has always coexisted with her path as an activist for human rights with a focus on race and gender. Carneiro notes how da Silva gave up the comfort of being a well-known activist with the Instituto Geledés to devote all of her attention to writing, thereby developing into a Black intellectual figure.[7] Just as she found success in her activist work, da Silva's career as a writer has had similar outcomes, with the publication of seventeen books that range from short story collections, poetry, theatrical pieces, to children's books, as well as edited volumes on affirmative action and anti-racism polices in the education system. Additionally, she has become a prolific writer of *crônicas*, having published seven collections: *Cada Tridente em seu lugar e outras crônicas* (2007), *Oh, margem! Reinventa os Rios!* (2011), *Racismo no Brasil e afetos correlatos* (2013), *Baú de miudezas, sol e chuva* (2014), *Sobre-viventes* (2016), *#Parem de nos matar* (2016), *O homem azul do deserto* (2018), and most recently *Exuzilhar: As melhores crônicas da Cidinha da Silva Vol. I and II* (2019). The unifying themes in these *crônicas* is Black culture, politics, and history, both in Brazil and in the larger African diaspora.

This idea of the "alvo," or target, found in Ricardo Aleixo's poem, which serves as inspiration for *#Parem de nos matar*, hearkens to the historical nature of violence against Black Brazilians. Importantly, the *crônicas* in the volume demonstrate that the violence in contemporary society can be traced back to a Brazilian state rooted in necropolitics, a term understood by Achille Mbembe as the "ultimate expression of sovereignty [which] resides, to a large degree, in the power and capacity to decide who may live or must die."[8] The theory of necropolitics builds on Michel Foucault's notion of biopower and Giorgio Agamben's ideas related to the state of exception. However, Mbembe questions whether biopower is sufficient to explain how the political, under the guise of war and fight against terror, makes murder of the enemy its primary and absolute objective.[9] In the context of Brazil, those who must die, as determined by the state, are disproportionally individuals and communities of African descent. Therefore, for this chapter, I will use the framework of necropolitics to undertake an analysis of Cidinha da Silva's *#Parem de nos matar* and to understand how an analysis of Black genocide in Brazil raises questions regarding citizenship for Afro-Brazilians who continually face the threat of social and physical death. While Cidinha da Silva covers a wide range of social issues in her book, including police brutality, poverty, and black beauty, all of her essays center around the question of the social, cultural, and political value of Afro-Brazilians in contemporary society. The volume thus engages with discussions on the possibility of political mobilization and social empowerment in the face of state violence and repression.

This chapter discusses the instances of violence—from the murder of Black youth by police to Afro-Brazilian celebrities targeted by online racist attacks—captured in da Silva's *crônicas*. I argue that the mechanisms of necropolitics manifest through two forms of violence, symbolic and material, which provide a way to understand why and how genocide is being enacted against Afro-Brazilians. I use the definition of genocide adopted by Black scholars, who apply the term to cases involving Afrodescendant peoples in the Americas, and in line with William Patterson's *We Charge Genocide: The Historic Petition to the United Nations for Relief from a Crime of the United States Government Against the Negro People* (1951). Patterson draws on the United Nations General Assembly Resolution of December 9, 1948, which defines genocide as:

> Any of the following acts committed with intent to destroy, in whole, or in part, a national, ethnic, racial, or religious groups as such:
> a) Killing members of the group;
> b) Causing serious bodily or mental harm to members of the group;
> c) Deliberately inflicting on the group conditions of life calculated to bring about its physical destruction in whole or in part;
> d) Imposing measures intended to prevent births within a group;
> e) Forcibly transferring children of the group to another group.[10]

In the context of Brazil, João H. Costa Vargas provides an additional definition regarding the complex ways genocide can manifest in Brazilian society, which builds on Abdias do Nascimento's concepts in *Brazil, Mixture or Massacre?: Essays in the Genocide of a Black People* (1989): "Black genocide in Brazil is multifaceted and is part of a continuum. The various dimensions of Black genocide can be schematized into two sets of events—all of which are perpetrated and (at least tacitly supported) by the wider society: material and ideological."[11] While there are debates about how genocide should be defined and enforced, the focus of this chapter demonstrates that Cidinha da Silva provides the reader with an archive of the accumulation of different violent acts against Black Brazilians, both symbolic and material, to illustrate that anti-Black racism and violence are indeed a reality that needs to be recognized and addressed in the public sphere.

Material Violence: Killing the Black Body

Cidinha da Silva documents in her book the current crisis unfolding in Brazil regarding the high rate of homicides among Afro-Brazilians, in particular young adult males from Brazil's major urban centers, like São Paulo, Rio de Janeiro, and Salvador. In 2017, Brazil recorded over 65,000 homicides, with 75 percent of those killed being Black citizens, and over half of this number were individuals between the ages of 15 and 29.[12] In *#Parem de nos matar*, da Silva transforms these sobering statistics into detailed accounts on high profile cases to discuss how and why Black youth are being targeted for death at high rates by the police, private citizens, and vigilantes.

Of all the stark images tied to the legacy of slavery and racial violence, lynching is a powerful metaphor, which da Silva uses to address the targeting of Black citizens on Brazil's city streets. In the *crônica* "O recado dos linchamentos" (Memo on Lynchings), the author begins her text by noting the recent rise in the number of Black Brazilians killed by *justiceiros*, or vigilantes: "recolham-se ao lugar de negros ou serão vocês o próximo alvo" (return to your proper place as Blacks or you will be the next target).[13] She calls upon Ricardo Aleixo's imagery of the target, as framed by his poem and used as the epigraph to this chapter, to emphasize how these deaths are not accidental or random but intentional. Extrajudicial killings have become frequent practices in Brazilian society and have been justified by elected officials, conservative media pundits, and parts of civil society as necessary due to a failed justice system.[14] The targets of these executions are disproportionately Black males, and the persistent killing of these youth is enacted by a "system that works by devaluing the lives of non-Whites and perceiving their autonomous and legitimate organizations as threats."[15] Da Silva argues that modern day lynchings extend beyond vigilantes to actions by individuals from Brazil's rich, upper-class society, many of whom are rarely featured in the media for their criminal behavior. Rarely are they publicly disclosed as agents of physical violence enacted on working-class, Black bodies, seen as less than human and as a threat to the safety and order of civil society. The actions of rich, young, white men—called by the well-known Brazilian term *playboys*—whose careless driving results in the killing of innocent Black pedestrians and Black workers are reframed by the author as perpetuations of the violent history of lynching against Brazil's Black population. "O recado dos linchamentos" features three instances in which young Black men are targeted by these drivers. In the first, a son of a multi-millionaire runs over a black cyclist. In the second, a drunk playboy runs over a worker riding home on his bicycle, resulting in the cyclist's arm being torn from his body and stuck to the car. The driver eventually stops his vehicle and throws the arm into a creek as if to discard evidence of the crime. In yet a third case, a medical school student runs over a *gari* and flees the scene without rendering aid.[16] Da Silva's decision to label these three cases "lynching" brings attention to the long history of white individuals and mobs killing Black individuals in public spaces with little or no legal consequences.

The leniency with which the criminal justice system dealt with these three young, white men raises questions regarding the privileged rights of white citizens in contrast to Black citizens. Cidinha da Silva unequivocally categorizes the three drivers as criminals but observes how they are protected by the law rather than being subjected to it. James Holston would classify her observations of these cases as a form of "differentiated citizenship," or immunity from the law. For Holston, all Brazilians are citizens of the nation state; however, categories of rights are applied differently depending on a person's race, social class, gender, and education. Therefore, the white drivers are afforded more rights and protections than the Black victims due to their privileged social status in Brazilian society. Holston argues that Brazilians "always promote the person at the expense of the individual. Thus, the person demands that the law be bent especially for him, that he obtain a singular application of law."[17] The law is adapted to the needs of the individual defendant, with particular regard to said person's origins and phenotype. In return, the victims, the three Black men, have their rights sacrificed as exceptions to the rights given to the drivers. This immunity from the law can be seen in the case of the drunk playboy who discarded the victim's arm in a creek. Originally given a sentence of six years in a *semiaberto* (semi-open) prison,[8] a suspended license for five years, and damages in the amount of sixty minimum salaries to the victim[9], the judge reduced the driver's sentence to two years of house arrest, a suspended license for eight months, and payment of damages in the amount of ten minimum salaries.[18] The judge's actions—issued after the publication of the *crônica*—strongly reinforce da Silva's argument that Afro-Brazilians are denied rights as legal persons and as human beings because the legal recourse they are entitled to as citizens insufficiently addresses the violence perpetuated against them, which is in itself not fully acknowledged by the legal system.

The genocide of Black youth, however, is not limited to the actions of private citizens. Most of the *crônicas* included in *#Parem de nos matar* address the pressing issue of the genocide of Black Brazilians and find the state to be the main perpetrator of violence via the police. For Jaime Alves, killings carried out by the police in Brazil reflect broader state ideologies that deal with domination, crime, order, justice, and "value judgements on who deserves to live."[19] The necropolitical logic of the state regarding who should live and who should die disproportionately impacts Black youth from Brazil's urban, working-class peripheries and *favelas*, or shantytowns. As previously noted, João Vargas observes that Black youth are viewed by the state and the ruling class as non-human and a threat to the existing social order when they decide to organize or congregate.

The right to life and impartiality before the law are questions that Cidinha da Silva raises in the *crônica* "Os meninos do Morro da Lagartixa" (The Boys from Gecko Hill), which critiques the police massacre of five Black teenagers and how the state handled the ensuing controversy. On November 28, 2015, Roberto, 16 years old, along with four of his friends, decided to celebrate his first paycheck from his job in a local supermarket at Madureira Park. That same evening, as they returned home to Morro da Lagartixa, in the *Zona Norte* of Rio de Janeiro, they came upon a squad of four military police officers who were searching for a group of assailants who had robbed a truck transporting beer.[20] Even though the five teenagers obeyed the police order to stop and identify themselves as residents of the neighborhood, they were still fired upon, with the police firing 111 bullets at the five unarmed youth. The police initially claimed self-defense, even though none of the young men were armed, none had criminal records, and all worked and studied in the local area.[21] In the conclusion to this *crônica*, Cidinha da Silva makes a scathing observation about this *chacina*, or police massacre: "Ocorre que discutir a violência, apenas, não resolve. É preciso problematizar o racismo estrutural da sociedade brasileira que gera violência e avaliza o extermínio de jovens negros, comemorado por governantes como gols de placa" (It so happens that merely discussing violence does not solve the problem. It is necessary to problematize the structural racism of Brazilian society that generates violence and guarantees the extermination of Black youth, celebrated by politicians like goals on the scoreboard).[22] The metaphor of the scoreboard has a poignant effect as soccer plays a central role in Brazilian society. Instead of players compiling records and accolades, it is the state recording another number to add to its sobering statistics in its war against poor communities of color. For da Silva, white supremacy is the root of state violence because, using the framework of Mbembe's necropolitics, it places certain individuals under the category of those who must die, which in the framework of modernity is non-white persons not seen as fully human and not given the same civil rights as other citizens.

The *chacina* is also a reflection of the state of exception, as defined by Giorgio Agamben. Achille Mbembe builds on Agamben's concept that the state of exception is not limited to atrocities like the Jewish Holocaust and that the first manifestations of biopower and state of exception in modernity occurred with the rise of the trans-Atlantic slave trade. For Mbembe, the "slave condition results from a triple loss: loss of a 'home,' loss of rights over his or her body, and loss of political status."[23] Scholars like João H. Costa Vargas and Jaime Alves argue that this loss on multiple fronts of a person's existence still occurs today in Brazil and other nations with significant Afrodescendant populations. This state of exception for the Black body, therefore, continues as a legacy of post-slavery societies, as Afro-Brazilians were never seen as fully human. Therefore, state institutions and their agents frequently suspend the rule of law when dealing with Afrodescendant communities.

The loss of home and life becomes a salient point for da Silva as she questions whether these five young men, representative of Black youth throughout Brazil, can freely move about their own community in Rio de Janeiro. In the opening section of the *crônica*, the author references the hit song from the mid-1990s that has become a classic in the *funk carioca* genre, "Rap da Felicidade" (Happiness Rap).[24] Recorded by Wilton Esteves and Wesley Castro Rodrigues in 1995, the song's refrain offers a powerful message from the perspective of a young, Black man from the *favela*:

> Eu só quero é ser feliz
> > andar tranquilamente na favela onde eu nasci
>
> e poder me ogulhar
> > e ter a consciência que o pobre tem seu lugar.
>
> *I just want to be happy / walk calmly in the favela where I was born / and be proud of myself / and be aware that the poor has a place too.*

Roberto and his four friends, all killed by the police, were walking through their own neighborhood and having a good time, echoing the sentiment of the song. Its lyrics contain an important political message relating to urban space and who is permitted to move in, through, and out of certain spaces of the city. The *favelas* in the *Zona Norte* of Rio de Janeiro are heavily policed, with frequent shootouts and blitzes, or checkpoints, that commonly result in excessive force by the police as residents try to leave and return to their homes. In the face of state-sanctioned surveillance and violence, the narrator of the song has one simple request: to be able to live in peace like anyone else and enjoy the banality of everyday life that is missing from his community. The final line of the refrain is particularly important. Here, the singer puts forth the argument that *favela* residents have a right to the city, a right that has been denied to them since these makeshift communities started to emerge soon after the abolition of slavery in 1888. Cidinha da

Silva echoes the sentiments of the lyrics by observing that "a liberdade de ir e vir não é facultada aos jovens negros sequer na favela onde nasceram" (the freedom to come and go is not given to Black youth, including in the favela where they were born).²⁵ This loss of home then translates into an increased likelihood of a loss of citizenship and, ultimately, the loss of one's life.

The massacre of the five Black youth is not only a material genocide but a symbolic one as well. The symbolic genocide here is rooted in the state's attempts to exonerate itself from any responsibility for the action taken by the police. Da Silva notes how the state government of Rio de Janeiro made every effort to blame the massacre on the individual officers instead of on the institutionalization of racism in the police force: "O Secretário de Segurança do Estado do Rio de Janeiro, José Mariano Beltrame se pronunciou e eximiu a Corporacão Militar de responsabilidades, haja vista que em sua opinião não se trata de um problema de despreparo professional dos responsáveis pela matança. Trata-se de um problema de caráter dos matadores" (The Secretary of Security for the State of Rio de Janeiro, José Mariano Beltrame made a public announcement absolving the Military Police Force of any responsibility, because in his opinion it's not a problem of professional unpreparedness of those responsible for the killing. It is a problem to do with the character of the killers).²⁶ The argument that the police who committed the heinous act of killing the five Black youth did so because of a moral defect serves as a strategy to remove all blame from the state. The secretary's explanation echoes a pattern by Brazilian state authorities to argue that the causes of societal violence are linked to the crime, drugs, and poverty found in margins of society. Marilena Chauí categorizes this meta-narrative as the myth of non-violence in Brazil. However, Chauí argues, the state is in reality the main source of violence in contemporary society, enacted through policies that increase socio-economic inequality and legitimize the use of force to control the general population.²⁷ Jaime Alves builds on Chauí's framework by making a direct connection between police terror in Brazil's major cities and the interests and policies formulated and enacted by politicians, state institutions, and powerful individuals with direct access to the state. Ultimately, these theories explain da Silva's use of the image of the police as the "armed hand of the state."²⁸

Symbolic Violence: Silencing Black Women in the Public Sphere

As João H. Costa Vargas has stated, genocide is not only material but ideological as well. In the case of Brazil, the ideology of racial democracy perpetuates the belief that racial miscegenation and flexible racial categories leads to a post-racial society where no one sees race. Thomas Skidmore has argued that the Brazilian white elite has promoted racial democracy throughout the twentieth century as a strategy to obscure real forms of racial oppression.[29] This ideology works to appropriate pieces of Black culture and repackage it as part of Brazil's national identity, reinforce the unspoken social contract that everyone lives in harmony as long as people know their place, and ultimately espouse *branqueamento,* or racial whitening. Cidinha da Silva documents in her *crônicas* the visceral reactions Brazilians express when Afro-Brazilians not only occupy highly visible spaces in the media but do so in a way that challenges the social norms that have developed due to the ideology of racial democracy. Da Silva focuses in particular on attacks made in the public and digital spheres against successful Black women, namely the actress Taís Araújo and the news anchor Maria Júlia Coutinho, and what these episodes of anti-Black racism uncover about the relationship between race, gender, and class. The racially charged and misogynistic posts shared by participants in online forums and the strategies employed by media conglomerates to discount and ultimately silence Maju and Taís are attempts at a symbolic violence—defined by Pierre Bourdieu as a gentle or invisible violence meant to reinforce relations of domination—which, in the context of Brazil, relates to the mythos of racial democracy and to social relations rooted in cordiality.[30]

The function of the token minority figure in silencing Black women and perpetuating the myth of racial democracy comes up in the title of the *crônica,* "Uma Michelle incomoda muita gente, duas Michelles incomodam muito mais..." (One Michelle Makes a Lot of People Uncomfortable, Two Michelles Even More So...). Michelle refers to Taís Araújo's character in the 2015 Globo series *Mr. Brau,* which she portrayed alongside her real-life husband Lázaro Ramos.[31] In the TV show, Araújo and Ramos portray a Black power couple, a famous singer and choreographer/businesswoman. The second Michelle in the title refers to Michelle Obama, a powerful Black woman that Michelle, the character, emulates. The question of how many non-white actors or other successful public figures will be allowed to inhabit these normative white spaces is the real question that da Silva is trying to address. The author describes the impactful image Araújo has in the show: "Taís Araújo radicalizou no visual para caracterizar o poderio professional e econômico da personagem. Abusou do volume, das cores, e do brilho de um cabelo crespo que lhe emprestou o ar felino que seu rosto delicado desconhecia, e que deve deixar os racistas em pânico" (Taís Araújo radicalized herself through the visual to characterize the professional and economic force for the character. She overdid volume, colors, and the shine of a frizzy hair that gave her a catlike vibe unfamiliar to her delicate face, and that probably put the racists in a panic).[32] As the author notes later in her text, not only did the role of a powerful successful woman make people uncomfortable, but using hair styles rooted in an Afro-centric aesthetic also caused many Internet users to react negatively.

On October 31, 2015, the actress's Facebook page was the subject of racist comments. In response, she stated in a post: "I will not be intimated, I will not lower my head either."[33] The hashtag #SomosTodosTaísAraujo (#WeAreAll-TaísAraujo) became a trending topic on the morning of November 1. The social media attacks against Taís Araújo could be interpreted as a form of violence meant to silence her and other Black women wanting to publicly express their identity. Yet, da Silva problematizes this incident by critiquing the politics of representation as dictated by the media, which prefers the token Black actor that makes white spectators comfortable and does not disrupt the legacy of Brazil's racial democracy.

Cidinha da Silva closes the *crônica* by commenting how both the real success of Taís and the portrayal of a successful Black women on TV reignited the never-ending debate about the subservient place of the Black woman in Brazilian society: "Nada de novo no front. Só a velha reificação do lugar da mulher negra no discurso e no imaginário da casa-grande recalcitrant e ressentida" (Nothing new on the front lines. Only the old reification of the place of the Black woman in the discourse and imagination of the recalcitrant and resentful casa-grande [big house])."[34] The reference to the *casa grande* points to the legacy of slavery, which Vargas observes as the symbolic violence of racial democracy, as outlined in Gilberto Freyre's study *A Casa Grande e a Senzala*, where racial relations in Brazil remain in harmony with each other at the expense of those in subaltern roles, namely Black women. Additionally, this dynamic of race and gender in relation to servitude has been critiqued by Kia Lilly Caldwell, who observes that, throughout the twentieth century in Brazil, Black women have been viewed in the main role of domestic workers who serve the powerful and are not considered capable of being in positions of power themselves in larger Brazilian society.[35] As the author argues in "Mr. Brau e Michelle, o casal odara" (Mr. Brau and Michelle, the Odara Couple), the *crônica* that serves as a sequel to the aforementioned piece, there is not necessarily a problem of Black actresses interpreting roles as maids or other menial labor positions.[36] The issue, instead, is the preponderance of Black characters without a voice, who are seen but not heard in scenes and who are only there to serve and clean in the background but are never able to articulate their own experiences, their feelings, and what their lives are like beyond white, hegemonic spaces. There exists a violence in that silence, she observes, which leads to the social death of Black women who are not seen as full citizens or even human. This is, as Jaime Alves observes, the double negation of Black life.[37]

The specter of the *casa grande* haunts other successful Black women in Brazil, in particular Maria Júlia Coutinho, a weather anchor for Rede Globo. Cidinha da Silva devotes four *crônicas* in her book to analyze the anchorwoman's experiences with racism in the workplace and in the public sphere. In April 2015, Maria Júlia Coutinho, also known as Maju Coutinho, was hired to be the weather anchor on *Jornal Nacional*, the most popular evening news program on Brazil's most powerful TV Network, Rede Globo. In July of that same year, like Taís Araújo, Maju was subject to racist attacks on Facebook. Da Silva uses the metaphor of the *casa grande* in the *crônica* titled "O espírito dos ataques raciais à jornalista Maria Júlia Coutinho" (The Spirit of Racist Attacks Against Maria Júlia Coutinho) to describe the online attacks: "A casa-grande desconfiada acende o sinal amarelo. Os ataques racistas são iniciados, sempre ardilosos e escancarados, mas em menor número. Querem intimidá-la. É a primeira parte da estratégia. A casa-grande dá o sinal vermelho. Recomenda-se lançar mão de piadas, granadas sórdidas, armas químicas de desagregação molecular da humanidade de uma pessoa negra" (The suspicious big house signals the yellow light. The racist attacks commence, always underhanded and blatant, but in few numbers. They want to intimidate her. It's the first part of the strategy. The big house gives the red light. It recommends to hurl jokes, sordid grenades, chemical weapons for the molecular disintegration of Black person's humanity).[38] Da Silva's allusions to war tactics parallel Achille Mbembe's argument that the state's ultimate goal is the extermination of peoples and communities it considers to be an enemy. In the cases of Maju and Taís, both are categorized as threats to the existing social order by positioning themselves as symbols of Black excellence; therefore, the symbolic violence tied to white supremacy taking place in cyberspace has the intended effect to discredit and invalidate the ontological selves of these women.

Da Silva notes that Rede Globo is also guilty of espousing white supremacist ideas. João Vargas argues that the hyperconsciousness of race in Brazil is a way to negate racism and racial inequality. This, in turn, contributes to the mobs of people online who are upset that Black women now occupy more visible roles in the news and media. In particular, the author targets the head of Rede Globo's news division for contributing to the myth that affirmative action policies and other equality laws means racism is no longer an issue: "E agora Ali Kamel? Os ataque racistas à jornalista e às atrizes deixaram a Rede Globo de calças na mão, pois colocaram em cheque sua posição de inexistência do racismo, expressado no livro *Não somos racistas* do diretor de jornalismo do corporação" (And now what Ali Kamel? The racist attacks against the journalist and the actresses caught Rede Globo with their pants down, because they put in check their own positioning of the inexistence of racism, expressed in the book *We Are Not Racists*, written by the network's news director).[39]

The book *We Are Not Racists* (2006) is not an academic study, though it attempts to present itself as such by collecting articles published in the *O Globo* newspaper since 2003, with the central thesis that racism is not a characterizing trait of Brazil because there no longer exists institutional barriers for the progress and social ascension of Black Brazilians. Kamel does not completely reject the assertion that racism exists in the country but diminishes its impact by arguing that there exists far more prejudice due to social class than race. Therefore, the ensuing attacks on Maju Coutinho, a successful Black woman, can be connected to the ideas of the non-existence of racism in Brazil, which her employer had promoted for many years.

How Rede Globo and Maju's fellow anchors decided to respond to the attacks points to the symbolic violence of Black women who are seen but rarely heard. The hashtag #SomosTodoMaju (#WeAreAllMaju) started to circulate, with notable anchors like William Bonner going on air during *Jornal Nacional* to hold up a handwritten sign with the hashtag. The act of supposed solidarity by the anchors generated controversy, which Cidinha da Silva aptly describes as she considers such a public act by a white anchor: "A pergunta reverbra: Somos todos Maju ou não somos? Sim, somos! O problem são eles! Ou seja, nós somos Maju porque vivemos e enfrentamos a discriminação racial cotidiana, em diversos níveis. Da morte simbólica que tentaram impingir à jornalista, ao extermínio físico imposto a Cláudia Ferreira e a 82 jovens negros por dia no Brasil" (The question reverberates: Are we all Maju or are we not? Yes, we are! They are the problem! Or, in other words, we are Maju because we live and face daily racial discrimination, on multiple levels. From the symbolic death that they attempted to impose on the journalist, to the physical extermination imposed on Cláudia Ferreira and the 82 Black youth per day in Brazil).[40]

The author explains that the hashtag represents the experiences of Black women and aims to problematize the violence imposed on them, whether symbolically, in the case of Maju, or physically in the case of Claudia Ferreira, a mother of four who was caught in police crossfire, subsequently placed in the back of a police SUV, and dragged by the vehicle for several blocks when the back door flew open as the police were taking her to the hospital. When William Bonner used the hashtag, he was engaging in what da Silva categorizes as: "pessoas que escolhem uma mulher negra única para respeitar, até para endeusar. Isso é muito comum entre os discípulos brancos e suas mestras negras: Iyalorixás, professors, regentes de grupos, companheiras de trabalho, como Maju" (people who choose a single

Black woman to respect, even to deify. That is very common among the white disciples and their Black female masters: Iyalorixás, professors, group leaders, work colleagues, like Maju).[41] Such Black women are objectified and come to serve the interests of a white, hegemonic society. They are not allowed to speak their truth, which becomes evident when Maju went on air to address the racists attacks and could only use the terms like prejudice, rather than accurately describe what truly happened to her, which were acts of anti-Black racism.

Cidinha da Silva closes one of the *crônicas* with an important question: "Toda vez que vejo a Globo fazendo coisas que parecem avanço, me pergunto o que eles querem com isso?" (Every time that I see Globo doing things that seem like progress, I ask myself, what do they really want with that?). The author's self-reflective interrogation on the controversy surrounding Maju points to the illusion of progress dictated by the metaphor of the *casa grande* that is referenced frequently throughout the book. This episode of online racist attacks directed at Maju again points to the lingering symbolic violence surrounding racial relations in Brazil, as institutions with power, like Rede Globo, lead discourses of "progress" in the workplace.

Conclusion

The genocide of Black individuals and groups continues today in Brazil through the manifestations of both material and symbolic violence. However, the use of necropolitics as a theoretical framework to explain how and why these different forms of violence have been directed at a demographic that constitutes over half of the population of the country is key to deconstructing the practice. Identifying the operative variables in such cases allows Cidinha da Silva in her anthology *#Parem de nos matar* to condemn the systematic destruction of Black communities. The author's work, therefore, contributes to current efforts by Black activists, community leaders, and public figures to affirm the existence of these violent experiences. Each *crônica* challenges the hyperconsciousness of race in Brazil, so well described by João H. Costa Vargas, as well as the Black necropolis of Brazilian cities, as identified by Jaime Alves. The timeliness and urgency of Cidinha da Silva in bringing attention to the *alvo* (target) of symbolic and physical violence directed at Black populations in Brazil—so poignantly visualized in Ricardo Aleixo's poem—reverberates in the Brazilian literary field.

NOTES

1. The *crônica* is a Brazilian literary genre like the American op-ed but which incorporates more creative writing elements, like a short story. *Crônicas* typically comment on cultural and political issues related to everyday life. Historically, they were published in newspapers and magazines, but now they are found in blogs and other online media outlets. Authors typically republish their *crônicas* as anthologies, which Cidinha da Silva did with the book *#Parem de nós matar*.
2. The *Portal Geledés* is an online portal managed by Geledés—Instituto da Mulher Negra (Geledés Black Woman Institute), an NGO founded in 1988 by Sueli Carneiro and one of the largest non-profits that focuses on Black feminism in Brazil. The *Portal Geledés* publishes articles, interviews, op-eds, and other information related to Black culture, politics, and history. For da Silva's blog, see Cidinha da Silva, *Blog da Cidinha*, accessed March 2021, http://cidinhadasilva.blogspot.com.
3. The author intentionally used all lower-case letters for the title of the poem. The poem can be found in the anthology Ricardo Aleixo, *Trívio: Poemas* (Belo Horizonte: Scriptum Livros, 2001). All translations from Portuguese to English in this chapter are my own.
4. Daniel Cerqueira et al., *Atlas da Violência 2017* (Rio de Janeiro: IPEA, 2017), 30.
5. Cidinha da Silva, *#Parem de nos matar* (São Paulo: Ijumaa, 2016), 166.
6. See Jaime Alves, *The Anti-Black City: Police Terror and Black Urban Life in Brazil* (Minneapolis: University of Minnesota Press, 2018); and João H. Costa Vargas, *Never Meant to Survive: Genocide and Utopias in Black Diaspora Communities* (Lanham, MD: Rowman and Littlefield Publishers, 2010).
7. Sueli Carneiro, "Prefácio," in *#Parem de nos matar*, Cidinha da Silva (São Paulo: Ijumaa, 2016), 12–14.
8. Achille Mbembe, "Necropolitics," *Public Culture*, vol. 15, no. 1 (Winter 2003): 11.
9. Ibid., 12.
10. João H. Costa Vargas, "Genocide in the African Diaspora: United States, Brazil, and the Need for a Holistic Research and Political Method," *Cultural Dynamics* 17, no. 3 (2005): 267–68.
11. Ibid., 280.
12. Cerqueira et al., *Atlas da Violência 2017*, 8.
13. da Silva, *#Parem de nos matar*, 21.
14. Alves, *The Anti-Black City*, 61–63. Alves categorizes the killing of black youth in the urban peripheries of Brazil's major cities as a form of domination and control known as the black necropolis. Alves provides examples of this macabre state logic, including local business owners and off-duty police officers being involved in many homicides, as well as former police offers being elected to city, state, and federal positions by promoting themselves as the "killers of bandits." Contemporary Brazilian literature from the 1990s was effective in problematizing the necropolitics of the Brazilian state. In Patricia Melo's 1995 novel *O matador* (The Killer), for example, the protagonist runs

a "security" business with full police cooperation to carry out extrajudicial killings throughout São Paulo.
15. Vargas, *Never Meant to Survive*, 13.
16. da Silva, *#Parem de nos matar*, 21–22. *Garis* are sanitation workers responsible for cleaning the streets and removing trash from public spaces. They are recognized by their distinct orange suits.
17. James Holston, *Insurgent Citizenship: Disjunctions of Democracy and Modernity in Brazil* (Princeton: Princeton University Press, 2008), 20.
18. In a sentence of *prisão semiaberto*, the condemned can study and go to work during the day but must report to the prison every evening, where they must sleep and reside at all other times. In Brazil, minimum salary refers to the national monthly minimum wage an individual may earn from an employer. In 2019, the monthly minimum salary was 998 Brazilian reais, or approximately $247.40. "Motorista Que Atropelou e Jogou Braço de Ciclista Tem Pena Reduzida," *G1 São Paulo*, May 4, 2016, accessed August 2019, https://g1.globo.com/sao-paulo/noticia/2016/04/motorista-que-atropelou-e-jogou-braco-de-ciclista-tem-pena-reduzida.html.
19. Alves, *The Anti-Black City*, 50.
20. Many *favelas* in Rio de Janeiro use the term *morro*, or hill, in their name since many *favelas* in the city are built on hills and other high points.
21. Cassiano Martines Bovo, "3 anos da Chacina de Costa Barros: 5 jovens mortos, 111 tiros," *Justificando*, November 9, 2018, accessed August 2019, https://www.justificando.com/2018/11/09/3-anos-da-chacina-de-costa-barros-5-jovens-mortos-111-tiros/.
22. da Silva, *#Parem de nos matar*, 36.
23. Mbembe, "Necropolitics," 21–22.
24. Funk music emerged in the mid 1980s in the *favelas* of Rio de Janeiro but did not gain mainstream traction until the 1990s.
25. da Silva, *#Parem de nos matar*, 34.
26. Ibid., 35.
27. Marilena Chauí, "A Não-Violência Do Brasileiro, Um Mito Interessantíssimo," In *1 Conferência Brasileira de Educação* (São Paulo: Secretaria Municipal de Educação de São Paulo 1980), 3–5.
28. da Silva, *#Parem de nos matar*, 35.
29. Thomas Skidmore, *Black into White: Race and Nationality in Brazilian Thought* (Durham: Duke University Press, 1992), 217.
30. Pierre Bourdieu, *Language and Symbolic Power*, ed. John Thompson, trans. Gino Raymond and Matthew Adamson (Malden, MA: Polity, 1991), 24.
31. The fact that *Mr. Brau* was a landmark TV series in 2015 for showcasing a lead cast of two Afro-Brazilian actors, Taís Araújo and Lázaro Ramos, highlights the continued symbolic violence of Brazil's racial hierarchies that Afro-Brazilians are not capable of occupying positions of importance in the public sphere. The actors are a married power couple, frequently drawing comparisons to African American power couples like Jay-Z and Beyoncé or Will Smith and Jada Pinkett Smith.

32. da Silva, *#Parem de nos matar*, 66.
33. "Taís Araújo Posta Desabafo Após Ser Vítima de Racismo Na Web: 'Não Vou Me Intimidar,'" *Extra*, January 11, 2015, accessed September 2019, https://extra.globo.com/famosos/tais-araujo-posta-desabafo-apos-ser-vitima-de-racismo-na-web-nao-vou-me-intimidar-17940557.html.
34. da Silva, *#Parem de nos matar*, 66.
35. See Kia Lilly Caldwell, *Negras in Brazil: Re-Envisioning Black Women, Citizenship, and the Politics of Identity* (New Brunswick, NJ: Rutgers University Press, 2007).
36. Odara is a Yoruba word frequently used in Afro-Brazilian religions like Candomblé that means beautiful, good, positive.
37. See Alves, *The Anti-Black City*.
38. da Silva, *#Parem de nos matar*, 76–77.
39. Ibid., 88–89.
40. Ibid., 77.
41. Ibid., 77.

WORKS CITED

Agamben, Giorgio. *Homo Sacer, Sovereign Power and Bare Life*. Stanford: Stanford University Press, 1998.
———. *State of Exception*. Chicago: University of Chicago Press, 2008.
Aleixo, Ricardo. *Trívio: Poemas*. Belo Horizonte: Scriptum Livros, 2001.
Alves, Jaime. *The Anti-Black City: Police Terror and Black Urban Life in Brazil*. Minneapolis: University of Minnesota Press, 2018.
———. "Neither Humans nor Rights: Some Notes on the Double Negation of Black Life in Brazil." *Journal of Black Studies* 45, no. 2 (2014): 143–62.
Bourdieu, Pierre. *Language and Symbolic Power*. Edited by John Thompson. Translated by Gino Raymond and Matthew Adamson. Malden, MA: Polity, 1991.
Caldwell, Kia Lilly. *Negras in Brazil: Re-Envisioning Black Women, Citizenship, and the Politics of Identity*. New Brunswick, NJ: Rutgers University Press, 2007.
Cerqueira, Daniel, Renato Sergio de Lima, Samira Bueno, Luis Iván Valencia, Olaya Hanashiro, Pedro Henrique G. Machado, and Adriana dos Santos Lima. *Atlas da Violência 2017*. Rio de Janeiro: IPEA, 2017.
Chauí, Marilena. "A Não-Violência Do Brasileiro, Um Mito Interessantíssimo." In *1 Conferência Brasileira de Educação*. São Paulo: Secretaria Municipal de Educação de São Paulo 1980.
da Silva, Cidinha. *Blog da Cidinha*. Accessed March 2021. http://cidinhadasilva.blogspot.com.
———. *#Parem de nos matar*. São Paulo: Ijumaa, 2016.
Freyre, Gilberto. *Casa-grande and senzala: Formação da família brasileira sob o regime da economia patriarchal*. São Paulo: Jose Olympio, 1977.

Holston, James. *Insurgent Citizenship: Disjunctions of Democracy and Modernity in Brazil.* Princeton: Princeton University Press, 2008.

Kamel, Ali. *Não somos racistas: Uma reação aos que querem nos transformar numa nação bicolor.* Rio de Janeiro: Nova Fronteira, 2006.

Martines Bovo, Cassiano. "3 anos da Chacina de Costa Barros: 5 jovens mortos, 111 tiros." *Justificando.* November 9, 2018. Accessed August 2019. https://www.justificando.com/2018/11/09/3-anos-da-chacina-de-costa-barros-5-jovens-mortos-111-tiros/.

Mbembe, Achille. "Necropolitics." *Public Culture,* vol. 15, no. 1 (Winter 2003): 11–40.

Melo, Patricia. *O matador.* São Paulo: Companhia das Letras, 1995.

"Motorista Que Atropelou e Jogou Braço de Ciclista Tem Pena Reduzida." *G1 São Paulo.* May 4, 2016. Accessed August 2019. https://g1.globo.com/sao-paulo/noticia/2016/04/motorista-que-atropelou-e-jogou-braco-de-ciclista-tem-pena-reduzida.html.

Nascimento, Abdias do. *Brazil, Mixture or Massacre?: Essays in the Genocide of a Black People.* Dover, MA: Majority Press, 1989.

Skidmore, Thomas. *Black into White: Race and Nationality in Brazilian Thought.* Durham: Duke University Press, 1992.

"Taís Araújo Posta Desabafo Após Ser Vítima de Racismo Na Web: 'Não Vou Me Intimidar.' " *Extra.* January 11, 2015. Accessed September 2019. https://extra.globo.com/famosos/tais-araujo-posta-desabafo-apos-ser-vitima-de-racismo-na-web-nao-vou-me-intimidar-17940557.html.

Vargas, João H. Costa. "Genocide in the African Diaspora: United States, Brazil, and the Need for a Holistic Research and Political Method." *Cultural Dynamics* 17, no. 3 (2005): 267–90.

———. *Never Meant to Survive: Genocide and Utopias in Black Diaspora Communities.* Lanham, MD: Rowman and Littlefield Publishers, 2010.

Part III: Intellectual Sonar

◆ CHAPTER 7
Other Forests
The Afro-Brazilian Literary Archive

Isis Barra Costa

O manual da floresta pede não olhá-la
nem o que nela forme inseto fumo água.
Pede não pedindo reeducação dos olhos
outras hipóteses no entendimento dos fatos.
Não está em códice o mundo transitivo
de rios e sacerdotes.
Das gentes tão gente que dói pensá-las
com nossas palavras.
O manual da floresta segue outro alfabeto.
Para ler seu texto pouco valem os expertos.
Sua linguagem é cálculo
um saber em metáforas número
—EDIMILSON DE ALMEIDA PEREIRA, "CONTAS"

The handbook for the forest asks one not to look at it / nor what in it becomes insect smoke water. / It asks without asking reeducation for the eyes / other hypotheses / on an understanding of facts. / It is not in codex the transitive world / of rivers and priests. / Of people so people that it hurts to think them / in our words. / The handbook for the forest follows another alphabet. / To read its text, experts are of little use. / Its language is calculus / a knowledge in number-metaphors.

To speak of paradigms is to speak of a unifying package of practices and concepts, of a conceptual structure of beliefs and sciences that opens a community's field of vision and informs its worldview.[1] It has to do with a pact, a social agreement that illuminates our field of vision by graying out other fields. Through paradigms, we see what we see by virtue of what we render invisible. As Edgar Morin explains, a paradigm carries out a selection and a determination of logical operations, it designates fundamental categories of intelligibility and controls their usage, allowing "os indivíduos conhecem, pensam e agem segundo paradigmas inscritos culturalmente neles" (individuals know, think, and act according to paradigms that are culturally inscribed into them).[2] Paradigms are at once subterranean and sovereign, as maintained by Maria Zilda da Cunha, in that they organize "todo o pensar, o sentir e o querer do homem" (all of man's thoughts, feelings, and desires).[3]

The purpose of this chapter is to conceive of the Afro-Brazilian literary archive, a long repertoire of diverse textualities, and from there to imagine the weaving of other paradigms. Only through a historical overview of the formation of Afro-Brazilian literature, from its roots in *oralitura* (orature) and its poetic and political unfoldings, can we begin to envision Afro-Brazilian literary production as part and parcel of its transcontinental diasporic tradition.[4]

Literary paradigms are patterns turned into conventional models that feed into notions of a literary tradition. They are standards elected by literary critics from the West. The concept of tradition encompasses, among other matters, the bibliography that a generation of writers receives from its predecessors. This ensemble forms repertoires of possibilities that are accessible to generations and communities of writers. It is impossible to think of literary paradigms without evoking the concept of a canon and its respective ideological baggage. Let us recall that the idea of a canon as we understand it carries ingrained in its history the medieval church that used the term to homologate sacred Christian books and reject apocryphal texts; in other words, to determine which texts truly came from God and which ones should be eliminated as "imposters." *Canon*: from the Latin, measuring line, ruler; from the Greek, measuring stick. In an ecclesiastic sense, canon is related to decrees. With the secularization of culture, the term "canon" began to be applied to the realm of literature in the sense of a standard of excellence, a standard for judgment and comparison.

Literature is a European cultural product, as Antonio Risério aptly warns us: "com sua marca ideológica de nascença, seu vasto e dinâmico repertório formal, suas técnicas e truques, gramáticas e matrizes, variando escalas em função de escolas. E literatura brasileira é a soma das modificações históricas que uma forma cultural europeia experimentou em sua inserção na realidade tropical sob domínio lusitano" (with its ideological birthmark, its vast and dynamic formal repertoire, its techniques and tricks, grammars and matrices, varying scales according to movements. Brazilian literature is the sum of the historical modifications that a European cultural form experienced upon its insertion into a tropical reality under Portuguese dominion).[5] The question of canon became central to the agenda of comparative literature because it constituted, as noted by Eduardo Coutinho, "uma das instâncias mais vitais da luta contra o eurocentrismo que vem sendo travada nos meios acadêmicos" (one of the most vital instances of the fight against Eurocentrism that has been bogged down in academic circles).[6] Resistance to this concept, as well as its reworking, is key, because simply discussing it "nada mais é do que por em xeque um sistema de valores instituídos por grupos detentores de poder, que legitimaram decisões particulares com um discurso globalizante" (defies a value system that is instituted by groups that wield power and legitimate particular decisions with a globalizing discourse).[7]

Since the 1980s, Afro-Brazilian literature has acquired greater visibility and claimed some space in literary canons. With the return to democracy, demands dating back to at least the 1930s from the Frente Negra Brasileira (Black Brazilian Front) were taken up and used to open the gates of school and university curricula. Some of the fruits of these demands include the legally binding curricular reform and the institutionalization of African studies in schools (Lei 10.639/03 "Diretrizes Curriculares Nacionais para Educação das Relações Étnico-raciais e para o Ensino de História e Cultura Afro-Brasileira e Africana").[8] We are conscious in Brazil of the role curriculum has in the construction of symbolic boundaries that reflect power relations. Tomaz Tadeu da Silva synthesizes:

> O currículo é um dos locais privilegiados onde se entrecruzam saber e poder, representação e domínio, discurso e regulação. É também no currículo que se condensam relações de poder que são cruciais para o processo de formação de subjetividades sociais. Em suma, currículo, poder e identidades sociais estão mutuamente implicados. O currículo corporifica relações sociais.[9]

> *The curriculum is one of the privileged locales where knowledge and power intersect, as do representation and dominance, discourse and regulation. It is also in the curriculum that power relations are condensed, ones that are crucial to the formation process of social subjectivities. In sum, curriculum, power, and social identities are mutually implicated. The curriculum embodies social relations.*

The legalization of curricular reform represents an instance of fracture in hegemonic power relations, something like burning an effigy, if we are to view the curricular instrument as an embodiment of social relations. Despite their incipience, we are witnessing the adoption of new policies of desegregation and affirmative action and a policy of seeking out new pedagogical materials and methodologies.

In the second decade of the twenty-first century, roughly ten years after the sanctioning of the curricular reform, Eduardo de Assis Duarte published a set of two pivotal anthologies—*Literatura afro-brasileira: 100 autores do século XVIII ao XX* (*Afro-Brazilian Literature: 100 Authors from the 18th to the 20th Century*) and *Literatura afro-brasileira: Abordagens na sala de aula* (*Afro-Brazilian Literature: Classroom Approaches*). Anthologies have the fundamental role of reconfiguring the canon and systematizing a body of literary works that share an array of common characteristics. The curatorial task of the compiler reflects selections often already established by generations of readers. Duarte's anthologies can be considered a landmark in the history of Afro-Brazilian literature. They can also be perceived as the culmination of engaged achievements articulated by Afro-Brazilian writers, critics, and readers that steadily intensified from the 1980s to the present.

Consequent achievements are currently under threat by the present sociopolitical situation. It is a classic backlash. The times in which we are living in Brazil highlight the need to reorganize networks of action and forge new tools that follow another logic, other ways of seeing the world, other forms of knowledge. The present moment brings demands that make us think of Audre Lorde's text "The Master's Tools Will Never Dismantle the Master's House." Back in the 1980s, she declared: "In a world of possibilities for all of us, our personal visions help establish bases for political action. The failure of feminist academics to recognize difference as a crucial force is the failure to transcend the first lesson of patriarchy. In our world, divide and conquer must become define and empower."[10] Considering that what was achieved in recent decades has been followed by setbacks, it becomes necessary to revisit demands.[11]

Let us recall that the period of re-democratization and implementation of social demands coincided with the development of new media in Brazil. It is in this context that we witnessed advances in new media with all their potential to empower and restructure the hierarchical paradigms of a society that bears the scars of a slaveholding system and a military dictatorship, followed by bilateral amnesty. Today we see movements (not just a singular movement) of Black youth, militants, and artists articulated with new breath. The political role previously taken on by poetry—think of the publications of the original *Menelick* and those of "Segundo Ato"—is nowadays largely fulfilled by the visual arts.[12] The printed image (whether in virtual space or physical publications) is by nature more permeable than the printed word, and the Wi-Fi diaspora has been a media platform of high political and artistic potential.[13]

The challenge at hand is that, beyond existing and future reflections (on specific textual systems, discursive strategies, ideological, and aesthetic effects), we must not lose sight of what is most crucial: the search for new critical paradigms that pass identity-themed reflections through the filter of articulation among specific textual systems and elements of reception that sustain and legitimate them. That challenge raises the following questions: How can we learn to see what has been made invisible for centuries? How can we escape exclusivist literate Western logic? How can we flee from Western machinations and their categories? How can we relearn the world? How can we go beyond fragmentary analysis? Well beyond belonging or not belonging to the canon (or canons), what can we create to avoid getting stuck at the crossroads? What risks are we willing to take? How can we outline a bigger whole, a great interwoven web, and manage to discern it with the mandatory humility of those who are conscious of how little we know? With the awareness that it takes time and patience to unlearn and relearn the word? How can we imagine the Afro-Brazilian literary archive?

Preliminary Answers

"Reeducação dos olhos" (re-education for the eyes) is what Edimilson de Almeida Pereira points us to in the poem "Contas" (Beads) in this chapter's epigraph. The imagination that informs literature is a concept, a process, a space that has always attracted me, ever since I enrolled as a graduate student in a New York University Comparative Literature course entitled "Topics of Imagination." Due to a printing error in the catalog, I could not read the subtitle that clarified the course would focus on Caribbean literature. The name of the instructor of record was unknown to me: Kamau Brathwaite. I remember thinking of "breath" and "wait" and liking it. It was through my studies and interaction with the poet and historian from Barbados, who would eventually become my mentor, that I began to forge tools to access personal archives that had been censored from me. I left on a journey in search of knowledge about time and space built by the poetics of the African Brazilian diaspora. I came across initiations. I lost and found meaning. I created and shattered fantasies. I aligned myself with the minority line of combat within the ranks of US academia, and I made a home out of that space in the crossroads (despite and due to the grief, itself).

When positioning oneself in the crossroads, everything depends on how one approaches, how one imagines, and how one chooses. Exu Elegba is the divinized gatekeeper of paths and crossroads of the Yoruba diaspora. Exu is *Elegbará*: *Elé* (owner) of *agbará* (force). *Agbará* differs from *axé* (the power to make things happen, to fulfill a potential). While *axé* is an orientation, *agbará* is a force of reaction that allows us to achieve and maintain *axé*. These are interdependent Afro-diasporic concepts of resistance that translate as the struggle for life as life can and should be. Written, narrated, and sung Afro-Brazilian textuality is a performance of the African-derived *agbará* and is potentially a conduit for healing. They are textualities soaked in *axé* and *ngolo*. To be prepared, a *futu* first requires a creator (individual or collective) capable of decoding and coding.[14] Second, it requires a *ngaga/bamba* who knows how to tie the *futu* and protect its contents, its *nkisi*. Finally, decoding and recoding (or *kanga*) a prepared *futu* (think of Afro-Brazilian texts) is the task of a reader, a critic, who is another *ngaga/bamba* and who knows how to untie and release the flow of a canal of epistemic symbols into its textuality.

This is re-education for the eyes. With Kamau Brathwaite, I came to see the slave ship (*tumbeiro*) as a kind of space capsule. In his study of Afro-Jamaican popular culture, Brathwaite analyzes the decisive role played by the immanent character of African cultures that were transported to the Americas. He says:

> What contemporary white commentators saw was what they wanted to see (and hear), what they were trained by prejudice and education to see and hear. As far as most Europeans during the period of slavery where concerned, slaves/Africans had no culture ... To try to understand the nature and reality of the slave's religion in Jamaica (and the Caribbean/New World), we have to begin with an understanding of the nature and reality of religion in Africa, where, as Herskovits and others have conceptualized it, *the culture focus is religious*, i.e., that African culture, like most pre-literate/oral, pre-industrial folk culture is what Europeans call theocentric: all aspects of life have religious reference and meaning; all artifacts and customs are based on or come out of religious belief, practice and symbolism; there is no real distinction between "secular" and "sacred," and the priest, who is essentially the center of the culture, is concerned with and/or is capable of more than "priestly" (sacerdotal) function, but is/can be healer/physician (physical and psychological), artist (as, among other things, dancer/choreographer), the maker/designer of symbolic cloth (*adire, adinkera*), the carver of stools, statutes and "fetishes," historian (the griot's function is a religious one), storyteller/poet, diviner/prophet, politician (the chief and *okomfo* [priest] [Baba/Iya/lalorixá] are always closely associated, often indistinguishable), warrior, philosopher, etc.[15]

It was the power of cultures sustained in cultural archives that remained invisible to the European world that allowed agents involved in this long process to maintain the power of their civilizations' legacies. Brathwaite explains the nature of this process:

> The significant feature of this African (religious) culture was that it was (is) *immanent*: carried within the individual/community, not (as in Europe) existentially externalized in buildings, monuments, books, "the artifacts of civilization"; so that in a sense, African societies *did* appear to European observers "to have no culture," because there is no externally visible signs of "civilization." That dance was African architecture, that history was not printed but recited, contemporary Prospero could not understand. And yet it was the immanent nature of this culture which made it amazing and successful ("miraculous") transfer from Africa to the New World/ Caribbean, even under the extraordinary conditions of slave trade/ slavery, possible.
>
> The slave ship became a kind of psycho-physical space capsule, carrying intact the carriers of the kind of invisible/ atomic culture I have described; so that every African on those ships had within him/herself the potential of reconstruction; every mortal individual African (now slave), blessed with religious gift, carried within himself the potential of explosion: the ability to use, starting with nothing more than his nakedness and breath, a whole wide range of remarkable resources.[16]

For us to start envisioning African diasporic literary archives, we need to undergo a re-education (or de-education) process so as to be able to recognize a millenary artistic repertoire that colonial and contemporary Prosperos were never able to acknowledge.

In a text dedicated to, among others, Kamau Brathwaite, Danny Dawson imagines what I refer to as literary and cultural archive as "treasure in the terror." Regarding the "extensive arsenal" mentioned by Brathwaite, Dawson explains:

> Africans brought with them to the Americas their most important possessions, their minds. Those minds were and are essential in the formation of the world we now inhabit. Those minds, functioning under the terror of slavery and continued oppression, also contained the treasure of African (i.e., Yoruba, Kongo, Mande, etc.) art, cultural contributions as nonexistent, or at best, deficient. This treasure, although often unacknowledged, misattributed or seen as only popular culture without specific historical or cultural connection to an African root, has become the vibrant enlivener of world culture. As we shall see, much of the planet thinks, prays, plays, dances and sings using the models created, established and disseminated by Africans and the African diaspora.[17]

This rich legacy never remained unclaimed. The fact that Afro-Brazilian literary archive remains invisible and unacknowledged by the canon does not translate into its nonexistence. If anything, this characteristic supported its blossoming according to its own volition. The potential for reconstruction that Brathwaite refers to manifested itself in continuous developments, creations, and recreations of artistic (as well as philosophic, culinary, medicinal, and cultural) expressions.

We must learn to see what has been made invisible. We suffer, as Dawson elucidates, "a continuous generational amnesia regarding Africans and their place in American societies." Using a concept elaborated with Robert Farris Thompson in lectures and conversations, Dawson aptly describes our condition. He states:

> Much of the scholarship concerning Africans in the Americas has functioned under the myopia of the "Deficit Model," a term frequently used by Robert Farris Thompson to explain the tendency of scholars to view African cultural contributions as nonexistent, or at best, deficient. The Deficit Model presumes that because of their lack of material goods and deprived social conditions under the yoke of chattel slavery, Africans were unable to contribute in any significant way, other than their labor, to the formation of the cultures in the Americas.[18]

Afro-Brazilian literary contributions, particularly the vast corpus of oral literature, remain as a rule erased by the historiography of Brazilian literature. In cases where they are perceived, they are either revealed as a "muse"—as thematic inspiration (rarely formal) to literate culture—or as a corpus that does not manage to measure up to the discursive strategies characterized by hegemonic literary paradigms.

How can we conceive of Afro-Brazilian literature in its diasporic historical context? From where and when do we trace its history? How can we first rethink Afro-Brazilian textuality in its context and then rethink Brazilian literature with its gaps and blinders? In her 1987 dissertation, Zilá Bernd pointed to some of the main constants that characterized "a literatura negra brasileira" (Black Brazilian literature). Among them was: "a existência foira da legitimidade conferida pelo campo literário instituído" (an existence outside of the legitimacy conferred by the institution of literature).[19] Reflecting on her dissertation in 2010, Bernd mentions that "é possível apontar tendências distintas de construção identitária que não se apresentam em termos diacrônicos ... que por vezes se entrecruzam" (it is possible to observe distinct tendencies of identity construction that are not presented in diachronic terms ... that sometimes cross over one another).[20] In search of an analogy for the concept of Afro-Brazilian literature, Eduardo de

Assis Duarte highlights the rich historical moment of "realizações e descobertas da literatura afro-brasileira" (achievements and discoveries of Afro-Brazilian literature) that had already been widening its corpus, and its "consolidação acadêmica enquanto campo específico de produção literária—distinto, porém em permanente diálogo com a literatura brasileira *tout court*" (academic consolidation as a specific field of literary production—distinct, but nevertheless in permanent dialog with Brazilian literature *tout court*).[21]

To understand the development of Afro-Brazilian literature, we must contextualize these achievements and discoveries. What first comes to mind is the critical literary movement that, starting in the 1970s, launched a radical questioning of the universalizing postures of Eurocentric canonic literary paradigms to demystify the supposedly apolitical nature of textual reading and production. Eduardo Coutinho considers this movement the highlight of contemporary comparative literature. Until the 1970s, according to Coutinho:

> Em nome de uma pseudo-democracia das letras, que pretendia construir uma História Geral da Literatura ou uma poética universal, desenvolvendo um instrumental comum para a abordagem do fenômeno literário, independente de circunstâncias específicas, os comparatistas, provenientes na maioria do contexto euro-norte-americano, o que fizeram, conscientemente ou não, foi estender a outras literaturas os parâmetros instituídos a partir de reflexões desenvolvidas sobre o cânone literário europeu.[22]

> *In the name of a literate pseudo-democracy that claimed to establish a General History of Literature or a universal poetics, developing a common instrument for an approach to the phenomenon of literature, independent of specific circumstances, what the comparative lit scholars ended up doing, consciously or not [the majority coming from the Euro-North-American context], was to project onto other literatures the institutionalized parameters that came from reflections developed for the European literary canon.*

Coutinho adds that a linear perspective of historicism "cedeu lugar a uma visão múltipla e móvel, capaz de dar conta das diferenças específicas, das formas disjuntivas de representação que significam um povo, uma nação, uma cultura, e os conjuntos ou séries literárias passaram a ser vistos por uma óptica plural" (gave way to a multiple and mobile vision, capable of noticing specific differences and disjunctive forms of representation that signify a people, a nation, a culture, and the ensemble or literary series came to be seen through a plural optic).[23]

From T. S. Eliot to Antonio Candido: Under the Sign of the Acid

I propose that we trace some of the footprints of this long movement that ebbs with the radical questioning of comparative literature in the 1970s and flows toward the first decades of the twenty-first century with the "realizações e descobertas da literatura afro-brasileira" (achievements and discoveries of Afro-Brazilian literature). The intention is one of metonymically revealing that this questioning, unconsciously and inevitably, would hardly be able to see beyond "subterranean and sovereign" hegemonic paradigms. It is here that I choose two iconic metaphors by T. S. Eliot and Antonio Candido. They deal with images that seem to reveal the DNA of Eurocentric canonic literary paradigms.

In one of the most controversial essays of Western literature, "Tradition and the Individual Talent" (1918), T. S. Eliot suggests the image of a perpetually moving loop, in which the totality of European literary production is simultaneously and productively active in the poetics of the present. In this essay, which the author himself situates "at the frontier of metaphysics or mysticism," Eliot reupholsters the concept of tradition with a historical perception that involves the past as a present element.[24] Within a principle of critical aesthetic, every new artist is situated in contrast and comparison to the past, inevitably modifying the totality of previously existing order. The meaning and appreciation of a poet, says Eliot, need to be situated: "His significance, his appreciation is the appreciation of his relation to the dead poets and artists. You cannot value him alone; you must set him, for contrast and comparison, among the dead."[25]

Eliot affirms this process is not about an evolution but merely about an awareness that the substance of art is translated in the constant flow and changing outlook of the country represented by the poet, "the mind of his own country." "Every nation, every race," says Eliot, "has not only its own creative, but its own critical turn of mind."[26] The historical sense leads the poet to express himself not merely within the boundaries of the generation to which he belongs, but also with an attitude in which the totality of European literary production is simultaneously and productively active in the poetics of the present.

Eliot's essay recalls a literary family tree, a large *padê* of the poet with his Western ancestors. The best part of a poetic work, says Eliot, occurs when "the dead poets, the poets' ancestors, assert their immortality most vigorously."[27] In his 2017 work on Bantu-Catholic poetics, Edimilson de Almeida Pereira intersects with Eliot in certain aspects. In *A saliva da fala* (*The Spit of Speech*), Pereira observes: "os cantopoetas simultaneamente interpretam o presente como futuro dos antepassados, e passado dinâmico, de si mesmo" (singer-poets simultaneously interpret the present as the ancestors' future and their own dynamic past).[28] *Different literary family trees. Different forests.* Referring to fundamentally oral textualities that are based on non-European aesthetics, Edimilson de Almeida Pereira puts forth: "para apreendê-las é necessário reconhecer outra dinâmica histórica (a dos grupos marginalizados durante e após a colonização) que se desenrolou paralelamente ao recorte histórico considerado oficial" (to apprehend them it is necessary to recognize another historical dynamic [that of marginalized groups during and after colonization] that rolled out parallel to the historical revisionism considered to be official).[29] *Other histories. Other ancestors.*

When elaborating his impersonal theory between poetry, author, and poem, Eliot uses an analogy between poetic production and the formation of sulfuric acid to describe how the poet becomes aware that he lives in the "present moment of the past."[30] The poet is the catalyzing fiber. The poem is the sulfuric acid. I will quote Eliot's curious passage about what takes place when a bit of finely filiated platinum is introduced into a chamber containing oxygen and sulfur dioxide:

> The analogy was that of the catalyst. When the two gases previously mentioned are mixed in the presence of filament of platinum, they form sulphurous acid. This combination takes place only if the platinum is present; nevertheless, the newly formed acid contains no trace of platinum, and the platinum itself is apparently unaffected: has remained inert, neutral, and unchanged. The mind of the poet is the shred of platinum. It may partly or exclusively operate upon the experience of the man himself; but, the more perfect the artist, the more completely separate in him will be the man who suffers and the mind which creates; the more perfectly will the mind digest and transmute the passions which are its material.[31]

Sulfuric acid is industry's most used chemical, used in everything from fertilizers and car batteries to oil refineries. It is the most utilized compound after water.[32] It is indicative of an economy. A country's economic development can be measured by its per capita consumption of sulfuric acid and by the product's importance in heavy industry. The metaphor that serves—in Eliot's conception—to separate the tares from the wheat (the poet from the ego's emotions)—is impregnated, on the one hand, by the destructive power of the mineral acid's extreme corrosive energy, and, on the other hand, by the chemical element's power to serve as an indicator of a country's industrial development.

The image we are left with is reminiscent of Claude Lévi-Strauss's "A Writing Lesson," in which, reflecting on an "extraordinary incident" on Nambikwara land, he formulates his hypothesis on the role of writing and empires. Writing, says Lévi-Strauss, "is a strange thing." He ponders: "If my hypothesis is correct, the primary function of writing, as a means of communication, is to facilitate the enslavement of other human beings. The use of writing for disinterested ends, and with a view to satisfactions of the mind in the fields either of science or the arts, is a secondary result of its invention and may even be no more than a way of reinforcing, justifying, or dissimulating its primary function."[33] *Other histories. Other ancestors.*

In 1959, Antonio Candido published the classic *Formação da literatura brasileira* (*Formation of Brazilian Literature*), in which he retrieves concepts proposed by Eliot to study the formation of Brazilian literature. Rather than proposing Eliot's metaphor of a literary circle, Candido leans more toward the other image, that of sulfuric acid. Seeing the ensemble of literary producers and receptors supplied with a transmitting mechanism, Candido imagines literary continuity as the passing of the torch between runners.[34] Thus, he evokes the Olympic Games, with its history of world powers flexing their muscles. Regardless of the results of Candido's criticism, some of the most crucial (and perhaps fertile) elements in Eliot's matrix are lost. Candido's study reveals a supposedly Brazilian tradition (no longer Western) and its "casualidade interna" (internal causality).[35] Whereas Eliot uses the concept of historical sense to situate English literature within the belly of the global West, Candido uses his concept of the historical point of view to withdraw Brazilian literature from the Western belly and insert it into an exclusively Brazilian "sistema articulado" (articulated system).[36] Thus, Candido abandons Eliot's transnational ancestral perspective.

From Antonio Candido to Edimilson de Almeida Pereira: Other Forests

Within the national literary system articulated by Candido—baggage we have long inherited—I think of the place occupied by textualities that were, as pointed out by Edimilson de Almeida Pereira, "exiladas" (exiled). Pereira observes how "cantopoetas" (singer–poets) have been treated "priva-os, inclusive, da marginalidade literária" (to deprive them even of literary marginality).[37] Those poets, representatives of oral African traditions from Minas Gerais, are, as Pereira indicates, "relegados a outro espaço além da margem" (relegated to another space beyond the margin)."[38] He adds: "ao invés de dizer que essa textualidade perdeu o seu lugar no campo da literatura legitimada, vale mudar a espessura das lentes analíticas e observar que ela se encontra em uma situação de exílio" (rather than say this textuality lost its place in the field of legitimate literature, it is better to change the thickness of the analytic lens and observe that it is actually in a situation of exile)."[39] Different from other Afro-Brazilian literary forms, oral textualities from the Bantu-Catholic archive end up occupying an extraordinary situation and space. Pereira analyzes: "sua exclusão dos jogos de formas literárias levou-os a delinear o seu próprio campo de jogo, ainda que não tenham descartado a possibilidade de diálogo com as outras textualidades" (their exclusion from the literary canon with its forms and rules, allowed them to delineate their own field of play without dismissing the possibility of dialogue with other textualities).[40] Borrowing Antonio Risério's terms "poemúsica" and "literatura subterrâneas" (poemusic and underground literature), adding Leda Maria Martins's "oralitura" (orature), and contributing his own "cantopoema" and "literaturas silenciosas" (song–poem and silent literatures), Pereira observes that these are textualities that "apesar de terem sido lançadas ao fundo do labirinto dos cânones literários ocidentais . . . demonstram uma expressiva capacidade de interferência social" (despite having been tossed to the back of the maze of Western literary canons, . . . demonstrate an expressive capacity for social interference).[41]

Thus, to formulate other literary paradigms, identitarian concepts that go beyond the national and ethnic emerge as necessary axes. It is not a matter of looking for evidence to justify the inclusion of these textualities and their poets to established canons, but rather, as Pereira says: "mas em ocupar outros ângulos de análise que nos permitam compreender [como] essa poética é capaz de dialogar com o cânone literário brasileiro" (more a matter of occupying other angles of analysis that allow us to understand [how] this poetics is capable of dialog with the Brazilian literary canon).[42] A big question remains: which other paradigms, which other models could serve as supports for the reading, for the outline and comprehension of a corpus that could never simply be added to the Western canon—a corpus that by its nature is anti-canonic? How can we defend getting over graphocentrism—discrimination based on the belief that written textualities are superior to others?[43] How do we evade the ease with which texts that follow the direction of a Pan-African *négritude*, or a Spanish-American *negrismo*, or an Afro-Brazilian Yoruba-centrism render other textualities and epistemological worldviews invisible?

As for the aesthetic sources of Black cultures, there has been little advancement to include Bantu poetics. As Pereira reminds us, Yoruba-derived textualities received more attention than those of Bantu origin, even gaining some projection in the realm of canonic literature, despite not having the autonomy of a literary system as such. Textualities woven "com fios dos mundos banto e católico" (with threads from the Bantu and Catholic worlds), Pereira points out, were not considered "como fonte de diálogo e inspiração para a formação do repertório poético brasileiro" (as a source of dialog and inspiration for the formation of a Brazilian poetic repertoire).[44] This intervention reminds us that it is important to pay close attention to a rather vulnerable issue. We run the risk of repeating the model imposed by Euro-Western paradigms that, by outlining and consolidating a body of literature, silenced values proposed by other axes of representation. Pereira comments on the existence of particular African languages that "atravessaram mares e terras longínquas para reconstituírem na América, de maneira nova, as antigas expectativas do ser humano de manter sua ligação com o divino" (crossed remote lands and seas to reconstitute in a new way in the Americas ancient human hopes of maintaining a connection to the divine).[45] These life experiences generated philosophical, poetic, and cultural repertoires. Pereira asserts that the repertoires of Bantu-Catholic interfaces present themselves as some of the most challenging. The character of this hybrid text, perceived as enigmatic, is linked as much to its linguistic structure as it is to its cultural practices and the value systems that inform its worldview. Such a textuality, says Pereira, in this sense, "é tão enigmática e tão compreensível quanto as linguagens produzidas por outros grupos, pois essas noções se relativizam de acordo com o grau de inserção do sujeito no mundo de uma determinada forma de linguagem" (is as enigmatic and as comprehensible as the languages produced by other groups, since these notions are relativized according to the degree of the subject's immersion within a determined form of language).[46]

Afro-Brazilian identities process themselves at crossroads of codes and symbolic systems that confront and weave each other. As Leda Maria Martins analyzes in *Afrografias da memória* (*Afrographies of Memory*), we are dealing with an "identidade que pode ser pensada como um tecido e uma textura, nas quais as falas e gestos mnemônicos dos arquivos orais africanos, no processo dinâmico de interação com o outro, transformam-se e reatualizam-se continuamente, em novos e diferenciados rituais de linguagem e de expressão, coreografando a singularidade e alteridades negras" (identity that can be thought of as a fabric and a texture in which the mnemonic gestures and speech of African oral archives, in the dynamic process of interacting with one another, continuously transform and update each other in newly differentiated rituals of language and expression, choreographing the singularity of Black alterities).[47]

For Afro-Brazilian literary production to be understood not as a modality of the Brazilian canon but as a tradition rooted in its diasporic forest with its own epistemological paradigms and worldviews, I propose the delineation of an inclusive hermeneutics emerging from the roots of oral literature. Only then will we be able to recognize the poetic forms that African ancestors brought to Brazil. Only then can we weave other paradigms that will allow us to conceptualize the great Afro-Brazilian literary archive within its own literary historical foliage. Only then will we be able to render visible multiple spheres of communication and diasporic convergences. It is necessary to cast out sulfuric paradigms, to reconjure what has been silenced, and to enter other forests.

NOTES

1. A version of part of this chapter was originally published in Portuguese as an homage to poet and researcher of Afro-Brazilian religiosity and culture Edimilson de Almeida Pereira in *Brasiliana: Journal for Brazilian Studies*.
2. Edgar Morin, ed., *Educar na era planetária: O pensamento complexo como método de aprendizagem pelo erro e incerteza humana* (São Paulo: Cortez/UNESCO, 2007), 58. Unless otherwise noted, all translations are mine.
3. According to Maria Zilda da Cunha: "Um paradigma constitui-se como uma lógica organizadora composta por conceitos ideologicamente selecionados, com os quais se lê o mundo e nele se atua. Portanto, subterrâneo e, ao mesmo tempo, soberano, o paradigma organiza e controla o pensar, o sentir e o querer do homem" (A paradigm establishes itself as an organizing logic composed of ideologically selected concepts used to read the world and act within it. Consequently, subterranean while also sovereign, paradigms organize and control man's thoughts, feelings, and desires). Maria Zilda da Cunha, "Naus frágeis e novos paradigmas em literatura e educação," *Perspectiva*, 30, no. 3 (2012): 775.
4. The term "oralitura" (the Portuguese equivalent of "orature" or "oral literature") gained traction in Brazil through the work of Leda Maria Martins. According to the author, the concept of orature, or "oralitura," invites (and incites) us to think of performative cultural traditions, in their verbal and performative forms, as it "indica a presença de um traço residual, estilístico, mnemônico, culturalmente constituinte, inscrito na grafia do corpo em movimento e na vocalidade" (indicates the presence of a residual trace, stylistic and mnemonic, culturally constitutive, inscribed in the grammar of body movement and utterance). Leda Maria Martins, "Performances do tempo espiralar." In *Performance, exílio, fronteiras: Errâncias territoriais e textuais*, edited by Graciella Ravetti and Márcia Arbex (Belo Horizonte: Editora UFMG, 2002), 88–89.
5. Antonio Risério, *Textos e tribos: Poéticas extra-ocidentais nos trópicos brasileiros* (Rio de Janeiro: Imago, 1993), 38.
6. Eduardo F. Coutinho, "A literatura comparada e o contexto latino-americano," *Raído* 2, no. 3 (2008): 24.
7. Ibid., 24.
8. Bill 10.639/03 "National Curricular Directives for the Education of Ethnic/Racial Relations and the Teaching of African and Afro-Brazilian History and Culture." It is important to recognize the advances that have been made since then, notwithstanding the stumbling blocks that hinder the implementation of these achievements in school

settings. Despite the setbacks that make change difficult, social gains have begun to have long-term repercussions.

9. Tomaz Tadeu da Silva, *Territórios conte stados: O currículo e os novos mapas políticos e culturais* (Petrópolis: Vozes, 1993), 23.

10. Audre Lorde, "The Master's Tools Will Never Dismantle the Master's House," in *Sister Outsider: Essays and Speeches* (Berkeley: Crossing Press, 2007), 112.

11. While this chapter specifically addresses the literary canon, other questions relate to us, academic critics, researchers, and educators. How should we conceive of an African-derived literary corpus? The challenge that has been put to the centers of knowledge production is not only to expand the canon but also to change teaching methods and approaches. What are the possible roles of centers of learning in a context marked by social and technological change?

12. *O Menelick 2º Ato* is a magazine that pays homage to the newspaper with the same name that marked the birth of São Paulo's Black press. It began with a blog and later became a physical magazine. It is important to note that, while the original *O Menelick* had poet Deocleciano Nascimento as its editor-in-chief, *O Menelick 2º Ato* was founded by photojournalist Nabor Jr. Whereas the original *O Menelick* had a team of editors and reporters (such as Geraldino do Amaral, Theophilo Gonçalves de Freitas, José Luiz Sampaio, and José Paulino, among others), *O Menelick 2º Ato* has a team of anthropologists, art critics, and cultural movers in the areas of dance and performance (Luciane Ramos Silva, Alexandre Bispo, and Christiane Gomes). According to *O Menelick 2º Ato*'s publisher, the magazine "é um projeto editorial de reflexão e valorização da produção cultural e artística da diáspora negra com destaque para o Brasil. O projeto foi criado em 2007, e inicialmente restringia-se a ocupar o sítio virtual: omenelicksegundoato.blogspot.com. Em maio de 2010, após quatro anos de estudo sobre uma estética editorial que pudesse aproximar o novo negro urbano do século XXI as raízes ancestrais responsáveis por moldar a sua identidade cultural, foi publicada a primeira edição impressa da revista. Com tiragem trimestral, a publicação é distribuída gratuitamente em eventos culturais, shows, espetáculos, galerias de arte, lojas, bibliotecas e zonas de conflito da cidade de São Paulo" (is an editorial project of reflection and valuation of the artistic and cultural production of the Black diaspora with an emphasis on Brazil. The project was created in 2007 and was initially confined to cyberspace at omenelicksegundoato.blogspot.com. In May of 2010, after four years of studying an editorial esthetic that could bring the new urban Blackness of the twenty-first century closer to the ancestral roots responsible for molding its cultural identity, the first printed edition of the magazine was published. With trimestral editions, the publication is distributed without charge at cultural events, shows, performances, art galleries, shops, libraries and conflict zones in the city of São Paulo). See "A revista," *O Menelick 2º Ato*, www.omenelick2ato.com/a-revista.

13. I use the term "Wi-Fi diaspora" to refer to contemporary exchanges and creations of Black cultures that happen in the digital realm. Anthropologist Goli Guerreiro uses the term "third diaspora" to refer to the same phenomenon. Guerreiro refers to

the First Diaspora as the period that embraces the trans-Atlantic slave trade and the return of the formerly enslaved to Africa; the Second Diaspora embraces the period of voluntary migrations (Jamaicans to London, Puerto Ricans to New York, Beninese to Paris, Cape Verdian to Lisbon and New York, Angolans to Brazil); while the Third Diaspora refers to the contemporary African diasporic digital circuit of communication (connecting cities such as Salvador, Kingston, Havana, New York, New Orleans, London, Lisbon, Dakar, and Luanda). See Goli Guerreiro, *Terceira diáspora, culturas negras no mundo atlântico* (Salvador: Corrupio, 2010).

14. In the cosmology that dates back to the former Kingdom of Kongo, a *futu* refers to a parcel of sacred medicine (or *bilôngo*). It is generally known in Portuguese as a *patuá*, a form of amulet usually made of cloth or leather that contains protective power. For a *futu* to be activated, it needs to be prepared and tied up. Tying up, or *kanga*, is the act of coding or activating one such personal amulet. For more information, see Kimbwandènde Kia Bunseki Fu-Kiau, *Self-Healing Power and Therapy: Old Teachings from Africa* (New York: Vintage Press, 1991).

15. Kamau Brathwaite, *Folk Culture of the Slaves in Jamaica* (London: New Beacon Books, 1981), 12.

16. Ibid., 13–14.

17. Dawson's text has no pagination and is no longer online. See C. Daniel Dawson, "Treasure in the Terror: The African Cultural Legacy in the Americas," *The Freedom Chronicle*, Northern Kentucky University's Institute for Freedom Studies, 2002, accessed April 2015.

18. Ibid.

19. Zilá Bernd, "Vozes negras na poesia brasileira: Contraponto com a poesia de língua francesa do Caribe" (PhD diss., Universidade de São Paulo, 1987), 279.

20. "Relendo a produção poética afro-brasileira—desde suas origens com Luís Gama em 1859 até os dias atuais—, é possível apontar tendências distintas de construção identitária que não se apresentam em termos diacrônicos, isto é, em uma perspectiva de 'evolução' no tempo, mas que por vezes se entrecruzam e convivem no âmbito da poética de um mesmo autor" (Re-reading Afro-Brazilian poetic production—from its origins with Luís Gama in 1859 until the present day—it is possible to observe distinct tendencies of identity construction that are not presented in diachronic terms, that is to say, in a perspective of 'evolution' in time, but that sometimes cross over one another and cohabitate within a single author's range of poetics." Zilá Bernd, "Da voz à letra: itinerários da literatura afro-brasileira," *Via Atlântica*, 18 (2010): 33.

21. Eduardo de Assis Duarte, "Literatura afro-brasileira: um conceito em construção." *Estudos de Literatura Brasileira Contemporânea* 31 (2008): 11.

22. Coutinho, "A literatura comparada," 22–23.

23. Ibid., 24.

24. T. S. Eliot, "Tradition and The Individual Talent," in *Selected Essays* (London: Faber and Faber, 1932), 21.

25. Ibid., 15.
26. Ibid., 13.
27. Ibid., 14.
28. Edimilson de Almeida Pereira, *A saliva da fala: Notas sobre a poética banto-católica no Brasil* (Rio de Janeiro: Azougue, 2017), 173.
29. Ibid., 49.
30. "The emotion of art is impersonal. And the poet cannot reach thus impersonality without surrendering himself wholly to the work to be done. And he is not likely to know what is to be done unless he lives in what is not merely the present, but the present moment of the past, unless he is conscious, not of what is dead, but of what is already living." Eliot, "Tradition and The Individual Talent," 22.
31. Ibid., 16.
32. Victor Ricardo Ferreira, "Uso do ácido sulfúrico pela indústria," *Brasil Escola*, accessed April 2019, https://brasilescola.uol.com.br/quimica/uso-Acido-sulfurico-pela-industria.htm.
33. Claude Lévi-Strauss, "A Writing Lesson," in *Tristes Tropiques*, trans. John Russell (New York: Criterion Books, 1961), 288, 291–92. Lévi-Strauss posits that writing arrives "the formation of cities and empires: the integration into a political system, that is to say, of a considerable number of individuals, and the distribution of those individuals into a hierarchy of castes and classes" (292). Writing, he continues: "seems to favour rather the exploitation than the enlightenment of mankind . . . If my hypothesis is correct, the primary function of writing, as a means of communication, is to facilitate the enslavement of other human beings. The use of writing for disinterested ends, and with a view to satisfactions of the mind in the fields either of science or the arts, is a secondary result of its invention and may even be no more than a way of reinforcing, justifying, or dissimulating its primary function" (292).

    Lévi-Strauss's theory on writing is later visited by Jacques Derrida in "The Violence of the Letter: From Lévi-Strauss to Rousseau," in *Of Grammatology*, trans. Gayatri Spivak (Baltimore: John Hopkins University Press, 1997). Derrida analyzes Lévi-Strauss's hypothesis: "The Nambikwara chief learns writing from the anthropologist, at first without comprehension, he mimics writing before he understands its function as language; or rather he understands its profoundly enslaving function before understanding its function, here accessory, of communication, signification, of the tradition of a signified" (121–22). One could observe that the lesson of writing no longer involves the experience lived by the anthropologist and the chief, but rather with the "rememoration of the scene" when the anthropologist reflects on the incident at night by himself (126). It is a lesson of the lesson. The "instantaneous appearance of writing" is not the origin/invention of writing, but rather its imitation, its "artificial borrowing" (126–27).
34. According to Antonio Candido: "Quando a atividade dos escritores de um dado período se integra em tal sistema, ocorre outro elemento decisivo: a formação da continuidade literária,–espécie de transmissão da tocha entre corredores, que assegura no tempo

o movimento conjunto, definindo os lineamentos de um todo. É uma tradição, no sentido completo do termo, isto é, transmissão de algo entre os homens, e o conjunto de elementos transmitidos, formando padrões que se impõem ao pensamento ou ao comportamento, e aos quais somos obrigados a nos referir, para aceitar ou rejeitar. Sem esta tradição, não há literatura, como fenómeno de civilização" (When the activity of writers from a given period integrate themselves into such a system, another decisive element occurs: the formation of a literary continuity—a kind of passing of the torch between runners, that ensures collective movement through time, defining the lineaments of a whole. It is a tradition, in the full sense of the word, that is to say, a transmission of something between men, with the totality of transmitted elements forming patterns that impose themselves on thought and behavior and to which we are obligated to refer for acceptance or rejection. Without this tradition, there is no literature as a phenomenon of civilization). Antonio Candido, *Formação da literatura brasileira: Momentos decisivos* (São Paulo: FAPESP; Rio de Janeiro: Ouro sobre Azul, 2009), 24.
35. Ibid., 153.
36. Ibid., 24.
37. Edimilson de Almeida Pereira, *A saliva da fala*, 32.
38. Ibid., 144.
39. Ibid., 23.
40. Ibid., 145.
41. Ibid., 23.
42. Ibid., 151.
43. Risério comments that to appreciate texts of non-European extraction analysts trained in mainstream literary tradition need to overcome some prejudices, mainly "o preconceito da escrita" (the literate prejudice). Risério, *Textos e tribos*, 51.
44. Pereira, *A saliva da fala*, 16.
45. Ibid., 67.
46. Ibid., 149–50.
47. Leda Maria Martins, *Afrografias da memória: O reinado do Rosário no Jatobá* (São Paulo: Editora Perspectiva; Belo Horizonte: Mazza Edições, 1997), 26.

WORKS CITED

Barra Costa, Isis. "Por um arquivo literário afro-brasileiro: Uma introdução à obra de Edimilson de Almeida Pereira." *Brasiliana: Journal for Brazilian Studies* 8, no. 1–2 (2019): 394–400.

Bernd, Zilá. "Da voz à letra: Itinerários da literatura afro-brasileira." *Via Atlântica*, 18 (2010): 29–41.

———. "Vozes negras na poesia brasileira: Contraponto com a poesia de língua francesa do Caribe." PhD diss., Universidade de São Paulo, 1987.
Brathwaite, Kamau. *Folk Culture of the Slaves in Jamaica*. London: New Beacon Books, 1981.
Candido, Antonio. *Formação da literatura brasileira: Momentos decisivos*. São Paulo: FAPESP; Rio de Janeiro: Ouro sobre Azul, 2009.
———. "Literatura e subdesenvolvimento." In *A educação pela noite e outros ensaios*, 140–62. São Paulo: Editora Ática, 1989.
Coutinho, Eduardo F. "A literatura comparada e o contexto latino-americano." *Raído* 2, no. 3 (2008): 21–31.
Cunha, Maria Zilda da. "Naus frágeis e novos paradigmas em literatura e educação." *Perspectiva*, 30, no. 3 (2012): 771–88.
Dawson, C. Daniel. "Treasure in the Terror: The African Cultural Legacy in the Americas." *The Freedom Chronicle*. Northern Kentucky University's Institute for Freedom Studies website (discontinued). 2002. Accessed April 2015.
Derrida, Jacques. "The Violence of the Letter: From Lévi-Strauss to Rousseau." In *Of Grammatology*, translated by Gayatri Spivak, 101–140. Baltimore: John Hopkins University Press, 1997.
Duarte, Eduardo de Assis. *Literatura afro-brasileira: 100 autores do século XVIII ao XXI*. Rio de Janeiro: Pallas, 2014.
———. *Literatura afro-brasileira: Abordagens na sala de aula*. Rio de Janeiro: Pallas, 2014.
———. "Literatura afro-brasileira: Um conceito em construção." *Estudos de Literatura Brasileira Contemporânea* 31 (2008): 11–23.
———. *Literatura e afrodescendência no Brasil: Antologia crítica*. Belo Horizonte: Editora UFMG, 2011.
———. "Por um conceito de literatura afro-brasileira." *Revista de Crítica Literaria Latino-americana* 41, no. 81 (2015): 19–43.
Eliot, T. S. "Tradition and the Individual Talent." In *Selected Essays*. London: Faber and Faber, 1932.
Ferreira, Victor Ricardo. "Uso do ácido sulfúrico pela indústria." *Brasil Escola*. Accessed April 2019. https://brasilescola.uol.com.br/quimica/uso-Acido-sulfurico-pela-industria.htm.
Fu-Kiau, Kimbwandènde Kia Bunseki. *Self-Healing Power and Therapy: Old Teachings from Africa*. New York: Vintage Press, 1991.
Guerreiro, Goli. *Terceira diáspora, culturas negras no mundo atlântico*. Salvador: Corrupio, 2010.
Lévi-Strauss, Claude. "A Writing Lesson." In *Tristes Tropiques*, 290–93. Translated by John Russell. New York: Criterion Books, 1961.
Lorde, Audre. "The Master's Tools Will Never Dismantle the Master's House." In *Sister Outsider: Essays and Speeches*, 110–14. Berkeley: Crossing Press, 2007.
Martins, Leda Maria. *Afrografias da memória: O reinado do Rosário no Jatobá*. São Paulo: Editora Perspectiva; Belo Horizonte: Mazza Edições, 1997.
———. "Performances do tempo espiralar." In *Performance, exílio, fronteiras: Errâncias territoriais e textuais*, edited by Graciella Ravetti and Márcia Arbex, 69–91. Belo Horizonte: Editora UFMG, 2002.

Morin, Edgar, ed. *Educar na era planetária: O pensamento complexo como método de aprendizagem pelo erro e incerteza humana.* São Paulo: Cortez/UNESCO, 2007.
Pereira, Edimilson de Almeida. *Lugares ares: Obra poética 2.* Belo Horizonte: Mazza Edições, 2003.
———. *A saliva da fala: Notas sobre a poética banto-católica no Brasil.* Rio de Janeiro: Azougue, 2017.
Risério, Antonio. *Textos e tribos: Poéticas extra-ocidentais nos trópicos brasileiros.* Rio de Janeiro: Imago, 1993.
Silva, Tomaz Tadeu da. *Territórios contestados: O currículo e os novos mapas políticos e culturais.* Petrópolis: Vozes, 1993.

◆ CHAPTER 8

Dismantling Coloniality via the Vocabulary of Afro-Chilean and Afro-Puerto Rican Music-Dance

Juan Eduardo Wolf

In the canyon forged by the river San José, which flows just inside Chile's northern border, lies the sanctuary of the *Virgen de las Peñas*. For over a century, dance troupes called *morenos de paso* have performed in front of the image of the Virgin that emerged out of the canyon's rock face.[1] Members of these troupes sacrifice time, physical effort, and financial expenditure to supplicate or thank the Virgin for a favor. Researchers like Zoila Mendoza and Juan Van Kessel have described these dances, known locally as *bailes religiosos*, as *mestizo* or Indigenous expressions.[2] Indeed, the use of panpipes or Andean brass bands as accompaniment contributes to this idea, as do the Aymara family names of well-known troupes, like the *Sociedad Religiosa de Morenos Hilario Ayca*. Other *moreno de paso* troupes, however, trace their heritage to the families of descendants of enslaved Africans in the region. These troupes are among the oldest officially registered in the *bailes religiosos* association, and they can trace their history to a time before the association's existence, when troupes like the *Compañía de don Andrés Baluarte* were assembled on three-year terms of sponsorship by individuals.[3] While troupe membership is open to anyone devoted to the Virgin, many Afrodescendant participants also dance because of this family tradition. Yet, the fact that *bailes religiosos* are usually associated with other ethnic groups has meant that this music-dance expression has often been overlooked as part of the African diasporic experience until recently, when Afrodescendant activists drew attention to this fact.[4]

The opposite is true for the music-dance collectively known as *bomba* from the island of Puerto Rico. Today, one can find *bomba* performed as entertainment in bars, as staged folklore for municipal festivals, as community practice at neighborhood gatherings, and even as classroom material for music and dance classes. For centuries, however, the expression's use of hide-head drums and these instruments' connection to *negros bozales* meant that the island's elite deemed it primitive and barbaric.[5] Furthermore, because slaves occasionally used *bomba* events as a space to plan rebellions, the colonial government placed restrictions on when and where the drums could be played during the nineteenth century. Nevertheless, in the mid- to late-twentieth century, responding to the political left's growing interest in promoting folklore, the Puerto Rican government's cultural institutions began to suggest that *bomba* could be considered a national expression, part of the tri-partite Spanish, Indigenous, and African heritage of Puerto Rican culture.[6] The government offered limited support for certain families associated with *bomba* practice to perform it on stage, and, with time, many Puerto Ricans accepted this staged version as a timeless, reified part of their national culture—the most explicit expression of the island's African heritage. Over the last two decades, a revival has taken place, both on the island and among the Puerto Rican population in the United States, promoting the role of *bomba* in creating community, bending gender expectations, and instilling pride in one's African heritage.[7] The African diasporic nature of *bomba*, an awareness of which was always present, went from its negative associations to one that could be positive.

The histories of the *morenos de paso* and the practice of *bomba* reflect the variety of stances that societies in the Americas have taken toward Afrodescendant expressions. Whether viewed and judged negatively like *bomba* or subsumed and ignored like the *morenos de paso*, these social attitudes toward the presence of Afrodescendants are a direct result of the way power was structured during the colonial era.[8] As historian Enrique Dussel has argued, Europe's reaction to the encounter with the Americas was to declare itself superior, the pinnacle of intellectual and technological development.[9] Colonization of the Americas thus took place with the idea of molding the Americas into Europe's image, while simultaneously extracting American resources to maintain European superiority. This sociocultural orientation that assumed the need for endless development and extraction in the name of intellectual and economic progress as defined by the West is one way we can define the concept of modernity. The colonial elites used categories of difference to rationalize the position of ethno-racial groups within the emergent power structure, based on how much these elites deemed the presumably inherent behavioral characteristics of each group to be worthwhile to the ostensibly universal orientation of modernity. The two music-dance genres described above illustrate how two Afrodescendant communities experienced this "modern" colonial system differently depending upon their context. In both cases, however, a fundamental consequence of such colonial social stances was to deny or suppress the ways that Afrodescendant perspectives and values could contribute to those societies by offering an alternate to modernity.

Despite the formal end of a major era of colonialism, contemporary societies still function under the influence of these colonial structures, ideas, and behaviors—a condition that can be referred to as coloniality.[10] The persistence of coloniality perpetuates certain injustices of that era, especially given the global reach of modernity today. One result is economic inequity. Despite the adoption of state multicultural policies and the efforts of Afrodescendant activists, the World Bank reports that, when considering the combined population of six Latin American countries in 2015, Afrodescendants represented 38 percent of that total population but also disproportionately made-up 47 percent of its poor and 49 percent of its extreme poor.[11] One way of responding to these injustices is to consider what Walter D. Mignolo and Catherine E. Walsh have called the "decolonial option," the choice to seek "understanding and affirming subjectivities that have been devalued by narratives of modernity that are constitutive of the colonial matrix of power."[12] Ascribing value to these subjectivities can then serve as the first in a series of actions to address social inequities, not at a global or universal level, but within a specific, localized context.

In this chapter, then, I choose this option to examine the Afrodescendant music-dance expressions discussed above, seeking out those perspectives that narratives of modernity have refused to recognize. I take inspiration in this task from Silvia Rivera Cusicanqui's anti-colonial *ch'ixi* methodology, which assumes that subjects can take part in colonial activities while maintaining an alternate set of values than those presumed by modernity. Rivera Cusicanqui uses word interplay rooted in Indigenous languages to illustrate what these alternate perspectives might be. With this methodology in mind, I look to the movement vocabularies and other performance practices within these expressions to offer various possible alternate subjectivities to those presumed by modernity. My goal is not to construct an objective history of these music-dance genres. Beyond being difficult to accomplish, such an endeavor feeds into the discourse of authenticity that limits certain values to the colonially different. Instead, I propose to assess concepts that may have connections to the Afrodescendant experience, with the intention that they might be considered as real, alternative modes of thought and, if appropriately resonant with cultural memory, become part of local solutions to the inequities created by coloniality.[13]

Adopting a *Ch'ixi* Perspective and Methodological Challenges

The Aymara word *ch'ixi* can mean "motley" or "stained," and Rivera Cusicanqui uses it to describe both her understanding of the world and her own mixed, *mestiza* heritage.[14] She wants to avoid using the infertile connotations of hybridity, so she prefers to think with the Indigenous concept of *ch'ixi*.[15] Rivera Cusicanqui invokes the metaphor of a tapestry that looks motley and stained from a distance but in which the individually spun threads of warp and weft can be distinguished upon closer examination. Furthermore, the *ch'ixi* nature of the tapestry can also apply to the individual spun tapestry threads to reveal multiple interlocked perspectives. When the threads in this metaphor are understood to be strands of culture, one has a new perspective of how different lines of thought can participate in the same expression, with the Indigenous perspectives given equal weight with those of the colonizer.

Rivera Cusicanqui considers Indigenous languages a critical tool in the assumption of a *ch'ixi* orientation. She has demonstrated how Andean languages, like Aymara and Quechua, offer dialectical pairs of heteronyms that give insight into worldviews that differ from the dominant hegemony. The simple change of vowel or phoneme from one descriptive term to another can suggest how an action that is commonly interpreted as complicit with coloniality can instead be undertaken with a different spirit. One example that Rivera Cusicanqui uses is the Aymara word pair *khiyki-kirki*, which mean singing and complaining, respectively.[16] While the cosmopolitan world might consider Indigenous singing a quaint part of staged multicultural folklore, Rivera Cusicanqui notes that music-dance can be cathartic for the struggles of Indigenous peoples, their complaints often voiced in these expressions. This language-based hermeneutic then contributes to a paradigm shift for mainstream understandings of culture, suggestive of other ways of dealing with contemporary challenges.

While I am attracted to the potential of Rivera Cusicanqui's *ch'ixi* techniques, some questions arise when taking Afrodescendants into consideration. To her credit, Rivera Cusicanqui does recognize Afrodescendant communities as First Nations due to their foundational role in the contemporary Americas, and her recognition of that role suggests that their voices should be included in anti-colonial dialogues. Unfortunately, her emphasis on the "re-appropriation of bilingualism" with an Indigenous language focus in her analysis tends to overlook the challenges Afrodescendants face. While this bilingual approach can work using words or ideas from African languages that have worked themselves into local vocabularies, many Afrodescendant communities do not have access to a clearly delineated language that they can point to as a starting point for "re-appropriation." Such is largely the case for the communities in Puerto Rico and Chile I am considering here. Given this limitation, I propose supplementing spoken language ideas with movement vocabularies and performance practices of Afrodescendant expressions within the Americas. Assuming *ch'ixi* hermeneutics means that, on the one hand, I acknowledge that this music-dance has developed under coloniality but that, on the other, I can also seek out how those same expressions might be reinterpreted through a consideration of a broad range of practices and ideas within those African cultures known to have been involved in the Atlantic slave trade. This approach may serve as the frame needed to arrive at different possible orientations toward Afrodescendant music-dance than those coloniality offers.

Inherent in adopting a *ch'ixi* perspective to Afrodescendant cultures in the Americas is a recognition of Africa's own pluriversality—that Africa is not the monolithic universe of the colonial imaginary but a plethora of cultures, each a universe unto itself.[17] Even limiting the cultures under consideration to those involved in the Atlantic slave trade is a daunting task. Here I must pragmatically simplify to a limited number of culture groups, reminding myself of the methodological caveats mentioned earlier. The historiography of the slave trade has divided the geographic regions from which slaves were taken into anywhere from three to six general areas. Thornton's three basic categories include the Western coast (which includes ports in current day Senegal to Sierra Leone), the Gulf of Guinea (roughly coinciding with ports along contemporary Liberia to Cameroon), and the Western central region (south of Cameroon to the Cape). Although numbers are difficult to estimate, and people from all three regions were enslaved throughout the era, the earlier period (1500–1650) consistently saw more slaves taken from the Western central region than from the Gulf of Guinea, which saw an increase beginning in 1700.[18] The overall number of slaves taken continued through the middle of the nineteenth century, with a sub-region of the Gulf of Guinea region known as the Blight of Benin providing the largest number of slaves, followed by the Western Central region.[19] These numbers demonstrate that the distribution of cultural influences arriving in the Americas changed over time, but other processes were also at play. As Gwendolyn Midlo Hall asserts, often the influence of the first cultural group that historically arrived in a region played a significant role in the way local culture continued to develop over time, even with the arrival of large numbers of slaves from other cultural groups.[20] Yvonne Daniel has further observed how, in Africa, individuals may have multiple religious loyalties due the proximity and shared qualities of neighboring religions. In the Americas, these religious interactions can result in mixtures of terminology or concepts applied in ways that are related but do not duplicate the African religions.[21] Acknowledging the complexity of these interactions, I also note the influence of major kingdoms within each of three regions above can help to identify trends or commonalities of thought between multiple cultures. These include the Mandinka for the Western Coast, the Akan and Lucumi for the Gulf of Guinea, and the Kongo-Bantu for the West Central region. Thus, I undertake this analysis of *morenos de paso* and *bomba* practice by attempting to balance the understanding of these complex cultural interactions with the need to consider specific alternatives from a limited number of cultures.

Arica's *Morenos de Paso*

The *morenos de paso* are part of a larger phenomenon of ritual dance-dramas throughout Latin America. They are most commonly linked to Iberian models of religious festival performance that include theatrical reenactments of Reconquista Era battles between the Spanish and Moors, as well as processions in which troupes of dancers put on elaborately costumed displays in honor of a patron saint. In the latter case, these troupes could represent themselves either by dressing elegantly in formal regalia or by dressing as an exotic costumed Other, like Africans or Native Americans. The majority of *bailes religiosos* in northern Chile seem to follow this exoticizing model, as dancers dressed as *turbantes* (in turbans), *gitanos* (Gypsies), or characters from Andean (often Bolivian) folklore. Within this context, the term *moreno* can be taken either literally as "Moorish" or, following more common usage, a respectable way of referencing a person's skin tone and complexion (as opposed to *negro*, Black, or *indio*, Indian, both which tend to be understood more negatively). All the *bailes religosos*, however, are stamped with a sense of religious devotion on the part of the dancers, most of whom will state that they are "dancing for the Virgin."

The *morenos de paso* distinguish themselves within this setting in at least two ways. First, they do not dress exotically but, rather, in what might be considered "business attire." Generally, they wear a dark suit jacket, a white collared shirt, a tie, and pressed pants or a knee-length skirt—topped off with an over-the-shoulder sash upon which is embroidered a phrase like "Viva Maria." This regalia suggests that the troupes have followed the model of dressing elegantly to represent themselves. A long-time member of the troupe *Los Hijos de Azapa* has stated that this style of dress was his elders' way of imitating the style of the Spaniards who dressed in dark uniforms for ceremonies.[22] In another fieldwork interview, I even saw an older photo in which *morenos de paso* dancers wore plumed, wide-brimmed cavalier hats.[23]

The second way that the *morenos de paso* stand out is, as their name suggests, the pacing step they use. Dances like the *gitanos* and *turbantes* are also referred to as *morenos de salto*, because dancers perform sequences in which they hop for extended periods as individual dancers switch places between the rows they have formed. The Andean folkloric dances are often performed to popular rhythms like *huayno* or *waka-waka*, which already have basic steps that could be described as bouncy and lively. The *morenos de paso*, meanwhile, keep a steady pace to the strains of a march. As they keep time on their *matracas* (ratchets), they create formations in a manner like marching or military bands, whether dancing in the church, in the plaza, or in procession.

Morenos de Paso: Considering the Kongolese in their Devotional Practice

Another name for the *morenos de paso* is the *morenos pitucos*. In the past, *pituco* referred to people who were finely dressed, but today the term more commonly has a negative connotation of being "snobbish." While I never got the impression that locals thought of these troupes as haughty, their use of the term at least means that the troupes called attention to the care and pride that they took in their uniform. After all, to reach the sanctuary, one must hike several miles through a dusty canyon. Keeping shoes shined and neat and clothes pressed and clean within such an environment demands extra effort. While all the *baile religoso* troupes want their regalia to leave an impression, the *morenos de paso* do not wear overly bright colors or have sequins to distract from their elegance and tidiness, which means that these traits must be their forte.

Clothing, then, becomes an especially important vehicle through which *morenos de paso* express their religious and social worth. While this observation may seem obvious given that the finery here is presumed to be cosmopolitan or in imitation of the Spanish, a multivocal perspective recognizes that this principle was not just held by Europeans. Cécile Fromont has explained how the Kongo kingdom's elite were quick to adopt European fashions into their established sartorial practices after contact.[24] Elites could signal wealth through the wearing of extensive European fabrics and by adding their own European-like symbols of royalty (such as family crests) onto those hats that were already recognized locally as icons of power. As Fromont demonstrates, these elite clothing practices conveyed messages of social capital both to locals and to European trading partners, and the value of such messages would have been recognized across much of the Black Atlantic.

This adoption of symbols was not just limited to clothing. As the Kongolese had made the spiritually practical and politically savvy decision to convert to Catholicism, the cross in multiple manifestations became a symbol of religious and educational wealth. One of these manifestations was a staff topped with a cross, which well-educated religious interlocutors called *mestres* carried to indicate their position.[25] The *caporal*, or dance captain, of a *morenos de paso* troupe carries an arm-length staff that merges with his right arm. These *caporales* present the staff to the Virgin as they enter with their troupes to sing to the Virgin in the church.

The cross also appears as one of the fundamental choreographic formations that a *morenos de paso* troupe performs. Once the dancers have entered the church and sung the greeting to the Virgin that corresponds to the time of day, they pace to the sound of a march until they stand in the shape of a cross. As one of the fundamental symbols of Christianity, the cross is mainly associated with having accompanied the conquistadors to the Americas. However, because the Kongolese had already adopted Christianity, the cross would have resonated with Africans from this region, and, furthermore, the Kongolese understandings of the cross would have been experienced with similar symbols that resembled the cross within native religions in the region.[26] The Kongo cosmogram, also known as the *yowa*, is a diagram that connects four evenly spaced points on a circle. The circle represents the daily motion of the sun, paying special attention to four important points: sunrise, noon, sunset, and midnight. The straight line that connects sunrise and sunset acts as a horizon and divides the world of the living from the kingdom of the dead, often understood as a river. A straight line connecting noon and midnight acts as a path from the dead, imagined below the earth, to the Supreme Deity, at the apex of the mountain of life. The circle also represents the trajectory of life, with the four points corresponding to birth, prime existence in the plane of life, dying, and prime existence in the plane of the dead. In this cosmology, a righteous person will always be traveling along this circle, dying only to be reborn.[27] To stand at the intersection of the two lines is to indicate a key point where, through an awareness of the sun's and life's trajectory, communication between the divine and earthly will happen, which is why certain Afrodescendant religious rites in the Americas involve drawing a cross

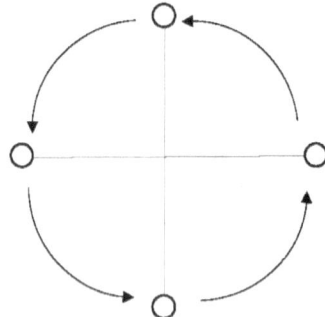

Figure 1. The Kongolese cosmogram, the Yowa. Courtesy of the author.

on the floor for the supplicant to position themselves in the most fortuitous way to achieve communication with the divine. The *morenos de paso* troupe's dancing into a cross formation not only symbolizes European idea of the cross but also resonates with Kongolese ideas surrounding the cosmogram.[28] A key difference between these two interpretations seems to be the Kongolese awareness of positionality within a circle of time, something that Congolese theologian Kiatezua Lubanzadio Luyaluka argues is actually the more important signifier here.[29]

Beyond the symbolic imagery of the cross formation, the dance figures that the troupes complete can also be analyzed for meaning. Following a study of Chile's *bailes religiosos*, and, in the highly symmetric choreography of *the morenos de paso* and *salto*, sociologist Juan Van Kessel sees a reflection of the highly symmetric Aymara concepts of space–time as well as the traditional divisions of labor.[30] Van Kessel also sees confirmation of the pervasiveness of these ideas in other Aymara cultural forms like weaving. In weaving, he correlates the two rows of dancers to threads that can either be woven back-and-forth in alternating patterns or as a contained pattern that then hierarchically gets duplicated through the rows. This latter idea appears in Kongolese forms as well, with a knot or cross-like form at the center of the pattern that either is replicated in a way that can go on indefinitely or, in basketry, uses alternating colors to emphasize a zig-zag, horizontal movement around the basket.[31]

While Van Kessel's dance figure argument applies to many of the troupes, a closer analysis of the individual steps of the *morenos de pasos*, specifically for the troupes that have a history of Afrodescendant participation, suggests a more unique set of aesthetics at play. In observing the older members of these troupes, I noticed that they rocked their shoulders when they stepped. I was especially drawn to a retired *caporal* who had years of experience dancing. As *caporal* he had the duty of pacing through the center of the two rows of facing dancers, following a zig-zag path. He would step forward with a straight leg across the body while raising his opposite shoulder, his staff arm accentuating the length of the line. While seeming to lean to one side, he never gave the impression of being out of control, particularly as he would change direction during his trajectory toward the front of the troupe. Upon asking several *morenos de paso* troupe members about these characteristics, they identified it as an older style of dancing, one that could still be associated with nearby Peruvian troupes who also had a long history of Afrodescendant family participation. This movement style displays many of the characteristics that Robert Farris Thompson has labeled the "aesthetic of the cool," in which value is placed on rhythm, control, angularity, and asymmetry.[32] Thompson has argued that this behavior reflects the integration of the body–mind, rather than the separation espoused by the classic Western mindset, and it is best observed when "ecstatic unions of sensuous pleasure and moral responsibility" occur.[33] He also has noted that, throughout West and Central Africa, these values are associated with a straight-faced ancestrality, so that in a "cool" performance, the wisdom of the aged appears alongside the vigorous dancing of youth. Generally, in the *bailes religiosos*, I often heard conservative dancers remind the others that they do not dance for attention but rather for the Virgin. This critique was often leveled at the dancers with more ostentatious regalia but could also be directed at dancers who critics thought might be too showy in their moves—perhaps even strutting. The performance of "coolness" by the older *morenos de paso* dancers here seems to push back against this critique of showing off by keeping a straight face while still performing these more angular steps. In performing in a *pituco* style, the dancers would appear to be accessing "a mode of asserting strength of self, broadly dovetailing with portions of the African mode of 'looking smart.'"[34]

What I hope is clear from these observations is that there are several resonances between the aesthetics involved in the *morenos de paso* expression and three major component cultures involved in this space. Outwardly, Iberian Catholic interpretations prevail because of the historical colonial power structure in the region. Noting the dominant Aymara and Quechua presence, however, Van Kessel and others have argued that how elements of Indigenous cosmology coincide with the *bailes religiosos* performance practices means that an Indigenous thread can be identified within this Andean *ch'ixi* expression. A larger anti-colonial gesture would consider the ways elements of African cosmology also constitute a thread within this practice due to the Afrodescendant presence in the region. Here, I have interpreted the *morenos de paso* from a generalized Western Central African perspective and found several possible resonances. Perhaps the connection with movement on the individual level—the aesthetic of the cool—is where the African thread in this *ch'ixi* practice is most apparent, given its difference from Iberian and Indigenous modes of movement practice. My idea here is not to suggest that this combination was the specific way the *moreno de paso* expression was created but rather that this expression offers the possibility of hearing the multiple voices needed to work in an anti-colonial fashion. The issue is not to argue about which culture contributed the most to the creation of the expression but rather what ideas that emerge from the expression might best be used in constructing a more equitable society.

The *morenos de paso* in northern Chile exemplify a case where the possibility of an Afrodescendant thread within a *ch'ixi* expression needs to be considered first. I now turn to the *bomba* in Puerto Rico, a situation where the variety of African influences at work over time needs to be re-emphasized.

Contemporary *Bomba* Narrative and Practice

Noel Allende-Gotia has argued recently that the Puerto Rican bomba involves a Bahktinian chronotype of historic inversion.[35] He notes how, over the last century, intellectuals and scholars have tended to read the contemporary understanding and practice of *bomba* back in time as a singular expression of Afrodescendant music-dance. In this reading, *bomba* arrived virtually intact from Africa and has continued to be performed in the same way from the moment the first Afrodescendants stepped foot on the island. The lack of information about the early history of *bomba* and the folklorization process that the expression has undergone during the twentieth century has contributed to this tendency.[36] Here I complement Allende's complex envisioning of *bomba* by suggesting how multiple African cosmologies can simultaneously resonate with *bomba* practice. From a *ch'ixi* perspective, the presence of these multiple cosmologies hints at the different influences on *bomba* over time.

Contemporary bomba practice consists of several elements. First, it requires the presence of at least two drums, generally referred to as barriles (barrels) due to their shape. These drums take on additional names depending upon their role: musicians keep the basic rhythm on the buleador (or multiple buleadores), while a single musician plays the generally higher-pitched primo or subidor. Another musician plays the cuá, a steady rhythm executed with sticks either on the side of a drum already being played or a miniature barrel created especially for this purpose. Every bomba has a song text, performed by a lead vocalist, who typically plays the maraca, as well as a chorus of singers that respond with a repeated phrase. Classic lyrics often reference historical situations that were familiar to a bomba community at some time, either as news stories or as personal situations between performers. At a bomba event, other participants sway, standing to form a semi-circle facing the musicians and creating the space called a batey or soberao that individual dancers then enter. The most striking feature of contemporary bomba practice happens when a dancer enters this space and salutes the primo drummer. At that point, this drummer is expected to play in a way that mimics the dancer's movements, acting as a medium for the music the dancer is improvising through their choreography. This interaction continues until the dancer salutes the drummer and leaves the space, ceding it to another dancer or for other musical interactions, like a *primo* solo.

Bomba: The Multiple Resonances with African Cultures

Unlike the *morenos de paso* case, *bomba* offers linguistic tools for thinking anti-colonially. In Manuel Álvarez's famous work on the African influences in Puerto Rican Spanish, he suggests that the name *bomba* derives from a Bantu word, *ngwoma*.[37] Nineteenth-century scholars conceived of Bantu as a large sub-Saharan language family, encompassing much of southern and central Africa, based on the presence of cognates. As one of these cognates, ngwoma or ngoma is a wide-spread word stem, often glossed generically as "drum" in various African languages. The term can also refer to a specific type (or types) of drum, a "community-based dance," and a set of music-dance practices associated with certain moieties or cults of healing.[38] This etymological interpretation resonates in Puerto Rico, where *bomba* has been used historically to refer to the drum in a general sense, as well as to song texts and dancing accompanied by drums.[39] As Allende suggests, however, contemporary use tends to focus on its reference to the dancing and song texts as a meta-genre, thereby reducing the multiple sub-genres of *bomba*, such as *sicá*, *holandés*, and *yubá*, to simply a number of rhythms to be executed within a standard practice. Following Allende's argument means recognizing that the drums are what group these multiple types of dances together, suggesting that these sub-genres initially had choreographies and functions different from contemporary practice.

Yet *bomba* is also a word that has been present in Afrodescendant practice in multiple areas of the Americas, dating back to the colonial period. Jeroen Dewulf has recently juxtaposed Afro-Puerto Ricans' use of the term with its presence on slave plantations in the Danish and Dutch West Indies, in Pinkster celebrations in New York, and *Vodou* ceremonies in Haiti.[40] He suggests that *bomba* derives from Kikongo culture—a possible reference to Mbumba, a Kongolese deity associated with snakes and water. In her dissertation, Christina Mobley has made a strong historical sociolinguistic argument to place this etymology of the deity Bomba/Mbumba even more specifically within the Kikongo dialects spoken in the Mayombe region.[41] Janzen has noted that, in this same region's variety of a historic cult known as Lemba, not only is Bomba one of the names given to a Kongo deity, but that miniature versions of the drums used in that cult's ceremonies were filled with potent plant substances to be hung around the neck as protective charms.[42] The drums in this cult were thought to contain the ancestors or mythic heroes, their voices, or the therapeutic power to set some affliction right.[43]

While this connection between Afro-Puerto Rican *bomba* with Kikongo culture is still speculative, it resonates with the growing academic literature asserting the need to examine the Kikongo influence on Afrodescendant culture in the Americas more closely. It also dovetails nicely with Rivera Cusicanqui's emphasis on language to discover the *ch'ixi* nature of cultural expressions. Through this particular lens, *bomba* practice takes on a religious character of protection and healing through the drums that scholars like Ashley Coleman Taylor have documented as part of some participants' experience of *bomba*.[44] Plus, this character is consistent with Mobley's interpretation of Kongolese influence on public music-dance in Haiti.[45] Finally, in keeping with Allende's vision of *bomba* practice as something always undergoing change, this connection would also suggest how a previously religious understanding of *bomba* has taken a more secular turn.

However, discussions about *bomba* have not given potential Kongolese influence much attention, in part because previous scholars have focused on possible influences from other parts of Africa. In his influential dissertation, Hector Vega-Drouet connects the *bomba* to Akan, particularly Ashanti, drumming.[46] While acknowledging that slaves arrived in Puerto Rico from all over Africa, he makes an extended argument to privilege connections between Ashanti and *bomba* drumming, largely based on the idea that a number of slaves arrived in Puerto Rico from the Dutch and British colonies in the Lesser Antilles. Assuming that Ashanti traditions had considerable influence in those islands, Vega-Drouet believes the same situation existed in Puerto Rico. He finds support for his ideas in the subgenre of *bomba* called *holandés* (presumably a reference to Holland) and in similarities he saw between *bomba* and Ashanti traditions during a visit to Ghana.[47] Vega-Drouet focuses particularly on: 1) the etymological similarity between *bomba* and the Ashanti royal rhythm called *bommae*; 2) the similar repetitive rhythmic pattern between a *bomba* and an Ashanti *mpintin*; and 3) the similar dancer-drum interactions found in *bomba* and the Ewe *vuga* (a rhythm the Ashanti presumably taught the Ewe). The first two set of similarities are weak, and I have already mentioned alternate, more methodologically sound sociolinguistic etymologies and the presence of multiple *bomba* rhythms, which Vega-Drouet ignores. The most promising idea that Vega-Drouet offers to think with is the Ashanti drum-dancer interaction—not in its similarity but in its difference to contemporary practice. He notes that, in the *vuga*, "the master drummer occasionally challenges and tests the dancer's acquaintance with the drum language."[48] This performance feature seems to reverse the idea found in the *bomba* and reinforces J. H. Nketia's suggestion that, more generally in Akan drumming, the master drummers are to be shown respect by dancers following their instructions expressed through a drum language.[49] Only when the drummer feels that the dancer deserves respect—through skill or social status—might the drummer follow a dancer's steps. If the dancer is disrespectful, the drummer will quote proverbs to humble the dancer. Preliminary research I have done suggests that similar attitudes can also be found among the Maninka of the Western Coast, so that multiple African cultures may have interpreted the drummer-dancer interaction this way, though not through the same drum language.

Perhaps the loss of tonal language in the diaspora has led to this change in the relationship between drummer-dancer, so that, although there is still a recognition of the mutual interaction needed in *bomba*, the dancer seems to be given the privilege of leading. Barton, however, has offered an anecdote of lead drummers in Loíza, who would *caminar el tambor*, or walk the drum, by holding it between their legs in search of a dancer to interact with, even forcing them to do so. Although not as commonly seen, Barton also noted that the complement to this drummer's walk is that a dancer performs so well, that the drummer acknowledges their skill by tilting the drum toward them.[50]

The case of the *bomba* has offered the opportunity to use signs within language to identify possible *ch'ixi* perspectives within Puerto Rican culture. Tracing an etymology through to Kongolese culture has suggested that the *bomba* drum may have served as an icon for divine power and that *bomba* events could be interpreted as a space of protection and healing. Turning to the movement practices within *bomba* for other ideas helped point to cultures within the Gulf of Guinea and Africa's Western coast that valued the drummer-dancer interaction in a different way than current practice. These included relying on a drum language and the use of community-based proverbs to ensure that protocols of respect were enforced. Adopting a *ch'ixi* perspective for *bomba* means metaphorically seeing these features as threads woven together that may not be discernable in the tapestry of a contemporary *bomba* performance but that, upon closer examination, can be spotted as possible individual threads to use in thinking against coloniality.

Circling Back to Dismantle Coloniality

Coloniality relies on the values of modernity—thinking in terms of constant forward progress, of development that requires constant consumption of resources. On the one hand, thinking in a *ch'ixi* mode with the *morenos de paso* expression suggests envisioning life in a cyclical fashion, one that will require a reckoning when an individual returns to any particular point on that cycle. The aesthetic of the cool that resonates with an individual's steps does not mean that individual remains static or unfluctuating as they move along the cycle. Instead, the movement comes with a controlled angularity that eventually suggests an alternate form of envisioning symmetry. This aesthetic even allows for an elegant or *pituco* style of addressing challenges. Thinking in a *ch'ixi* mode with *bomba*, on the other hand, can help one recognize the need for power or healing in the face of adversity or imbalance, respectively. This healing is not quiet and static but requires the proverbial language of communal wisdom that the drum calls an individual to interact with, actively and respectfully. Keeping these perspectives in mind when tackling difficult issues can help them become a more permanent part of the conversation.

More *ch'ixi* thinking can be done here: for example, teasing out threads of thought from other regions of Africa in the *morenos de paso* and recognizing the values of the Indigenous and European threads in *bomba*. Even with this additional work, however, it is important to remember that these ideas have emerged from two very specific contexts and may not always have value to those contexts today. Whether these alternate perspectives are of value depend upon whether they resonate with the cultural memory those who struggle within those contexts and what the society they create ultimately chooses to value. What I hope to have illustrated here is a mode of thinking that may prove useful to those working to dismantle coloniality, both in these two and many additional contexts.

NOTES

1. The author thanks the *morenos de paso* and *bomba* performers who have shared their knowledge with him, especially those cited here. Special thanks to Mintzi

Martinez-Rivera for her suggestions on an earlier draft of this chapter and to the editor of this volume for her patience and interest in the topic.
2. In Peru, Mendoza uses the phrase "ritual dances" for these expressions. *Mestizo* (literally mixture) was initially a colonial racial caste referring to the offspring of European and Native coupling, but it is now more broadly associated with a cultural mix of these heritages. Zoila S. Mendoza, *Shaping Society through Dance: Mestizo Ritual Performance in the Peruvian Andes* (Chicago: University of Chicago Press, 2000), 4.
3. Juan Van Kessel, *Aica y la Peña Sagrada* (Iquique, Chile: El Jote Errante, 1992), 24.
4. Throughout this chapter, I will use the hyphenated term "music-dance." While cosmopolitan culture continues to conceive and refer to these concepts separately, many cultures do not conceive of such a division, and indeed, have different perspectives on how sound and movement are organized. See also Juan Eduardo Wolf, *Styling Blackness in Chile: Music and Dance in the African Diaspora* (Bloomington: Indiana University Press, 2019), 13.
5. The term *negro bozal* was a colonial category used to indicate a slave that came directly from Africa with little to no knowledge of European language and culture.
6. Arlene M. Dávila, *Sponsored Identities: Cultural Politics in Puerto Rico* (Philadelphia: Temple University Press, 1997), 67–73.
7. See Jade Power-Sotomayor and Pablo Luis Rivera, "Puerto Rican Bomba: Syncopating Bodies, Histories, and Geographies," *CENTRO Journal* 31, no. 2 (2019): 5–39.
8. The primary era of colonialism referred to in this chapter is the Spanish colonial era in the Americas (1492–1898), although the current colonial condition of Puerto Rico remains relevant to this discussion. In the legal language of the United States, Puerto Rico is one of its unincorporated territories, while Puerto Rico's local government has used the phrase *estado de libre asociación* (a freely associated state) in its documents, which has often been translated as Commonwealth. Over the years, however, several United Nations committees have recognized that the process of decolonization in Puerto Rico is not complete.
9. Enrique Dussel, "Eurocentrism and Modernity (Introduction to the Frankfurt Lectures)," *boundary 2* 20, no. 1 (1993): 72.
10. Many Latin American scholars reference Aníbal Quijano's framing of coloniality, or the coloniality of power. See Walter D. Mignolo and Catherine E. Walsh, *On Decoloniality: Concepts, Analytics, Praxis* (Durham: Duke University Press, 2018). Meanwhile, Rivera Cusicanqui points out that other people were already discussing such issues. Silvia Rivera Cusicanqui, "*Ch'ixinakax utxiwa*: A Reflection on the Practices and Discourses of Decoloniality," *South Atlantic Quarterly* 111, no. 1 (2012): 103.
11. German Freire et al., *Afro-descendants in Latin America: Toward a Framework of Inclusion* (Washington, DC: World Bank, 2018), 71.
12. Mignolo and Walsh, *On Decoloniality*, 146.
13. "Cultural memory" is Samuel A. Floyd Jr.'s idea that members of a culture have a subjective knowledge that is not formally taught to them but that can serve as a basis

for judgment of whether a practice or event rings "true" or "right" for them. Samuel A. Floyd Jr., *The Power of Black Music: Interpreting Its History from Africa to the United States* (New York: Oxford University Press, 1995), 8.
14. Rivera Cusicanqui, "Ch'ixinakax utxiwa," 105. See note two for clarification of the *mestizo* category.
15. "Infertile" is Rivera Cusicanqui's descriptor for hybridity, rooted in genetic and racialized logic. Ibid., 105.
16. Sylvia Rivera Cusicanqui, "The Potosí Principle: Another View of Totality," *emisférica* 11, no. 1 (2014), https://hemisphericinstitute.org/en/emisferica-11-1-decolonial-gesture/11-1-essays/the-potosi-principle-another-view-of-totality.html.
17. For the fundamental idea that decoloniality requires rejecting the universal for the pluriversal, see Mignolo and Walsh, *On Decoloniality*.
18. John Thornton, *Africa and Africans in the Making of the Atlantic World, 1400–1800* (New York: Cambridge University Press, 2006), 118.
19. David Richardson, "Slave Exports from West and West-Central Africa. 1700–1810: New Estimates of Volume and Distribution," *The Journal of African History* 30, no. 1 (1989): 13.
20. Gwendolyn Midlo Hall, *Slavery and African Ethnicities in the Americas: Restoring the Links* (Chapel Hill: University of North Carolina Press, 2005), 192.
21. Yvonne Daniel, *Dancing Wisdom: Embodied Knowledge in Haitian Vodou, Cuban Yoruba, and Bahian Candomblé* (Urbana: University of Illinois Press, 2005), 2–3.
22. Miguel Zegarra Baluarte, in personal interview with the author, July 25, 2006.
23. Adolfo Aica, in personal interview with the author, May 29, 2009. These personal interviews, as well as my descriptions of *morenos de paso* performances, are a result of several years of fieldwork into Afrodescendant music-dance performance in and around Arica, Chile. For more details on the *moreno de paso*, see chapter 5 in Wolf's *Styling Blackness in Chile*. In contrast, while I have completed some preliminary fieldwork in Puerto Rico, the work on *bomba* that I present here is mostly literature based. Here I am beginning to lay the groundwork for contrasting two different pluriverses within the African diaspora.
24. See Cécile Fromont, *The Art of Conversion: Christian Visual Culture in the Kingdom of Kongo* (Chapel Hill: University of North Carolina Press, 2014), especially chapter 3.
25. Ibid., 21.
26. Both Thornton and Hall have argued for the need to take greater account of Kongolese culture in the Americas. See Thornton, *Africa and Africans*, 326; and Hall, *Slavery and African Ethnicities*, 149.
27. Robert Farris Thompson, *Flash of the Spirit: African and Afro-American Art and Philosophy* (New York: Vintage, 1984), 108–109.
28. To complement this idea even further, Van Kessel also makes notes of how Aymara ritual practices corresponded to the local agricultural cycle. See Juan Van Kessel, *Danzas y Estructuras Sociales de los Andes* (Cusco: Instituto de Pastoral Andina, 1981), 277.
29. Kiatezua Lubanzadio Luyaluka, "The Spiral as the Basic Semiotic of the Kongo Religion, the Bukongo," *Journal of Black Studies* 48, no. 1 (2017): 93.

30. Van Kessel, *Danzas y Estructuras Sociales de los Andes*, 301.
31. Els Cranshof, Nicolas Nikis, and Pierre de Marrt, "Ceramics Decorated with Woven Motifs: An Archaelogical Kongo Kingdom Identifier?," in *The Kongo Kingdom: The Origins, Dynamics, and Cosmopolitan Culture of an African Polity*, ed. Koen Bostoen and Inge Brinkman (New York: Cambridge University Press, 2018), 172–73.
32. Robert Farris Thompson, "An Aesthetic of the Cool," *African Arts* 7, no. 1 (1973): 41–42.
33. Ibid., 42.
34. Ibid., 45.
35. Noel Allende-Gotia, "Topografía social y cultural de las músicas africanas y afrodescendientes en el archipiélago puertorriqueño: la historia de las músicas afrodiaspóricas en Puerto Rico como antinomia de la historia folklorizada de la bomba," *CENTRO Journal* 31, no. 2 (2019): 59.
36. Mendoza has defined "folklorization" as the process "whereby public forms of expression are selected as being representative of a whole region or nation and are staged and promoted as such." Mendoza also illustrates how this process can be an interaction between multiple actors from different sectors of society rather than a simple imposition of elite values on staged performances of folk practices. Zoila S. Mendoza, *Creating Our Own: Folklore, Performance, and Identity in Cuzco, Peru* (Durham: Duke University Press, 2008), 6–7.
37. Manuel Álvarez Nazario, *El elemento afronegroide en el español de Puerto Rico: Contribución al estudio del negro en América* (San Juan, PR: Instituto de Cultura Puertorriqueña, 1974), 291.
38. John M. Janzen, *Ngoma: Discourses of Healing in Central and Southern Africa* (Berkeley: University of California Press, 1992), 74; Gerard Kubik, *Theory of African Music, Volume II* (Chicago: University of Chicago Press, 2010), 9–11.
39. Álvarez Nazario, *El elemento afronegroide*, 291–93, 297–300, 303–306.
40. Jeroen Dewulf, *The Pinkster King and the King of the Kongo: The Forgotten History of America's Dutch-Owned Slaves* (Jackson: University Press of Mississippi, 2017), 224–25.
41. Christina Mobley, "The Kongolese Atlantic: Central African Slavery and Culture from Mayombe to Haiti" (PhD diss., Duke University, 2015), 229–33.
42. John M. Janzen, *Lemba 1650–1930: A Drum of Affliction in Africa and the New World* (New York: Garland, 1982), 275.
43. Ibid., 256–57.
44. Ashley Coleman Taylor, " 'Water Overflows with Memory': Bomba, Healing, and the Archival Oceanic," *CENTRO Journal* 31, no. 2 (2019): 153–55.
45. Mobley, "The Kongolese Atlantic," 333–34.
46. Hector Vega-Drouet, "Historical and Ethnological Survey on Probable African Origins of the Puerto Rican Bomba, including a Description of Santiago Apostol Festivities at Loiza Aldea" (PhD diss., Wesleyan University, 1979), 53, 55.
47. Ibid., 39, 53–54.
48. Ibid., 64.
49. J. H. Nketia, "The Role of the Drummer in Akan Society," *African Music Society Journal* 1, no. 1 (1954): 43.

50. Halbert Barton, "The Challenges of Puerto Rican Bomba," in *Caribbean Dance: From Abakua to Zouk*, ed. Susanna Sloat (Gainesville: University Press of Florida, 2002), 185, 191.

WORKS CITED

Allende-Gotia, Noel. "Topografía social y cultural de las músicas africanas y afrodescendientes en el archipiélago puertorriqueño: La historia de las músicas afrodiaspóricas en Puerto Rico como antinomia de la historia folklorizada de la bomba." *CENTRO Journal* 31, no. 2 (2019): 58–85.

Álvarez Nazario, Manuel. *El Elemento Afronegroide en el Español de Puerto Rico: Contribución al Estudio del Negro en América*. San Juan, PR: Instituto de Cultura Puertorriqueña, 1974.

Basso Ortiz, Alessandra. "Los gangá longobá: El nacimiento de los dioses." *Boletín Antropológico* 20, no. 2 (2001):195–208.

Barton, Halbert. "The Challenges of Puerto Rican Bomba." In *Caribbean Dance: From Abakua to Zouk*, edited by Susanna Sloat, 183–96. Gainesville: University Press of Florida, 2002.

Coleman Taylor, Ashley. " 'Water Overflows with Memory': Bomba, Healing, and the Archival Oceanic," *CENTRO Journal* 31, no. 2 (2019): 137–160.

Cranshof, Els, Nicolas Nikis, and Pierre de Marrt. "Ceramics Decorated with Woven Motifs: An Archaelogical Kongo Kingdom Identifier?" In *The Kongo Kingdom: The Origins, Dynamics, and Cosmopolitan Culture of an African Polity*, edited by Koen Bostoen and Inge Brinkman, 165–196. New York: Cambridge University Press, 2018.

Daniel, Yvonne. *Dancing Wisdom: Embodied Knowledge in Haitian Vodou, Cuban Yoruba, and Bahian Candomblé*. Urbana: University of Illinois Press, 2005.

Dávila, Arlene M. *Sponsored Identities: Cultural Politics in Puerto Rico*. Philadelphia: Temple University Press, 1997.

Dewulf, Jeroen. *The Pinkster King and the King of the Kongo: The Forgotten History of America's Dutch-Owned Slaves*. Jackson: University Press of Mississippi, 2017.

Dussel, Enrique. "Eurocentrism and Modernity (Introduction to the Frankfurt Lectures)." *boundary 2* 20, no. 1 (1993): 65–76.

Floyd, Samuel A, Jr. *The Power of Black Music: Interpreting Its History from Africa to the United States*. New York: Oxford University Press, 1995.

Freire, German, Carolina Diaz-Bonilla, Steven Schwartz Orellana, Jorge Soler Lopez, and Flavia Carbonari. *Afro-descendants in Latin America: Toward a Framework of Inclusion*. Washington, DC: World Bank, 2018.

Fromont, Cécile. *The Art of Conversion: Christian Visual Culture in the Kingdom of Kongo*. Chapel Hill: University of North Carolina Press, 2014.

Hall, Gwendolyn Midlo. *Slavery and African Ethnicities in the Americas: Restoring the Links*. Chapel Hill: University of North Carolina Press, 2005.

Janzen, John M. *Lemba, 1650–1930: A Drum of Affliction in Africa and the New World*. New York: Garland, 1982.

———. *Ngoma: Discourses of Healing in Central and Southern Africa*. Berkeley: University of California Press, 1992.
Kubik, Gerard. *Theory of African Music, Volume II*. Chicago: University of Chicago Press, 2010.
Luyaluka, Kiatezua Lubanzadio. "The Spiral as the Basic Semiotic of the Kongo Religion, the Bukongo." *Journal of Black Studies* 48, no. 1 (2017): 91–112.
Mendoza, Zoila S. *Creating Our Own: Folklore, Performance, and Identity in Cuzco, Peru*. Durham: Duke University Press, 2008.
———. *Shaping Society through Dance: Mestizo Ritual Performance in the Peruvian Andes*. Chicago: University of Chicago Press, 2000.
Mignolo, Walter D., and Catherine E. Walsh. *On Decoloniality: Concepts, Analytics, Praxis*. Durham: Duke University Press, 2018.
Mobley, Christina. "The Kongolese Atlantic: Central African Slavery and Culture from Mayombe to Haiti." PhD diss., Duke University, 2015.
Nketia, J. H. "The Role of the Drummer in Akan Society." *African Music Society Journal* 1, no. 1 (1954): 34–43.
Ortiz, Fernando. *Los bailes y el teatro de los negros en el folkore de Cuba*. La Habana: Editorial Letras Cubanas, 1951.
Power-Sotomayor, Jade, and Pablo Luis Rivera. "Puerto Rican Bomba: Syncopating Bodies, Histories, and Geographies." *CENTRO Journal* 31, no. 2 (2019): 5–39.
Richardson, David. "Slave Exports from West and West-Central Africa. 1700–1810: New Estimates of Volume and Distribution." *Journal of African History* 30, no. 1 (1989): 1–22.
Rivera Cusicanqui, Silvia. "*Ch'ixinakax utxiwa*: A Reflection on the Practices and Discourses of Decoloniality." *South Atlantic Quarterly* 111, no. 1 (2012): 95–109.
———. "The Potosí Principle: Another View of Totality." *emisférica* 11, no. 1 (2014), https://hemisphericinstitute.org/en/emisferica-11-1-decolonial-gesture/11-1-essays/the-potosi-principle-another-view-of-totality.html.
Thompson, Robert Farris. "An Aesthetic of the Cool." *African Arts* 7, no. 1 (1973): 40–43, 64–67, 89–91.
———. *African Art in Motion: Icon and Act in the Collection of Katherine Coryton White*. Los Angeles: University of California Press, 1974.
———. *Flash of the Spirit: African and Afro-American Art and Philosophy*. New York: Vintage, 1984.
Thornton, John. *Africa and Africans in the Making of the Atlantic World, 1400–1800*. New York: Cambridge University Press, 2006.
Van Kessel, Juan. *Danzas y estructuras sociales de los Andes*. Cusco: Instituto de Pastoral Andina, 1981.
———. *Aica y la Peña Sagrada*. Iquique, Chile: El Jote Errante, 1992.
Vega-Drouet, Hector. "Historical and Ethnological Survey on Probable African Origins of the Puerto Rican Bomba, including a Description of Santiago Apostol Festivities at Loiza Aldea." PhD diss., Wesleyan University, 1979.
Wolf, Juan Eduardo. *Styling Blackness in Chile: Music and Dance in the African Diaspora*. Bloomington: Indiana University Press, 2019.

◆ CHAPTER 9

Xiomara Cacho Caballero

Linguistic Heritage and Afro-Indigenous Survivance on Roatán

Jennifer Carolina Gómez Menjívar

> ¿Cuál es el pasado
> De este presente que succiona
> Dejando en interrogante la sobrevivencia
> de la identidad?
> —XIOMARA CACHO CABALLERO, *TUMÁLALI NANÍGI:*
> *LA VOZ DEL CORAZÓN: THE VOICE OF THE HEART*

What is the past / of this present that suckles / leaving open the question of survivance / of identity?
Native survivance is an active sense of presence over absence, deracination, and oblivion ... Survivance stories are renunciations of dominance, detractions, obtrusions, the unbearable sentiments of tragedy, and the literary legacy of dominance and victimry.
—GERALD VIZENOR, *LITERARY CHANCE*

The number of Afro-Indigenous writers living in Améfrica has increased and, with them, attention to the marginal zones from whence they hail has also increased. This chapter examines Xiomara Cacho Caballero's work on Garifuna experience in Central America's Northern Triangle, a region frequently associated with violence and drug trafficking. Importantly, Cacho Caballero is from Roatán, the island to which British settlers deported Garifuna peoples in 1797.[1] Forced to leave their homeland of Yurumein (St. Vincent) and to board ships on a perilous journey, Cacho Caballero's ancestors arrived on the tiny island off the coast of Honduras with little besides the intangible culture—language, music, and dance—that centuries later the UNESCO would declare the Patrimony of Humanity. Cacho

Caballero is an Afro-Indigenous voice from the very island where survivors of the deportation disembarked and henceforth devised strategies to ensure the survival of their culture and community. Just as her ancestors did before her, Cacho Caballero examines the possibilities of survival on Roatán and finds in her intangible culture the spiritual and creative material necessary for the community's survival. As I demonstrate in this chapter, Cacho Caballero's work is a multimodal means of confronting the marginality and violence that Garifuna peoples are subjected to on the "narco islands" of Central America. The analysis begins with a discussion of Cacho Caballero's children's stories, follows with an analysis of her book-length essay, covers her trilingual (Garifuna, Spanish, English) poetry, and concludes with thoughts on Cacho Caballero's digital presence. Despite the limited circulation of her writing, I argue that Cacho Caballero's work occupies an important place in the panorama of contemporary Black letters. In her oeuvre, Cacho Caballero treats linguistic revitalization as a form of spiritual mending that—like ceremony and communion with one's ancestors—is critical for emerging from violence as a stronger Afro-Indigenous community.

Linguistic Revitalization and Young Garifuna Readers

Following the language of Garifuna people enables a richer analysis of the logocentric cultural products—such as poetry, short stories, film, music, and even newly written dictionaries—produced by members of the diaspora. By making "the [ancestral] word" dominant, Garifuna peoples divest whiteness from the concept of *logos* and invest in it an Afro-Indigenous epistemic. Garifuna cultural production possesses a historically validated linguistic core that many of its writers put at the center and which has been mistakenly put second in heavily quoted mainstream anthropological analyses that theorize "race" instead of Indigenous experience first. For that reason, I devote this section to the connections between the Garifuna legacy of survivance and the stories that Cacho Caballero writes invoking ancestral wisdom as a guide for Garifuna children. Her approach challenges the many texts that repeat Douglas Taylor's problematic characterization of this group as a "Negro cake composed of Amerindian ingredients."[2] Such framing not only omits the importance of the Indigenous language to the Garifuna community but also fails to capture the repeated subjections to ethnocide and linguicide that it has faced. To keep these principles in focus, I now move to a discussion of the Garifuna homeland during the colonial period.

When Garifuna writers recall and document their homeland as such, it is with the name "Yurumein," though maps continue to identify it as "St. Vincent." Located

596 miles, or 959 kilometers, away from Venezuela, it is an island in the Lesser Antilles that was long ago disputed by both the French and the British during their struggle for dominance in the Caribbean. Speakers of Arawak languages from mainland South America arrived on the island around 600 AD and were joined by speakers of Carib languages—who also hailed from mainland South America—about three centuries later.[3] As Afro-Caribbean linguist Michelle Ocasio tells us, the language spoken in Yurumein prior to the arrival of Europeans was *Kalípona*. Geneviève Escure describes *Kalípona* as possessing an "Arawakan morphosyntax, as well as lexical and morphological Carib elements."[4] *Kalípona* was the language spoken by many families on the island that became known as "St. Vincent" after the arrival of the British. The African men who escaped enslavement when the vessels that carried them as slave cargo were shipwrecked near the coast of Yurumein (St. Vincent) were welcomed into *Kalípona*-speaking families. The practice of calling kin those who married into the *Kalípona* community had been culturally established through the intermarriage of speakers of Arawak from the coastal Amazonian region and Carib languages from the Caribbean Basin many centuries prior. In these Afro-Indigenous unions, the language spoken in homes and the language that children used in community while their fathers went to sea to fish was their mother tongue: *Kalípona*. Thus, *Kalípona* became the second language of the former speakers of Indigenous West African languages and, consequently, it became the first language of their children.

Unlike West African slaves who were forced out of necessity to produce pidgin languages and whose children and descendants took these pidgins and transformed them into creole language varieties consisting of European substrates (like English or French) and West African lexical and morphological elements, babies and young children who learned *Kalípona* did so through their unfractured and un-enslaved kin networks. John Holm's *Central American English* and my own *Tropical Tongues* have examined the histories of creole languages and the unique history of the Garifuna language in the isthmus, though the field of Latin American cultural studies has yet to bring the conclusions from these analyses to bear on Garifuna cultural production. This is relevant because the linguistic genesis of the Afro-Indigenous language restricts the application of theories of Negritude, Antillanité, and Créolité that have been generally applied to Afrodescendant communities and their cultural production in the circum-Caribbean. Returning to Yurumein (St. Vincent) in the eighteenth century, when Europeans began to fight against each other for Indigenous lands, *Kalípona* speakers on the island were kin and a single linguistic community. They were, however, renamed "Caribs" and reclassified by the Europeans who sought to divide and conquer the

Indigenous peoples of the island on the basis of phenotype to better effectuate their program of settler colonialism.

As historian Peter Wade observes, "at the time when the Spanish and Portuguese arrived in the New World, Africans were a well-known category of a person. Some of this knowledge derived from classical texts, religious sources and traveler's tales; but some of it derived from direct contact with Africa, by virtue of voyages of exploration down the West African coast from the 1430s which had resulted in African slaves entering Lisbon from the 1440s."[5] After renaming speakers of *Kalípona* "Caribs," the French and the British subjected the Indigenous community to the racial taxonomies in vogue in Europe and reclassified them as "red" or "black" depending on their phenotype.[6] Europeans thus created a category they called *Charaibes Noirs* in French and *Karaib Negroes* in English, and they dealt with the group in a manner distinct from the way that they engaged with "Red" Caribs. After all, as Wade goes on to explain: "Indigenous people and Africans had different locations in the colonial order, both socially and conceptually. Indigenous people were, officially, to be protected as well as exploited; Africans were slaves and ... the main concern was with control, rather than protection."[7] The segmented approach to the community of *Kalípona* speakers came to a head in 1796, when the British on Yurumein (St. Vincent) accused those they called *Karaib Negroes* of conspiring against them with the French. After the charge, validated by fellow Europeans, they moved to establish punishment: banishment from Yurumein/St. Vincent.[8] The British destroyed provision grounds, putting the community on the brink of starvation, to drive them into surrendering. A total of 4,776 prisoners were taken to the island of Baliceaux, north of St. Vincent, where the Afro-Indigenous community was forced to await their deportation.[9]

The British settlers' deportation of the phenotypically Black speakers of *Kalípona* was due to three reasons well-summarized by anthropologist Nancie González: they desired the fertile lands of Yurumein (St. Vincent) for the establishment of export agriculture; they saw it as a means of establishing political advantage over their French adversaries; and they considered it a way of avoiding allegiances between those whom they called Black Caribs and the non-Carib Black slaves they brought to St. Vincent to overthrow them, as former slaves had done to the French in Haiti beginning in 1791.[10] After all, to Europeans, it was impossible to see Black Caribs as Indigenous peoples and it was impossible for them to see the linguistic and cultural patterns of kinship across phenotypes that were of Indigenous design. The tone of one British observer succinctly captures their insistence that this was a different "type" than the Indigenous peoples they were willing to tolerate:

the slaves who escaped from the wreck were received by the inhabitants as brethren. But this was not all, the Proprietors of the Island gave their daughters in marriage to these strangers, and the race which sprang from this mixture were called Black Caribs, having preserved more of the primitive colour of their fathers, than the lighter hue of their mothers. The Yellow Caribs are of a low stature, the black are tall and stout, and this doubly savage race speak with a degree of vehemence which seems like anger.[11]

Deportation ships were loaded in March 1797 with 2,248 Black speakers of *Kalípona*; the other 2,528 had perished in Baliceaux in the course of their imprisonment.[12] When the ships arrived at Roatán, a tiny island off the coast of Honduras, the number of people who ultimately survived imprisonment, forced voyage, and murder aboard the ships was recorded at a mere 2,026. As Charles Taylor notes, "this small band represented virtually all that was left of the Black Carib people, less than half of the number who had surrendered on St. Vincent just a few months earlier," and given estimates of the size of their community prior to the Black Carib Wars, "up to 77 percent of the population may have died in the space of two years."[13] These survivors carried with them cassava bread, which had been prepared in the traditional Arawak manner prior to ship embarkation, and their intangible heritage: their *Kalípona* language and Indigenous identity. As Afro-Caribbean linguist Michelle Forbes reminds us, the term *Kalípona* was then pronounced with an aspirated /p/, rendering the pronunciation [kalipʰona]. This language, like any other, continued to experience internal linguistic innovation and eventually became known as *Garifuna*.

According to *Ethnologue*, there are approximately 175,000 speakers of Garifuna in Central America today (Figure 2). The proficiency of its speakers is as varied as the degree of Garifuna language endangerment in the countries where it is spoken; it is considered nearly extinct in Nicaragua and highly threatened in Belize and Guatemala, but it is in a developing position in Honduras. This means that "the language is in vigorous use, with literature in a standardized form being used by some though this is not yet widespread or sustainable."[14] However, it should be noted that, even within a country like Honduras, there are places where members of the Garifuna have ceased to speak the language. This is the case in Roatán, the island on which Cacho Caballero's ancestors were deposited by the British and in which the author was raised. Conscious of the historical importance of her island to the Garifuna community and of the linguicide that is accelerating in the twenty-first century, Cacho Caballero produces literature for both younger and older readers. As Cacho Caballero demonstrates in her writings, preserving

Figure 2. Linguistic map of the Garifuna Language. Copyright: Ethnologue, 2019.

language and culture is a family matter. In line with initiatives to revitalize the Garifuna language, Cacho Caballero's work focuses on building cultural pride among young children. In doing so, her work, especially her children's stories, counters the legacy of European linguistic imperialism on Indigenous languages.

Many of the towns founded by Garifuna people as their families settled beyond the island of Roatán were renamed when they were incorporated into the independent republics of Central America. However, the impact of Hispanicization—the ideology largely responsible for the linguistic and cultural threat to other Indigenous communities in the isthmus—ended there. As the liberal push for public education overtook Indigenous languages elsewhere in the isthmus, it largely excised the Caribbean coast from its planning due to the lack of *mestizo* teachers interested in settling in northern Honduras. The ideology of Hispanicization and the mission of public education continued to hover over Indigenous communities in the Pacific coastal areas and in the highland interiors, but the first wave of Hispanicization would not fully hit areas like Roatán until the early twentieth century, when the growing banana trade led the influx of *mestizo* labor and settlement to the area.

The adoption of a Latin script to preserve a threatened Indigenous language—what we see elsewhere in Mesoamerica—was simply neither necessary nor available in these areas. The language remained a part of the oral tradition until religious and public schooling began to compete (and succeed) in leading children to shift away from the Garifuna language. Cacho Caballero's children's stories, *Wafien and his Maracas* (2000) and *Dios negro: Black Jesus: Búngiu Wuríti* (2003), directly address the situation. The first story involves a child named Wafien who wishes to learn how to make maracas out of gourds and seeds. He seeks assistance from a cousin who knows how to make them well, and, in turn, the cousin provides both instructions and motivation when Wafien fails on his first try. Wafien succeeds on his second try and is thrilled to have accomplished the feat of making this traditional instrument. The second story is set in a schoolroom led by a *mestiza* teacher who announces a drawing contest to her class. One of the children draws Jesus, just as he imagines him to be: Black. Both the teacher and the school principal insist that he change the skin color of the image and punish him when he refuses to do so. The child returns home despondent and shares his experience with his mother, who comforts him and reassures him that, yes, Jesus is indeed Black and that the young boy was right to refuse to "correct" his portrait.

These plots bring to bear the words of bell hooks with respect to Afro-Indigenous histories and kinship: "to understand fully how bonds with ancestors are broken, how our visions are lost, it is necessary that we name without shame or fear the way white supremacist domination and its ideological base, white supremacy, strategically work to sever bonds between Africans, African Americans, and Native Americans."[15] The messages in Cacho Caballero's trilingual books are straightforward, encouraging children to be proud of their traditions, of their skin color, and of their rural communities. The order of languages in which the stories appear in the same volume—Garifuna first, followed by Spanish and English—does not exclude young monolingual readers from this clear message. The trilingual encoding of the communication brings them closer to the written form of the language they might have perhaps only heard from elders in their community and provides them a translation in the language(s) they have learned in schools. Importantly, these books fill a void because, despite their limited circulation, they are two of the few, if not the only, books that center Garifuna language and culture in an accessible form for children. Their relatively simple plotlines explicitly advocate for the importance of Garifuna language and culture in the daily lives of children. By targeting this young readership as well as their caregivers and parents, Cacho Caballero defends the need for the youngest members of the Garifuna community to recover their ancestral language. Cacho Caballero understands that when a language is eliminated, the cultural knowledge of a people disappears. Her efforts further underscore the fact that, for many Indigenous writers, language has been inherited from ancestors, and these syllables form a link to tradition.[16] As I discuss next, another area of concern for Cacho Caballero is the extent to which the drug trade has impacted the land and traditions that Garifuna peoples have likewise inherited from their ancestors.

Drugs, Violence, and Adult Content

Cacho Caballero's book-length essay *Viaje, pisto, plomo y miedo* (2016) opens with an extensive reflection on the natural power of Honduras' Caribbean coast, a place in which the environment is more powerful than any human being. The conclusion is one that the author arrives at after being lost in the immensity of Pearl Lagoon while on a trip from Orinoco to Bluefields (Figure 3). After considering the omnipresent spirit of nature on this coast, Cacho Caballero thoroughly examines the contemporary challenges faced by her people. The coast itself is home to the many Garifuna villages established by the ancestors after their dispersal from Roatán, and the sea possesses a life-giving force to a people who depend on it for food and spiritual sustenance. Because there are no roads between the *mestizo* towns of Honduras and Nicaragua and the Garifuna towns, or even between the Garifuna towns themselves, nautical navigation has been the traditional means of travel between sites (Figure 3). However, as Cacho Caballero indicates, tourism and the drug trade have forever altered the towns on Garifuna ancestral lands.

When Cacho Caballero returns to her island Roatán after visiting Bluefields, she reflects on her town, a maritime community that is all at once rough and

Figure 3. Maritime route from Orinoco to Bluefields. Copyright: Google Maps, 2019.

melancholic, simultaneously loud and silent. Readers, Cacho Caballero asserts, might very well feel as if they find themselves in "en el África habitada por una sociedad totalmente nueva que trata de mantener sus costumbres y su cultura a toda costa" (in Africa, inhabited by a totally new society that tries to keep its customs and culture at any cost).[17] It is, she continues, an island full of history and culture, where, since 1797, when the first ancestors arrived, there have been no "personas ricas, sólo jornaleros, marinos cargando su anzuelo, agrupados en convoyes listos para emprender la marcha en lejanas pescas los días señalados, otros individuos circunstanciales necesitados de trabajo se unen a ellos y contribuyen a su tripulación marina" (rich people, only day laborers, fisherman casting their hooks, together in groups ready to take on the route to faraway fishing on designated days, other circumstantial individuals in need of work join them and complete their fishing crew).[18] The price for this tranquility and collaborative spirit has been extreme, however, as Garifuna people are: "víctimas de la sociedad consumista que nos aísla por su falta de oportunidades" (victims of a consumer society that isolates us as a result of its lack of opportunities).[19] While many of the values of the community are rooted in a shared experience of poverty, Cacho Caballero does not romanticize a situation that is clearly due to the exclusion and marginalization of Garifuna people from the dominant *mestizo* context.

While all generations have borne the effects of marginality, the young people of Roatán face challenges that are new to Roatán. As Cacho Caballero explains in a segment of the essay that depicts a fictional conversation between "grandmothers" and "aunts," the population between the ages of fifteen and thirty-five is lost and, as a consequence, the elders are at risk of losing the culture to which they have so carefully tended during their own lifetime. Written as a Socratic dialogue, the women share and debate positions regarding the situation. One fictional woman, Doña María, poignantly states: "la juventud en esa margen de edad está siendo asesinada en un 50%: uno de cada dos son drogadictos" (the youth in that age bracket are being murdered at a 50 percent rate: one in two is a drug addict).[20] The loss of half of the youth is taken as a sign that their culture is at a risk of disappearing. To exacerbate matters, unemployment in Garifuna communities has driven youth to seek employment in the United States, while many of those who have remained battle depression and despair. Due to the socio-economic context of Roatán—an island quickly transitioning into both a tourist and a drug-trafficking site in Central America's Northern Triangle— the despair experienced by Garifuna youth radiates to their loved ones.[21] As the "grandmothers" and "aunts" in Cacho Caballero's essay indicate, losing one's spirit is not merely a metaphysical experience but also the psychological effect of running out of options in a hostile socio-economic context. After all, for individuals between the ages of fifteen to thirty-five, educational attainment does not increase employment opportunities. Despite holding degrees in engineering, medicine, law, and other professions, these trained specialists "tendrán que hacer milagros para poder pagarse una casa; a vivir con los padres, con los abuelos. Tendrán que aceptar todo tipo de trabajos temporales. Tendrán que aprender a vivir, a convivir con el concepto de subsistencia . . . y a esperar que todo mejore" (will have to work a miracle to pay for a house; live with their parents or their grandparents. They'll have to learn to live with the concept of subsistence . . . and to wait for everything to get better).[22]

Elders like the fictional Doña Silvia observe that Garifuna youth are "en un punto donde 'no se puede estar,' 'no se puede vivir'" (at a point where 'it's impossible to be,' 'one can't go on living').[23] The lost generation—as Cacho Caballero describes it upon returning to the first-person narrative voice that opened the essay—cannot escape this predicament. The situation is aggravated by the fact that mafias control local businesses, including those that purportedly operate legally. One example, she states, is public transportation. While purportedly a non-illicit enterprise, it has become a monopoly and the most lucrative routes are held by insiders, which new transportation companies are not allowed to operate. Thus, any young Garifuna men who wish to make a living in this employment sector see all doors closed to them and, in effect, are impeded from improving their economic situation. The drug trade thus becomes one of the sole avenues for young men to make a living on an island that has been historically impoverished, despite being soulfully rich.

Continuing her gendered analysis of the effects of the drug trade and tourism on youth, Cacho Caballero finds that many of the young women of the lost generation engage in sex work. As in the case of illicit substances, she points to socio-economic causes: "el problema por el cual se da la explotación sexual es el turismo, es una actividad que durante el viaje, en lugares distintos al de su entorno habitual, el turista aprovecha para introducir a mujeres en estos mundos a través de la trata de blancas, prostíbulos ocultos, de los que el mundo exterior no tiene conocimiento y en los cuales estas mujeres se ven introducidas sin saberlo y sin poder salir del mismo" (the problem that leads to sexual exploitation is tourism, for it is an activity that occurs while the tourist, finding himself in places that are distinct from his own, takes advantage of the situation to introduce women from these contexts into prostitution, hidden brothels, which are unknown in the broader context [of the tourist destination] and in which these women are introduced without knowing and without being able to escape).[24] Roatán is no different than other Caribbean islands, which, since the 1960s, have been advertised as cheap escapes for North American and European tourists. Tourism and sex work in the Caribbean are concomitant, explains Kamala Kempadoo, and, for those who work in the field of sex tourism, "the encounters are not bound by monetary transactions, but flow from and into more general practices of hustling or making do, in countries where the informal economy is tightly interwoven with the formal, and sexuality with economics."[25] Cacho Caballero's essay thus echoes broader analyses of sexuality in tourist economies as one of many "survival strategies for making do."[26] Roatán is, Cacho Caballero emphasizes, a context in which very few employment opportunities are available to Garifuna youth outside of drug and tourist markets.

Garifuna peoples, like many other Indigenous peoples, have developed healing cultures that place an emphasis on the relationship between the living and the ancestral realm. It is thus not accidental that the essay ends with a statement made by a witness to the tragic events of a Holy Week that claimed the lives of a drug dealer, his wife, and his young children: "Esto que está pasando en este pueblo en estos momentos, aporta aprendizajes para retomar el camino de la sabiduría de los ancestros, comprender mejor la enseñanza de los abuelos cuando recomiendan vivir de acuerdo con la naturaleza en el poder de la razón, tal como el universo tiene una inteligencia que pone orden en el ambiente, también el hombre y la mujer que quiere alcanzar la sabiduría tiene que conseguir el orden en su vida por medio de su conciencia" (What is happening in this town in these moments contributes lessons for retaking the path of the wisdom of our ancestors, to better understand the teachings of the elders when they recommend that we live in harmony with nature in the power of reason, just as the universe has an intelligence that establishes order in the environment, so too, do the men and women who wish to reach wisdom need to obtain order in their lives through their conscience).[27] Cacho Caballero thus transmits the wishes of the Garifuna ancestors, who remind readers that their teachings can breathe life into the new generation and ensure Garifuna cultural survival on Roatán. In doing so, she likewise engages with a healing strategy that involves and directly depends on ancestral wisdom. In line with the healing practices developed through music and ceremony that Oliver N. Greene describes in his studies of *dügü* and Garifuna mass, Cacho Caballero's strategy for establishing a connection to ancestors relies on the use of the Garifuna mother tongue.[28]

Indigenous people in Abiayala continue to experience the consequences of repeated invasions, looting, and linguistic tyranny.[29] Consequently, Indigenous conceptions of well-being have come to represent an area of scholarly inquiry that encompasses practices as diverse as dance, ethnobotany, and language preservation, and many others, across Abiayala. As discussions of the language rights of Indigenous peoples have gained prominence, so have connections between the use of mother tongues and the well-being of entire communities. Indigenous writers like Xiomara Cacho Caballero (Garifuna), Wingston González (Garifuna), Calixta Gabriel Xiquín (Kaqchikel Maya), and Miguel Ángel Oxlaj Cúmez (Kaqchikel Maya)—all from the same Central American region—are aware that it is possible to heal through language. Quantitative socio-medical studies confirm what these authors strive to demonstrate through their poetry, namely that "language is medicine, recognizing that the health of an Indigenous language is reflected in the health of its people, [and] recognizing that using a suppressed ancestral language has health benefits for the individual descendants and their community."[30] In *Viaje, pisto, plomo y miedo*, Cacho Caballero establishes the root causes of the malaise of the Garifuna community in Roatán, while in the poetry that I examine in the next section, she develops her theory about the ethno-linguistic dimension of Garifuna well-being. As a Garifuna writer committed to her ancestors and community in Roatán—a homeland ravaged by the desperation caused by unemployment, drug trade, and the spoils of the tourist industry—she advocates for language maintenance and transmission to bring about healing for her community. This poetry completes a circle that returns us to the central premises of her children's stories: Garifuna culture is medicine, as well as a gift from the ancestors.

Writing to/for the Ancestors

The poetry that Cacho Caballero writes in Garifuna, Spanish, and English imparts the sense of writing as ceremony, as an offering to ancestors through metaphysical connection that is an important element of Indigenous well-being. Through a process closely related to *dügü*—a ceremony held by relatives to heal their loved ones through dance, drumming, and embodiment—Cacho Caballero's trilingual poetry reads like an invitation for the ancestors to speak to their descendants and bring healing to the community.[31] Belizean Garifuna anthropologist Joseph O. Palacio points out that a central belief in Garifuna spirituality is that the ancestors are always near and have a vested interest in protecting their loved ones. The songs and prayers spoken to them in the Garifuna language during *dügü* are precisely what activates the relationships between the living and the deceased through time and space, a process that reaches its peak when the ancestor possesses the body of a descendant during the two or three nights that the ceremony lasts.[32] The ancestors might communicate with their descendants through dreams or use the body of the possessed relative to issue their own voices, thereby explaining some particular circumstance to their family, revealing the future of a family member, advising someone who is about to make an important decision, or simply spending time with the family in the realm of the living. Notably, the ancestral lands of the Garifuna family are the only place the spiritual and physical planes can overlap to bring about such communion: "the village, as the incubator of Garifuna indigeneity, acquires its maximum significance through the insistence of the ancestors."[33] Ancestral communication thus supersedes the limits of time and space but only on the condition that it be carried out on Garifuna land and through the Garifuna language.

Cacho Caballero's first poetry collection, *Tumálili nanigi: La voz del corazón: The Voice of the Heart* (1998), is a trilingual volume that reads like a prayer asking for the intercession of the ancestors to see the community through the painful predicament of ethnocide and linguicide. The poetry is offered to the ancestors, who then use the poet to give council to their descendants. As observed in the works of other Indigenous poets of Abiayala—from Joy Harjo (Muscogee) in its northern reaches to Elicura Chihuailaf (Mapuche) at its southern tip—poetry is a ceremonial practice through which ancestors impart their wisdom. As poet Gaspar Pedro González (Maya Q'anjob'al) observes: "Our ancestors spoke and we continue their speech in the form of metaphors, symbolism, and images of concepts nonexistent in the realm of matter."[34] Furthermore, as Cacho Caballero's poetry and that of other Indigenous poets of her generation indicates, there is an important connection between native languages and the transmission of ancestral wisdom. It is through the deployment of the ancestral mother tongue that the ancestor is invoked and manifests in the plane of the living.

In her poetry, Cacho Caballero submits herself to the ancestors and entrusts her voice to them, just as one would receive the spirit of the ancestors during a *dügü* ceremony. The Garifuna language is used throughout the collection of poetry and becomes an object of essential value for the transnational and multigenerational Garifuna people. This is evident in "Garáwon–Scream–Tambor," the first trilingual poetic trio in the volume. To be clear, I use the term *trilingual poetic trio* because the three poems express distinct messages that are nonetheless intertwined; they are not simply translations of a singular poem. "Garáwon" and "Tambor" retain the same lexicon and structure, although their rhythm diverges naturally due to the prosody of the two languages.[35] The two poems work with the theme of Garifuna children while expressing appreciation for *both* the island of Roatán and Honduras in the first and second stanzas of the poems. In both the Garifuna and Spanish compositions, the repetition of the phrase "they play the drum" highlights the *garáwon* drum, an instrument inherited from the ancestors that is used to summon them to the plane of the living. Drum music is much more than a recreational activity; its rhythm is sacred and accompanies the sung and danced verses to receive the presence and message of the ancestors. Furthermore, "Garáwon" and "Tambor" affirm that, by participating in *dügü* ceremonies, offering food to ancestral spirits, assuming the responsibility of carving their land, and talking about their identity, the Garifuna children of Roatán bring joy to their ancestors.

GARÁWON	TAMBOR
Haneimeti hadonhani garáwon	¡Cómo tocan el tambor
Irahuñu nageirana	los niños de mi pueblo!
Areidahamuti wanichugu	Conservan sus costumbres
Ayanuha hagia luagu lanina dügü	y hablan del dugú.
Gundatiñu liraunana nageire	Muy felices
Dagagudatiñu hon wayuna	Ofrendan comidas a sus ancestros
Hinsieti sun huliligati hon	Aman la comunidad nacional
Adonha hamuttigien garáwon	También tocan el tambor[36]

Literal translation of "Tambor" (Drum): How they play the drum / the children of my village! / They preserve their customs / and speak about dügü. // Very happy / they offer food to their ancestors / they love the national community / they also play the drum.

The English composition in the same trilingual poetic trio is called "Scream" and is physically situated between the pages of "Garáwon" and "Tambor," though it fulfills an indisputably different function and has a three- instead of a two-stanza structure. The poem's title marks its engagement with pain, which is markedly absent in the compositions that immediately precede and follow it. Tellingly, the ancestors are absent in all the verses of the poem. Instead of the devotion found in "Garáwon" and "Tambor," the lines in "Scream" focus directly on a Black workforce that toils and experiences the humiliation of severe work. This, as well as the prohibition of the Garifuna language in public spaces and the hostility that speakers of the Garifuna face when they use their mother tongue, is the source of the pain in the poem. In the last verses of the poem, the poetic voice employs the second person to empathize with the ostracized speaker of Garifuna: "Seeking to replace / your Garifuna language / Where forbidden, / hostility, frustration, but / You are still here." Thus, by placing this poem between "Garáwon" and "Tambor," the trilingual poetic trio works with the themes of invocation–grief–invocation that mark Garifuna experience, as depicted in Cacho Caballero's *Viaje, pisto, plomo y medio*. Through its appeal to the ancestors for their intervention in earthly matters, the poetic voice closes the cycle and renews hope in the beat of the drums of the Garifuna children who continue to honor their ancestors.

This opening trilingual poetic trio is not an exception. "Uenedu–Dream–Sueño," for example, bears the same title across their three languages, but their structures in English and Spanish are distinct from the first composition in Garifuna. The presence of the ancestors is at the heart of all three, though "Uenedu" explicitly mentions Yurumein in its second stanza: "Lubaragien habúgun, Garinagu induroun / Yurumei bugaha wagiirabei."[37] The composition in Garifuna places the memory of the ancestors' exile from Yurumein at its center and appeals to the reader to never forget what happened in 1797: "Sianti labuleidunua yurumei / Irumu milu sedu san / Gádürü wein disi sedu san / Gádürü wein disi sedu / Hanüguni giounu yurumei / hóuniwagua."[38] Thus, the paradigm of ancestors whose dispossession resulted in the acquisition of a rich history of survival is established in the first poem of the trilingual poetic trio. The added value of the versions in English and Spanish is that it reminds those who read colonial tongues to revel in the gift of Blackness, to dream with and of her ancestors, and to fulfill her ancestors' dreams for their descendants.

All three compositions incorporate the image of a dream and repeat the image of the sky in the hands of the reader. "Uenedu" consists of just three stanzas and ends with this very concept; "Dream" and "Sueño," however, include a fourth and fifth stanza that poignantly arrest the reader:

DREAM	**SUEÑO**
The sky in your arms	El cielo en tus brazos
is the conscience of the colour	es la consciencia del color
of your skin	de tu piel
Before the eyes of society.	Ante los ojos de la Sociedad
And the freshness of your pigmentation	es la frescura de tu pigmentación.
What is marvelous is	Lo maravilloso es
the African blood.	La sangre africana.
The pain that was suffered	Es el dolor que sufrieron
by those who opened to you the doors of	aquellos que te abrieron
the Americas.	Las puertas a las Américas[39]

The trilingual poetic trio recognizes the agency of dreams, which are experienced somatically, in the apparent unconscious of the subject, permitting the body to generate and be impacted by the affective signifiers it generates. The reveries of the dreamer raise her above the materiality of earthly present, suspending it in a spiritual plane—that of the ancestors. The composition in Garifuna leaves the reader on this plane. Meanwhile, its English and Spanish counterparts take alienation as a given and endeavor to make a yet stronger statement by adding the additional stanzas relating to the reader's ancestors. The message that is imparted on the readers of the non-Garifuna language compositions is that the dream itself is the gift of their Blackness. Their ancestors—both those captured in Africa and those deported to Roatán—suffered to open the doors of the Americas to their descendants. This revelation, imparted in a dream, is a gift provided to the reader.

The trilingual poetic trio "Wayuna–Relying–Ancestros" issues a parallel thematic cycle. In "Wayuna," the word *Yurumein* is repeated almost in ceremonial fashion. Meanwhile, "Relying" engages with the socio-economic position of Garifuna people, who experience injustice in all the national contexts in which they reside. The poem's verses tell the story of a people who have been exploited in enclave work and on ship crews and are repeatedly forced to leave their villages in search of employment opportunities: "Then to the USA / Relying on dollar remittances / Supplementing earnings / putting values in our mind."[40] Living in the United States, the poetic voice states, leads these new Garifuna exiles to forgo their collective values and to succumb to the very consumerism that drives their oppression. For its part, "Ancestros" expresses an unrelenting anguish that is amplified each time the poetic voice repeats the question: "Cuántos de ellos murieron?" (How many of them died?).[41] Alluding to earlier trilingual poetic trios, this composition repeats the image of Garifuna ancestors opening the doors of the Americas to their descendants while reminding readers that only the sea was a witness to how many died as they were trafficked from the African continent and when they were deported from Yurumein. The poetic voice indicates that the Garifuna songs of today mark their arrival to the Americas and call on the reader to remember multiple instances of attempted ethnocide and linguicide. It declares that, while their ancestors were subjected to death, pain, and anguish at the hands of their torturers, today they have descendants who honor them and listen to them. The thematic cycle of the trilingual poetic trio thus closes the loop on the themes of homeland–loss–remembrance: the lead composition in Garifuna invokes the ancestors through the Garifuna language, the composition in English calls them out of the spiritual plane into the pain of the descendants in the present, and the composition in Spanish closes with the spiritual communion between the living and the remembered.

In Cacho Caballero's trilingual poetic trios, cultural survival depends entirely on absolute surrender to the ancestors. This is further evidenced in "Dimureba–Speak to Us–Alarido." The Garifuna and English compositions reflect on the impact of schooling on Garifuna children in a prayer to "Baba," a word that can mean either grandfather or God in Garifuna. This prayer implores for guidance out of darkness and specifically asks for intervention so that her brother does not to lose his identity. In both "Dimureba" and "Speak to Us," the brother appears as a metonym for those who have lost themselves because of formal education. These are the boys who—unlike the boys in Cacho Caballero's previously discussed children's stories—have succumbed to internalized shame because of the white teachers who humiliate them for their color and culture. Without a sense of *nati* (origin) and his language, the brother in these poems has become, as Garifuna thinker Rubén Reyes puts it, "an unidentifiable human being" without a place of origin and a community in which to belong.[42]

DIMUREBA	**SPEAK TO US**
Féridaguata luban furendei nati	My brother is not the same anymore
Bulieila hererun wayuna	He does not speak his language anymore
Kei saragu garínagu	Brush away,
Feridiguátia nati.	The misunderstanding from him.[43]

The poem in Spanish of this trilingual poetic trio, "Alarido," interrogates the brother's situation differently. In a philosophical manner, the first verse incorporates the image of a seedling and pairs it with the concept of the "prospective history that it keeps." The possibility of the small seed to take root, to grow, and to survive is met with the question: "¿Cuál es el pasado / De este presente que succiona / Dejando en interrogante la sobrevivencia / de la identidad?" (What is the past / of this present that suckles / leaving open the question of survivance / of identity?).[44] This composition, like the one in Garifuna and English with which it is grouped, examines the relationship between the present and the future, ultimately arguing that the future needs careful tending in the present. As in "Dimureba" and "Speak to Us" (and even like *Viaje, pisto, plomo y miedo* discussed earlier), this poem reflects on the conditions that take the breath of life away from the future itself. The poetic voice's concern is that Garifuna people have already experienced undeniable losses and that this weighs heavily on the youngest members of the community. The "alarido" (scream) of the title is not one of agony, but one which sounds the alarm on the threats to a Garifuna future. It issues a call to readers to ensure that the present nurtures the future, thereby safeguarding all that is needed for cultural survivance: "la profundización / de su contenido / la cautela / y sabiduría ancestral" (the deepening / of its very substance / forethought / and ancestral wisdom).[45] These last four verses of "Alarido," so lucid and succinct, allow the reader to understand what the poetic voice seeks to preserve each time she invokes the ancestors in her writing—whether children's stories, essays, or poetry. They poignantly highlight bell hooks' observation that "Nostalgia for a lost past is useless if it paralyzes and keeps us so trapped in the memory of grief that we cannot engage in active struggle. To allow our ancestors to dwell among us and to invite their wisdom to enter is powerful. We are nurtured by their presence."[46] With the vision of survivance through tides of change, hooks continues, "black and red people look once again to the spirit of our ancestors, recovering worldviews and life-sustaining values that renew our spirit and restore us the will to resist domination."[47]

Language for Posterity, Writing as Ceremony

In *The Ecology of Language Evolution*, Congolese linguist Salikoko Mufwene proposes that languages be viewed as species that bequeath codes to their descendants with respect to the previous generation's use or disuse. Recognizing the hereditary attributes of languages makes it possible to see mother tongues as living, active, and highly complex "species" that have a higher survival rate dependent on the frequency of their invocation. As Mufwene states, "The language-as-species analogy maintains that languages as complex adaptive systems have lives; some die while others come into existence, as a consequence of what their speakers qua hosts do."[48] Seen from this perspective, it is possible to understand that linguistic inheritance and language maintenance do not entail simply copying a language and putting it to rote use. Rather, linguistic ecology considers the bio-physical environment in which a language can thrive or die. Returning to the Garifuna language that has concerned this chapter, Roatán was the first island in which speakers of Garifuna lived after their deportation from Yurumein (St. Vincent). For centuries, the Garifuna communities' isolation from Central American hegemonic cultural centers meant that the language did not have to compete with either Spanish or English and could thus develop organically. The bio-physical environment of the language thus allowed it to thrive through uninterrupted transmission from one generation to another.

This is no longer the case. As Cacho Caballero demonstrates in her work, the socio-economic conditions of Roatán are a threat to its young people and hinder the transmission of the wise values and the ancestral language of the island community. Roatán is on the sea route of drug trafficking and is a tourist destination while its Indigenous people are subjected to the socio-economic impact of their illicit economies. While the power of the drug cartels on the island increases, the feeling that Roatán no longer belongs to the Garifuna community increases: "las personas sólo observan como las armas pasaban de mano en mano, adueñándose la dictadura de los narcos de la paz y tranquilidad" (people are left watching weapons pass from one person to another, with the narco dictatorships taking taking over the old peace and tranquility).[49] The impact that drug trafficking has had on the Garifuna community, on their culture, and on their language is profound. Anthropological and sociological research provides academic analyses of the extent to which Mexican drug cartels use the Central American isthmus as a production and warehouse area. Ana Lilia Pérez explains in *Mares de cocaína* that cartels have determined that the isthmus' lands are exceptional for cultivation and drug production; their oceans are splendid for their transport and, if the shipment is hot, for warehousing.[50] In response to this, Cacho Caballero issues the voice of Roatán, an Indigenous voice speaking ancestral wisdom, calling for resistance to the linguicide and ethnocide brought about by these newer threats to Garifuna language and culture.

For Cacho Caballero, like other Indigenous authors of Abiayala, writing with the health of her people and in the spiritual presence of the ancestors is critical to her poetic work. This was particularly evident during the COVID-19 pandemic, with Cacho Caballero's use of Facebook and YouTube as platforms to inspire and uplift her reader-followers with posts, memes, and virtual gatherings. The global pandemic took a grave toll on Indigenous communities worldwide, leading many of them to prioritize the safety of speakers of native languages within their communities. In this sense, we are reminded of Eliseo Jacob's discussion of the activist role of the *crônica* genre online in Chapter 6 of this book as well as Isis Barra Costa's assertion in Chapter 7 of this book that "the printed image (whether in virtual space or physical publications) is by nature more permeable than the printed word, and the Wi-Fi diaspora has been a media platform of high political and artistic potential." Writing to her Afro-Indigenous community on Facebook, Cacho Caballero urged Garifuna peoples to take precautionary measures for theirs and their elders' well-being. In those same years, her YouTube presence increased as she was invited to participate in writers' events like "Letras al Aire," "Voces al Viento," "Recital Afrobooktuber," released and archived on the same platform. These activities, as well as Cacho Caballero's interview for the Arte 504 television program on the Honduran Canal 8 (aired on 6 August 2021), illustrate that those who fight for Afro-Indigenous survivance must cover all the spaces—and most recently, lettered digital spaces—with decolonial strategies. As Alejandro de Oto observes: "La descolonización supone tramar el cuerpo de otro modo que la racialización, porque los cuerpos que se anudan en los esquemas raciales son aquellos en los que la experiencia ha sido substituida por la representación, y la materialidad ha sido remplazada por la reificación" (Decolonization supposes plotting the body in a different way than racialization, because bodies that are placed within racial frameworks are those whose experience has been substituted by representation, and materiality has been replaced by reification).[51] This requires receiving ancestors when writing. Ultimately, the act of producing children's stories, essays, poetry, cookbooks, and cultivating a digital presence is Cacho Caballero's ceremony, an offering to her own ancestors and an invocation that they join her in the twenty-first century Garifuna plane. With this invocation, she confronts the crises that endanger the Garifuna language and the lives of its speakers.

NOTES

1. For further research into the history of Garifuna peoples and what led to their deportation from the island of Roatán, see Christopher Taylor, *The Black Carib Wars: Freedom, Survival, and the Making of the Garifuna* (Jackson: University Press of Mississippi, 2012).
2. Douglas Taylor, *The Black Carib of British Honduras* (New York: Wenner-Gren Foundation, 1951), 143.
3. Geneviève Escure, "Garifuna in Belize and Honduras," in *Creoles, Contact, and Language Change: Linguistic and Social Implications*, ed. Geneviève Escure and Armin Schwegler (Amsterdam: John Benjamins, 2004), 37.
4. Ibid., 46.
5. Peter Wade, *Race and Ethnicity in Latin America* (New York: Pluto Press, 2010), 24.
6. Raymond Breton, *Dictionnaire caraibe-françois, meslé de quantité de remarques historiques pour l'ésclaircissement de la langue. Composé par le R. P. Raymond Breton, religieux de l'ordre des Fréres Prescheurs, et l'un des premiers missionnaires apostoliques en l'isle la Gardeloupe et autres circonvoisines de l'Amerique* (Auxerre: Gilles Bouquet, imprimeru ordinaire du ROY, 1665).
7. Wade, *Race and Ethnicity in Latin America*, 26.
8. Shephard, *An Historical Account of the Island of St. Vincent* (London: W. Nicol, Cleaveland Row, St. James, 1831), 161.
9. Taylor, *The Black Carib Wars*, 142.
10. Nancie L. Solien González, *Sojourners of the Caribbean: Ethnogenesis and Ethnohistory on the Garífuna* (Chicago: University of Illinois Press, 1988), 20.
11. Shephard, *Historical Account*, 22.
12. Taylor, *The Black Carib Wars*, 145.
13. Ibid., 146–47.
14. David M. Eberhard, Gary F. Simons, and Charles D. Fennig, eds., "Garifuna: A Language of Honduras," in *Ethnologue: Languages of the World*, 24 ed. (Dallas, Texas: SIL

International, 2021), https://www.ethnologue.com/language/cab. *Ethnologue* summarizes the status of each language in each country where it is used based on two types of information: (1) An estimate of the overall development versus endangerment of the language using the Expanded Graded Intergenerational Disruption Scale (EGIDS), and (2) a categorization of the official recognition given to a language within the country. The EGIDS consists of thirteen levels with each higher number on the scale representing a greater level of disruption to the intergenerational transmission of the language. For more information, see "Language Status," in *Ethnologue: Languages of the World*, 24 ed. (Dallas, Texas: SIL International, 2021), https://www.ethnologue.com/about/language-status.

15. bell hooks, "Revolutionary 'Renegades,'" in *Black Looks: Race and Representation*. (Boston: South End Press, 1992), 185.
16. Gilberto Giménez, "La moda de las identidades: Identidades y conflictos étnicos en México," in *La sociedad mexicana frente al tercer milenio*, ed. Humberto Muñoz García and Roberto Rodríguez (Mexico City: UNAM, 2002), 113.
17. Xiomara Cacho Caballero, *Viaje, pisto, plomo y miedo* (Tegucigalpa, Honduras: Guardabarranco, 2016), 29.
18. Ibid., 30.
19. Ibid., 34.
20. Ibid., 39.
21. Elisabeth Kirtsoglou and Dimitrios Theodossopoulos, " 'They Are Taking our Culture Away' Tourism and Culture Commodification in the Garifuna Community of Roatan," *Critique of Anthropology* 24, no. 2 (2004): 138.
22. Cacho Caballero, *Viaje, pisto, plomo y miedo*, 41.
23. Ibid., 40.
24. Ibid., 55.
25. Kamala Kempadoo, *Sexing the Caribbean: Gender, Race, and Sexual Labor* (New York: Routledge, 2004), 118–19.
26. Ibid., 191.
27. Cacho Caballero, *Viaje, pisto, plomo y miedo*, 80.
28. See Oliver N. Greene, "Music, Healing, and Transforming Identity in Lemesi Garifuna (the Garifuna Mass)," *Caribbean Quarterly* 60, no. 2 (2014): 88–109; and Oliver N. Greene, "The *Dügü* Ritual of the Garinagu of Belize: Reinforcing Values of Society Through Music and Spirit Possession," *Black Music Research Journal* (1998): 167–81.
29. Although the concept of Abiayala has existed for centuries, today it is being used more frequently with reference to the ancestral lands of all the Indigenous communities of the Americas, not just those of Latin America. Emil Keme establishes trans-Indigenous and multilingual connections among Indigenous peoples in the mostly Spanish-speaking, Portuguese-speaking, English-speaking, French-speaking, and Dutch countries of this hemisphere. Keme explains that rethinking the Americas in its entirety as a single Abiayala "thus offers us the possibility of articulating a place of collective enunciation that goes beyond the borders imposed by Europeans and

their descendants; the possibility of rethinking and recovering the world from our millenary epistemological legacies." Emil Keme, "Para que Abiayala viva, las Américas deben morir: Hacia una Indigeneidad transhemisférica," *NAIS: Native American and Indigenous Studies* 5, no. 1 (2018): 28.

30. Alice Taff et al., "Indigenous Language Use Impacts Wellness." In *The Oxford Handbook of Endangered Languages*, eds. Kenneth L. Rehg and Lyle Campbell (Oxford: Oxford University Press, 2018), 862.
31. There are three types of ceremonies related to this practice, but in all three, the relative of the sick individual receives the spirit of an ancestor (a process more commonly known as "possession" in Anglophone contexts) possession) to bring relief to a loved one or to bring clarity to an important situation faced by the family or community in question. The descendant who receives them during the ceremony adopts the voice of the ancestor while expressing their concerns or recommendations for the situation that has brought them together may improve. See Greene, "*Dügü* Ritual."
32. Joseph O. Palacio, "The Multifaceted Garifuna: Juggling Cultural Spaces in the 21st Century," in *The Garífuna, a Nation across Borders: Essays in Social Anthropology* (Belize City: Cubola Productions, 2013), 111.
33. Ibid., 112.
34. Gaspar Pedro González, *13 B'aktun: Mayan Visions of 2012 and Beyond* (Berkeley: North Atlantic Books, 2010), 89.
35. The literal translations of the poems in Garifuna were developed by using Roy Cayetano's *The People's Garifuna Dictionary* and Rubén Reyes's *Garüdia: Garifuna Trilingual Dictionary*. I am also grateful to Azucena Oro Álvarez, José Alfonso López Aguilar, Paul Joseph López Oro, Tomás Sánchez, Osbel Edilberto Lalín Ramírez, and Michelle Ocasio for their input on my translations of the verses.
36. Xiomara Cacho Caballero, *Tumálili nanigi: La voz del corazón: The Voice of the Heart*. Tegucigalpa: Graficentro, 1998), 1, 3.
37. Ibid., 4.
38. Ibid., 4.
39. Ibid., 5, 6.
40. Ibid., 11.
41. Ibid., 12.
42. See Rubén Reyes, *Garüdia: Garifuna Trilingual Dictionary (Garifuna–English–Spanish)*. Los Angeles: CreateSpace Independent Publishing Platform, 2012).
43. Cacho Caballero, *Tumálili nanigi*, 16–17.
44. Ibid., 18.
45. Ibid., 18.
46. hooks, "Revolutionary 'Renegades,' " 193.
47. Ibid., 194.
48. Salikoko S. Mufwene, *The Ecology of Language Evolution* (Cambridge: Cambridge University Press, 2001), 197.
49. Cacho Caballero, *Viaje, pisto, plomo y miedo*, 72.

50. See Ana Lilia Pérez, *Mares de cocaína: Las rutas náuticas del narcotráfico* (Mexico City: Grijalbo, 2014).
51. Alejandro de Oto, "Notas metodológicas sobre el humanismo en Frantz Fanon," in *La crítica en el margen: Hacia una cartografía conceptual para rediscutir la modernidad*, ed. José Guadalupe Gandarilla (Mexico: Akal, 2016), 144.

WORKS CITED

Breton, Raymond. *Dictionaire caraibe-françois, meslé de quantité de remarques historiques pour l'ésclaircissement de la langue. Composé par le R. P. Raymond Breton, religieux de l'ordre des Fréres Prescheurs, et l'un des premiers missionnaires apostoliques en l'isle la Gardeloupe et autres circonvoisines de l'Amerique*. Auxerre: Gilles Bouquet, imprimeru ordinaire du ROY, 1665.

Cacho Caballero, Xiomara. *Dios negro: Black Jesus: Bungiu Wuriti*. Tegucigalpa: Editorial Universitaria, Universidad Nacional Autónoma de Honduras, 2003.

———. *Tumálili nanigi: La voz del corazón: The Voice of the Heart*. Tegucigalpa: Graficentro, 1998.

———. *Viaje, pisto, plomo y miedo*. Tegucigalpa, Honduras: Guardabarranco, 2016.

———. *Wafien and his Maracas*. Tegucigalpa: Editorial Universitaria, Universidad Nacional Autónoma de Honduras, 2000.

Cayetano, Roy E. *The People's Garifuna Dictionary: Dimureiágei Garifuna*. National Garifuna Council of Belize, 1993.

de Oto, Alejandro. "Notas metodológicas sobre el humanismo en Frantz Fanon." In *La crítica en el margen: Hacia una cartografía conceptual para rediscutir la modernidad*, edited by José Guadalupe Gandarilla, 133–62. Mexico: Akal, 2016.

Eberhard, David M., Gary F. Simons, and Charles D. Fennig, eds. *Ethnologue: Languages of the World*. 24 ed. Dallas, Texas: SIL International, 2021. Online version: http://www.ethnologue.com.

Escure, Geneviève. "Garifuna in Belize and Honduras." In *Creoles, Contact, and Language Change: Linguistic and Social Implications*, edited by Geneviève Escure and Armin Schwegler, 35–65. Amsterdam: John Benjamins, 2004.

Forbes, Michelle Ann. "Garifuna: The Birth and Rise of an Identity through Contact Language and Contact Culture." PhD diss., University of Missouri, Columbia, 2011.

Giménez, Gilberto. "La moda de las identidades: Identidades y conflictos étnicos en México." In *La sociedad mexicana frente al tercer milenio*, edited by Humberto Muñoz García and Roberto Rodríguez. Mexico City: UNAM, 2002.

Gómez Menjívar, Jennifer Carolina, and William Noel Salmon. *Tropical Tongues: Language Ideologies, Endangerment, and Minority Languages in Belize*. Chapel Hill: University of North Carolina Press, 2018.

González, Gaspar Pedro. *13 B'aktun: Mayan Visions of 2012 and Beyond*. Berkeley: North Atlantic Books, 2010.

Greene, Oliver N. "The *Dügü* Ritual of the Garinagu of Belize: Reinforcing Values of Society Through Music and Spirit Possession." *Black Music Research Journal* (1998): 167–81.

———. "Music, Healing, and Transforming Identity in Lemesi Garifuna (the Garifuna Mass)." *Caribbean Quarterly* 60, no. 2 (2014): 88–109.

Holm, John. *Central American English*. Amsterdam: John Benjamins Publishing, 1982.

hooks, bell. *Black Looks: Race and Representation*. Boston: South End Press, 1992.

Keme, Emil. "Para que Abiayala viva, las Américas deben morir: Hacia una Indigeneidad transhemisférica." *NAIS: Native American and Indigenous Studies* 5, no. 1 (2018): 21–41.

Kempadoo, Kamala. *Sexing the Caribbean: Gender, Race, and Sexual Labor*. New York: Routledge, 2004.

Kirtsoglou, Elisabeth, and Dimitrios Theodossopoulos. " 'They Are Taking our Culture Away' Tourism and Culture Commodification in the Garifuna Community of Roatan." *Critique of Anthropology* 24, no. 2 (2004): 135–157.

Mufwene, Salikoko S. *The Ecology of Language Evolution*. Cambridge: Cambridge University Press, 2001.

Palacio, Joseph O. "The Multifaceted Garifuna: Juggling Cultural Spaces in the 21st Century." In *The Garifuna, a Nation across Borders: Essays in Social Anthropology*, 105–122. Belize City: Cubola Productions, 2013.

Pérez, Ana Lilia. *Mares de cocaína: Las rutas náuticas del narcotráfico*. Mexico City: Grijalbo, 2014.

Reyes, Rubén. *Garüdia: Garifuna Trilingual Dictionary (Garifuna–English–Spanish)*. Los Angeles: CreateSpace Independent Publishing Platform, 2012.

Shephard, Charles. *An Historical Account of the Island of St. Vincent*. London: W. Nicol, Cleaveland Row, St. James, 1831.

Taff, Alice, Melvatha Chee, Jaeci Hall, Millie Yéi Dulitseen Hall, Kawenniyóhstha Nicole Martin, and Annie Johnston. "Indigenous Language Use Impacts Wellness." In *The Oxford Handbook of Endangered Languages*, edited by Kenneth L. Rehg and Lyle Campbell, 862–84. Oxford: Oxford University Press, 2018.

Taylor, Christopher. *The Black Carib Wars: Freedom, Survival, and the Making of the Garifuna*. Jackson: University Press of Mississippi, 2012.

Taylor, Douglas. *The Black Carib of British Honduras*. New York: Wenner-Gren Foundation, 1951.

Vizenor, Gerald. *Literary Chance: Essays on Native American Survivance*. Valencia: Publicacions de la Universitat de València, 2007.

Wade, Peter. *Race and Ethnicity in Latin America*. New York: Pluto Press, 2010.

◆ CHAPTER 10

Reclaiming Lands, Identity, and Autonomy

Rapping Youth in Rural Chocó, Colombia

Diana Rodríguez Quevedo

On an ordinary February day, boys and teens living on the Pacific coast of Colombia are at school, doing chores at home or in the fields or enjoying some playtime outdoors. This was not the case for the children of twenty-three communities in the Chocó region in 1997.[1] On February 24 and 28, the national military, backed by paramilitary troops, attacked the area by land and air, forcing the inhabitants of Cacarica to abandon their homes, belongings, lands, crops, and livestock. Children and adults were taken to shelters in other towns while other people fled to Panama.[2] The vast majority of the displaced community was Afro-Colombian, primarily *campesinos* or peasants, who had lived on those lands for generations.[3] They were uprooted under the pretext that they were guerrilla sympathizers.[4] While some people were sheltered in the Coliseo de Turbo, others fled to small towns or cities. This study focuses on the songs of a group of boys and teenagers who returned with members of their families and their communities to the Cacarica region between the years 2000 and 2001.

The Colombian Pacific coast is an area of approximately ten million hectares that makes up 6.2 percent of the Colombian territory.[5] This region is characterized by a combination of tropical moisture and dry forests rich in biodiversity, along with extensive networks of rivers, mangroves, and other water systems.[6] The rivers are a valuable part of the daily transportation, communication, and economy of the region. They also serve as social and cultural spaces that define the local population. The media has focused the issue of forced internal displacement in Colombia as an urban problem because internally displaced people (IDPs) who have nowhere else to go ultimately occupy public spaces and change city landscapes. The "displaced" are a constructed category and "a normalised phenomenon in Colombian society."[7] The massive exoduses in the Pacific coast have transformed the region itself.[8]

Oral lore has been a significant component of Afro-Colombian traditional culture of the Pacific coast. According to political and cultural geographer Ulrich Oslender, oral tradition is a dynamic space to transmit and reproduce local history, morals, and ways of thinking, a task that corresponds to community elders, keepers of knowledge of the area and of nature.[9] Orality offers a perspective of "past-present-future," which is part of the reconstruction of collective memory that goes beyond nostalgia to foment a "re-narrating" of history.[10] Songs, dances, and theatre performances are part of the re-telling of collective history, and through "re-narrating," memory becomes a site of resistance. The displaced people of Cacarica—groups of adults and youth—chose music to tell their experiences, create awareness, and make demands about their socio-political situations. The elders resorted to *vallenato* music to share their experiences while a group of boys and male teens claimed rap to express, denounce, and resist the multiple acts of violence that were part of the forced mass displacement. The songs and dances shift from local folklore to becoming an integral means of a political plan. Creating and "re-narrating" collective memories through stories are an act that defies the erasure of the region and its people. These youth groups composed, performed, and recorded a total of twelve songs that are included on two separate CDs: the first disc features the children's rap band Grupo de Rap Infantil and is entitled *Óyeme Chocó: Melodías de la esperanza; comunidades en retorno al Cacarica, Chocó* (*Listen to me, Chocó: Melodies of Hope; Communities Returning to Cacarica, Chocó*, 1999), and the second CD features the youth band Renacientes and is entitled *A nuestros mártires: Comunidades en resistencia del Cacarica* (*To Our Martyrs: Cacarica Communities in Resistance*, 2002).[11] Along with the rap songs, both CDs contain *vallenato* songs performed by elder members of the communities, as well as instrumental *chirimía* tunes.[12] These songs were composed during and after the displacement, and they serve many purposes, one of which is to denounce the horrors of the exodus as well as the torture, rape, murder, disappearances, material loss and destruction, and economic blockades that led up to the displacement.[13] Aside from giving a testimony of the human rights violations that occurred, these young rappers affirm their Afro-cultural heritage and identity, and they demand justice, peace, reparation, land restitution, and an end to violence and impunity.[14] In 2001, the government conceded to return some lands in Cacarica to the displaced communities. The civilian population that was displaced and repatriated denominated themselves Comunidad de Autodeterminación, Vida y Dignidad, CAVIDA (Community of Self-Determination, Life and Dignity, CAVIDA) and proposed this territory as a *zona humanitaria y de biodiversidad* (a humanitarian and bio-diversity zone). In other words, this was to be a violence-free zone that prohibited the entry of armed agents.[15]

These songs, with titles such as "Tiempos difíciles" (Tough Times), "Maldita guerra" (Damn War), "Los sin futuro" (Those Without a Future), "No queremos más guerra" (We Don't Want Any More War), "A mi país" (To My Country), "Tierra querida" (Beloved Land), and "Tierra natal" (Birth Land), function to access personal and collective memory for communities subjected to armed conflict and displacement. These rap songs are part of what Stuart Hall calls a global postmodern counternarrative to national media and socio-political hegemony. This music is an appropriation, which transcodes African-American rap, the origins of which are in the margins but which has become highly popular.[16] Part of this black musical expression is a strategic contestation that incorporates and complements individual identity markers with collective ones by clearly highlighting a *yo*, or "I," and a *nosotros*, or "we," that extends beyond ethnic identity.

Forced Internal Displacement in Colombia

Colombia is currently the country with the highest number of forced internally displaced people in the world, of which the majority are Afrodescendants, Indigenous, and *mestizo* peasants. The latest statistics indicate some 7.7 million internally displaced Colombians, or *desplazados*.[17] Aside from displacing individuals, families, and entire communities, this phenomenon has also been responsible for high numbers of civilian casualties and material destruction. As the main survivors, Afro-Colombian and Indigenous women have been at the forefront of this struggle, as they are driven to take on leadership roles in their homes and communities.

In February 1997, a paramilitary operation backed by the national army carried out "Operación Génesis," forcibly displacing approximately ten thousand people from Colombia's Pacific coast, a region with a high concentration of Afrodescendants, to other parts of the region and the country.[18] The military invaded using aerial bombs, while the paramilitary took over on land.[19] Over the past thirty years, the Chocó region has become a war site due to high interests over the land's biodiversity, lumber exploitation, and other natural resources. Also, it is a refuge for drug traffickers, and it is a point of entry for contraband arms. In short, this land has been disputed by armed groups—which include two guerrilla groups, the Revolutionary Armed Forces of Colombia (FARC) and National Liberation Army (ELN)—drug traffickers, and paramilitary groups (AUC), who were active in the zone in the late twentieth century and in the early twenty-first century.[20] According to a member of the *Asociación Campesina Integral del Atrato* (Integrated Peasant Association of the Atrato, or ACIA), "the people in Atrato now live in fear, terror, because both groups (guerilla and paramilitary) threaten, torture and assassinate people, and set up check points. . . . there are also the economic blockades involved in this."[21] The northern part of the Colombian Pacific Coast is a geo-politically strategic area that has attracted transnational companies interested in establishing megaprojects in agriculture, lumber, mining, and tourism industries, as well as road and port infrastructure development programs.[22]

In her essay "Desterrados: Forced Displacement in Colombia," Mabel González Bustelos, a Spanish journalist and researcher with the Centro de la Investigación para la Paz (Peace Research Center), offers a succinct correlation of the situation of forced internal displacement to a neoliberal economic model in Colombia:

> Forced internal displacement is a phenomenon linked to the history of Colombia and to the country's unfinished historical processes. The economic and political elite have used displacement to "homogenize" the population in a given area and to maintain and expand large estates. Currently, the pressure exerted by the neoliberal model to increase capital circuits has made the process more difficult by introducing factors that change the value of the land. As such, people are not displaced "by violence"; rather, violence is the tool used to expel the population. The true causes for displacement are hidden behind the violence. The reasons for displacement include strategic control of military and political areas, restructuring of local and regional powers, control or disruption of social movements, control of production, extraction activities (of natural resources and minerals), megaprojects, expansion of stockbreeding estates and agricultural industry, control of illicit crops, etc.[23]

In response to this situation, the rap songs in the CDs *Óyeme Chocó* and *A nuestros mártires* call to specific politicians, denounce the exploitation of natural resources, and demand respect for the people and wildlife that occupy the land and the waterways.

Colombian society is multi-ethnic and pluricultural. Luís Evelis Andrade, a representative of the National Indigenous Organization of Colombia (ONIC), affirms that "Colombia es uno de los países de mayor reconocimiento legal para gente en base a su etnia, pero eso no se transfiere a la acción" (Colombia is one of the countries with the most legal recognition for people based on their ethnicity but that does not transfer to action).[24] Andrade explains that, despite the amendments to the Colombian Constitution in 1991, public policies continue to exclude Indigenous and Afro-Colombian communities from guaranteeing their rights, acknowledging their ethnic identities and particular ways of life, and accepting and supporting their forms of government. In *Evil Hour in Colombia*, ethnohistorian Forrest Hylton emphasizes that:

> According to the Colombian Constitution of 1991, considered one of the most progressive in the world, indigenous peoples have rights to autonomy—collective management of land and political as well as cultural self-determination through *cabildos*, cells of local government. In 1993, under Law 70, Afro-Colombians secured rights similar to those enshrined in the constitution for the indigenous peoples: inalienable collective land titles managed by community councils. Both Afro-Colombians and the indigenous people built on non-liberal traditions of constituting themselves as democratic citizens and communities . . . More than a decade after their conquest of citizenship, the Chocó department still had the highest rates of poverty and infant mortality, in a country in which more than half the population lived in poverty.[25]

The 2005 census completed by the Departamento Administrativo Nacional de Estadísticas (The National Administrative Department of Statistics, or DANE), indicated that Afro-Colombians comprise 26 percent of the total population, although, as Christopher Dennis mentions in *Afro-Colombian Hip-Hop*, "a little over ten percent of the population openly defines itself as black (over four million inhabitants), while approximately twenty-one percent of the population (over nine million) can claim some African ancestry." Dennis adds that "the departments with the highest concentration of Afro-Colombians are Chocó (82 percent), Valle del Cauca (27 percent), and Cauca (22 percent), all part of the Pacific littoral."[26] The Chocó department is home to the largest Afro-Colombian population. It is also among the departments that have suffered the most violence and forced internal displacement over the past fifteen years.[27]

Afro-Colombian Rap

Rap music has its origins in the United States, and as media professional S. Craig Watkins mentions in his book *Hip Hop Matters*, "most historians and cultural critics trace [rap] back to the early and middle 1970s, back to a time and place affectionately known as the 'Boogie Down Bronx.'"[28] Rap has developed from an underground form of expression to a powerful commercial industry with a long list of subgenres that include black nationalist rap, message rap, gangsta rap, freestyle rap, and jazz rap, to name a few.

In its roots, rap music was primarily associated with African American youth, and the hood was the space and place of representation and expression. Cheryl L. Keyes states that rap is "undoubtedly urban and a medium by which segments of a disenfranchised urban youth speak."[29] Murray Forman also affirms that "[r]ap music takes the city and its multiple spaces as the foundation of its cultural production. In the music and its lyrics, the city is an audible presence, explicitly cited and digitally sampled in the reproduction of the aural textures of the urban environment."[30] Rap also started as an underground musical expression in Colombia, and it continues to be so in many urban settings. While rap in Colombia has become commercialized, it is not to the extent as in the United States. However, the members of the bands Renacientes and Grupo de Rap Infantil occupy rural spaces, and the songs by these displaced Afro-Colombian youth represent a rural space as opposed to an urban one. The place or location of Cacarica, Chocó, goes well beyond the equivalent of the North American rap "hood," but it does align with the concept of "posse," which Oxford English Dictionary defines as a "group of people who have a common characteristic, occupation, or purpose." Within the Afro-Colombian cultural and socio-political context and within that of the broader Colombian context under a state of armed conflict, the term "posse" encompasses a broad sector of the population that has struggled and resisted to make claim and dominion of its territory, its history, and its culture. In this case, "posse" transcends generations and kinship in its identification of a collective united by occupation. Place, purpose, and identity are the elements that define "posse" for these young rappers and the communities they represent. Marie Boti and Malcolm Guy, directors of the documentary *Musiques Rebelles Americas*, describe their experience and reaction when they travelled to meet and document the music of the displaced communities in Cacarica after their return to the land:

> To reach the village we would have to travel by plane, taxi, boat, canoe, and foot through mosquito-infested jungle, with the paramilitary forces liable to turn up at any moment. But it was worth it: despite the obvious difficulties and fears of further attacks and possible displacements, music saturated the entire community, from the youngest child to the village elders. And everyone knew the lyrics, whether they were the vallenato songs of the elders, or the rap of the youth, because they told the stories of their lives.[31]

The quote illustrates the very particular relational ties created through the sharing of music across generations. The rap songs on both CDs highlight a strong social, cultural, and political content. None of them deal with romantic love themes nor glorify street violence, drugs, drug dealing, or gangster life. Furthermore, these lyrics do not include cussing nor do they denigrate women. Instead, these tracks focus on love of the land and community. These Afro-Colombian songs, like some subgenres of American rap, " 'keep it real' thematically, rapping about situations, scenes and sites that comprise the lived experience of the hood."[32] For these IDPs, the "hood" is recoded as the Cacarica River basin in the department of Chocó instead of an urban space. Moreover, the lyrics in these songs do not include any Spanglish as is common in rap music from barrios in big cities in Colombia, like Bogotá, Cali, Medellin, and in tracks by commercialized Afro-Colombian rap and Afro-Colombian reggae-rap artists and bands such as Ghettos Clan, Choc Quib Town, Voodoo Souldjahs, Profetas, Marcando Territorio, and Asilo 38.

Dennis states that "the implementation of neoliberal reform and economic restructuring only intensified the years following the writing of the new constitution, processes that essentially exasperated many of the social ills weighing on Afro-Colombian rural communities." These are the main topics that Afro-Colombian rappers sing about: "growing poverty, an escalating armed conflict, the expansion of the drug trade, displacement, mass urbanization, rising violence, mounting repression, and increased tension."[33] Since the early 1990s, Bogotá, Medellín, and Cali have been the main centers for rap music in Colombia. In the 1990s, Afro-Colombian rap bands sang about inequality, lack of opportunities, and "norteñismo." In the 1980s, stowaways brought rap music from the United States into Colombia through the port cities of Buenaventura in Valle del Cauca and Turbo in Antioquia. Going north to the United States was a very attractive venture for youth in Buenaventura and Turbo, and many songs dealt with that topic.

The first rap albums in Colombia were not recorded until the 1990s due to lack of financial investment, as well as a lack of understanding and support for this genre of music. The urban band Los Generales Rap y Reggae—an Afro-Colombian band—are credited with having recorded the first rap album in Buenaventura in 1991, while the band La Etnnia—a white and *mestizo* all-male band—recorded the first rap album in Bogotá in 1994 (Páez López). In Los Generales R&R's self-titled album, produced by Colmusica, the band sings about hunger, poverty, unemployment, and dreams of going to the United States. The band also covers original rap and reggae tunes. The combination of rap and reggae has been a common blend in Colombia. The bands Voodoo Souldjahs and

Profetas also combine rap with reggae in their songs.

Marcando Territorio is a band composed of Afro-Colombian youth and adult males and females. This band is from Buenaventura, and their songs reference racial oppression and struggles at global levels, while highlighting the ancestral and traditional legacy of Colombian Pacific folklore. A central theme in their work is achieving the dreams of youth and striving for a peaceful society.[34] Their song "Libertad" begins with references to leaders and activists such as Nelson Mandela, Malcolm X, and Martin Luther King Jr., and mentions many socio-economic and political issues affecting the black population in Colombia, including forced displacement.

Pablo Fortaleza from Puerto Tejada, Cauca, and Antombo Languagui from Central African Republic are the members of the band Profetas, which came together in 1997. Their music combines elements of Afro-Colombian rhythms, reggae, rock, and rap. The band has performed at many music festivals in Colombia and in Europe, where it has a large following and has won awards.

Choc Quib Town is a band composed of siblings Gloria Martínez Perea, known as "Goyo," and Miguel Martínez Perea, known as "Slow," from Condoto, Chocó, along with Carlos Valencia Ortiz, known as "Tostao," from Quibdó, Chocó. The band came together in the year 2000, and its music is a combination of various rhythms and genres, including funk, reggae, rap, electronic, and traditional rhythms from Colombia's Pacific coast, such as *currulao*, *bambazú*, and *bunde*, as well other Latin American rhythms, such as salsa. Choc Quib Town has been very prolific and successful in and outside of Colombia. The band has recorded nine albums, has received two Latin Grammy awards, and has been nominated for two Grammy awards. According to Dennis, "Choc Quib Town's growing success and popularity suggest that their musical amalgamations have the capacity to bridge, at least to some extent, the divides of that which is perceived as local and global, national and transnational, traditional and modern, black and non-black."[35]

Support for hip hop from local and state organizations began in the mid-1990s. The annual festival "Hip Hop al Parque" is part of the series "Festivales al Parque," and it is an international hip hop music celebration that takes place in Bogotá. Local governmental organizations, such as the Instituto Distrital de las Artes (IDARTES), the Secretaría de Patrimonio Cultural, and the Instituto Distrital de Turismo (IDT Bogotá) have sponsored the festival since its inception in 1996. "Bogotá Music Market" (BOmm) is another festival, which is also state sponsored through the Cámara de Comercio de Bogotá, with the support of the Instituto Distrital de las Artes (IDARTES). This festival takes place in Bogotá and the first installment took place in 2011. Centralization of financial funds and support to rap artists and bands affects musicians in the rest of Colombia, especially those in rural areas and those who have been forcibly displaced.

Los Generales R&R, Marcando Territorio, Profetas, and Choc Quib Town can be categorized as urban rap bands. They use musical instruments and pre-recorded tracks. They own or have access to recording studios, as well as equipment for concerts. Their sound is elaborate and polished in comparison to that of Grupo de Rap Infantil and Renacientes. A visual contrast is noticeable in videos and documentaries of these bands. Footage of Grupo de Rap Infantil and Renacientes in the documentary *Musiques Rebelles Americas*, directed by Boti and Guy, and in the documentary *Nunca más* (2001), directed by Marta Rodríguez and Fernando Restrepo Castañeda, depicts children standing barefoot in a field with livestock roaming while the boys sing their rap songs acapella style. The lyrics of their songs emphasize the land as key aspects of their identity and survival, as well as human rights violations and the causes and effects of forced internal displacement on their families and communities.

The songs by these young rappers from Cacarica accentuate a connection with the earth and with the land they inhabit. The land becomes a leitmotif in many of its interpretations: land as earth, territory, country, homeland, nation, ground, and even death. The song fragments "Tierra querida es el Chocó" (Beloved Land Is Chocó) and "Tierra natal es el Chocó" (Birth Land Is Chocó) exemplify different meanings of the term "land."

These lines personify the land and demonstrate empathy for its pain and suffering. The song highlights a hybrid relationship with the land, encapsulating emotion and connectedness by birth. The rappers who were forced to abandon the land, only to return years later, resist and re-territorialize the scarred place with their song. The struggle of this space as the place of origin, the place of birth, becomes a struggle of space as the place of destination from the perspective of forced internal displacement. Steve Pile explains the value of "micro-movements of resistance" in the spatiality of struggle.[36] These songs illustrate allegiance to the land and empower the people who were uprooted and displaced. Consider the following lines from the song "Mi tierra querida" (My Beloved Land) by the band Renacientes:

> Oh, patria querida
> Querida, ¿por qué sufres así?
> Con tantas cosas lindas que hay en mi país . . .
> Con las aguas de mi tierra, me cubro de pies a cabeza[37]

> *Oh, beloved homeland / Beloved, why do you suffer so? / With so many beautiful things in my country . . . / With waters in my land, I cover myself from head to toe*

This excerpt also emphasizes a personification of the land through suffering, and it repeats the concept of land as "home" and the place of origin. The song mentions land and water, both terrains of resistance and zones of knowledge for Afro-Colombians in the Pacific coast. The space represents beauty and commends authority for those who inhabit it. Just as fishing and working the land are necessary for everyday sustenance, so is singing about how the space is an intricate part of the identity of its people. The suffering is juxtaposed with the image of a country of "many beautiful things." The duplication of the possessive adjective "my" illustrates a body politic further compounded by the act of willingly engulfing oneself with water. Mangroves are complex root systems, and, as such, these songs emphasize the beauty, the pain, and the struggles of these spaces by presenting cross-sections of knowledge of the land and the waters that physically surround its people and that figuratively embody them. The actions in this song function as a praxis of identity that directly integrates land, water, and self.

For Afro-Colombians, the connection to land goes back centuries to the era of colonization, and in Colombia there are stereotypes associated with different regions and the ethnicity of the people who inhabit them.[38] The earth and the land hold a special value for Afro-Colombians because the survival, care, and respect of the land means that of its people as well. Ana Sofía Roa and Bernardo Vivas, both IDPs from Cacarica, mention in a radio interview that they and their fellow community members are peasants. As such, they belong to the land and that is where their roots lie and from whence their culture stems.[39] The physical, cultural, emotional, and spiritual ties with the land are representations of the people's identity, their sense of belonging, sustenance, and purpose of life. Although Afro-Colombians have been migrating to urban centres since the 1980s, and they have been moving away from the Pacific coast, anthropologist Peter Wade affirms that "blackness has been and still is a critical feature of regional history and identity" in the Chocó region.[40]

In this rural setting, threatened by armed groups and financially motivated companies, socio-sensitivities regarding space differ from those of the "hood," even though both urban and rural spaces connote an association with community. As Forman mentions, "a convention for the rapper [is] to be placed at the centre of the world, as the subject around which events unfold and who translate topophilia (love of place) or topophobia (fear of place) into lyrics for wider dissemination."⁴¹ The "hood" is the location where the four pillars of hip-hop are expressed and practiced: MCing or rapping, DJing, graffiti, and break dancing. In urban settings, graffiti serves as visual demarcation of territory primarily for gangs, and gangsta rappers often allude to territorialization aspects in their songs. Yet, for the rappers from Chocó, whose homes and belongings have been destroyed, graffiti is not a form of expression. For these displaced youth, the love and appreciation for the land and the constant fear of being uprooted again take on a whole other meaning regarding the topophilia and topophobia Forman mentions. According to Edward Said, "exile is a condition of terminal loss."⁴² Hence, returning to one's territory two, three, or four years after being displaced heightens the physical and metaphorical roots and links with the place and space that is considered home. Furthermore, in certain cultures, land is not considered home until there is a cemetery or until a member of the community has been laid to rest in the earth there. This is the case for some Afrodescendants. Consequently, the burial of loved ones in the earth, as mentioned in the song "¿Dónde están los mártires?" (Where Are the Martyrs?) by Renacientes, indicates another point of relation, transcendental to individuals and to a place for mourning.⁴³

When comparing the lyrics of songs by rappers from the *comunas* (ghettos) of Bosa or Ciudad Bolívar in Bogotá, the songs by Renacientes and Grupo de Rap Infantil not only speak to the issues of land from their own perspective, but they also recognize the difficulties in their community that extend beyond those of a "hood." This is evidenced in the verses of the song "No queremos más guerra" (We Don't Want Any More War) by Werlin Perea, a member of the band Renacientes:

> Estados Unidos va a cambiar nuestro pueblo
> Yo soy colombiano y no quiero más guerra
> Porque el Plan Colombia es pa' quitar la tierra...
> Nosotros sin esta tierra, no sabemos qué hacer⁴⁴

> *The United States is going to change our town / I am Colombian and I don't want any more war / Because Plan Colombia is to take away our land . . . / Without this land, we don't know what to do*

These lyrics affirm citizenship and a nation-based identity while denouncing the threat of another nation gaining control over the land.⁴⁵ Cacarica has been a contested space by military, guerrilla, and paramilitary groups, as well as by drug and arm traffickers. Its geographic location is strategic for illegal activities and exploitation of the land. Philosopher and sociologist Henri Lefebvre affirms that space is political and becomes "the locus and medium of Power."⁴⁶ Technologies of oppression of this Colombian territory include mining, large-scale monoculture, aerial pesticide spraying, and land mines and other explosives. Consequently, the people who occupy the land become commodities for those who claim control over them and their territory.

The messages in these verses demonstrate a high degree of urgency and commitment so that the victims and the events of forced internal displacement and its many repercussions, including hunger, unemployment, and physical and psycho-emotional violence, will not be forgotten and those responsible will be held accountable. The song "No queremos más guerra" (We Don't Want Any More War) by Werlin Perea mentions suffering of the land and of its people. The lyrics personify the land as "Mother Earth," contrasting this socio-political territory with a war space. This collection of songs functions as a catalyst for change. Many aspects of struggle and perseverance are highlighted in the song "La Guerra" (War) by Henry Angulo, a member of the band Grupo de Rap Infantil:

Durante treinta meses hemos padecido
de hambre, desnudez y desconsolación
y muchas amenazas contra la población[47]

For thirty months we suffered / hunger, nakedness, and disconsolation / and many threats to the population

In the song "Los sin futuro" (Those Without a Future) by Lewis Gómez, the rappers express a negative sentiment of going from a rural area to an urban one:

Del campo no' desplazan pa' los centro' urbano'
pa' que nuestros padres queden sin trabajo
Los ricos se ríen viéndonos así
pidiendo limosna pa' poder vivir[48]

They displace us from the countryside to urban centers / So that our parents end up jobless / The rich folks laugh seeing us like this / begging on the streets to make a living

Being displaced and homeless carries stigma, which adds to issues of racial discrimination. Together, these factors cause other civilians and armed agents to become suspicious of IDPs, assuming they are members or supporters of subversive groups like the guerrillas. Discrimination and stigmatization further complicate life for IDPs, as they struggle to find work or job training in other towns and in cities away from their homeland. Robert Harris, a journalist who specializes in music, comments in an interview on the Canadian Broadcasting Company radio that rap music, aside from transforming the personal into something social, political, and collective, focuses against the system and the ruling class.[49] This stance is relevant to the music by the youth from Cacarica, as they turn their strife into a larger act of resistance that includes their entire community, demanding attention and solidarity from the national authorities and from fellow Colombians at large.

These songs highlight threats to the integrity of Afro-Colombians. Safety and well-being are daily concerns for the inhabitants, young and old, of Cacarica. Guerrilla, paramilitary, and national army factions have penalized the cultural uniqueness and practices of these Afro-communities. Both José Santos Caicedo Cabezas and Marilyn Machado, representatives of the organization *Proceso de Comunidades Negras de Colombia, PCN* (Black Communities Process), assert that part of the social cleansing that has taken place in the Pacific region by the paramilitary and the national army is the imposition of normative forms of conduct that include the obstruction of cultural practices, including the use of dreadlocks and earrings among young men, and their performance of rap or *curralao* music. The authorities have also imposed behavior and relationship codes to control circulation and transportation schedules and to restrict individuals and communities from burying the dead or mourning the deceased in public.[50] Using music to express and celebrate special moments in life is very common for Afro-Colombians. Therefore, prohibiting expressions of mourning through song highly impacts historical cultural practices for both youth and elder members of the Cacarica communities.

In rap music, the "hood" as territory acquires a political dimension that corroborates senses of identity and agency. Marcela Ceballos explains that the neighbourhood as a social space and experience takes on the meaning of origin or of the place of belonging for the rapper, thereby giving meaning to who and what the rapper is.[51] Rap is undoubtedly a territorialized expression, following Ceballos, but for the young and displaced rappers from Chocó, the land (a communal possession) as home and sustenance acquires a broader dimension, especially considering how the territory is threatened by many groups and entities for its economic value of the land.

Beyond rapping about their "hood," these young Afro-Colombian rappers incorporate other identity markers in their music, such as the color of their skin, gender, occupation, age, and nationality, among others. The song "Tierra querida" (Beloved Land) by Pablo Salazar illustrates racial identifying element as follows: "Negro, negro soy / orgulloso me siento de mi color" (Black, black I am / proud I am of my color).[52] The denotation of blackness refers to an ideological framework that Victorien Lavou explains as "la existencia histórica del negro como categoría homogeneizante y supuestamente definitoria ... una categoría rentable porque lo negro era lo inferior, lo bárbaro, lo malo, lo que se tenía que educar o civilizar, el Otro por antonomasia" (the historical existence of the negro as a homogenizing category ... and a supposedly profitably defining category because black meant the inferior, the savage, the bad, that which had to be educated or civilized, the Other par excellence).[53] These young rappers from Cacarica cling to their racial features and highlight them to consolidate an identity that implies community and solidarity. Lavou further explains that "[l]a categoría 'negro' comporta una lucha de la reivindicación social y de construcción identitaria ... en al categoría 'negro' subyace una carga histórica, semántica e ideológica que la ha convertido en una apuesta epistemológica" (the category 'black' purports a struggle for social vindication and one of identity building ... where a historic, semantic and ideological charge underlies the category 'black' that has been turned into an epistemological challenge).[54] These rap songs illustrate part of the reality that Afro-Colombians have been disenfranchised for centuries and that they continue to demand equity and justice as per the Constitution of 1991. Youth are a part of a larger movement that works to gain visibility for Afro-Colombians and to demand basic human rights, including the right to live peacefully in their territories.

The songs "La Guerra" (War) by Henry Angulo and "Los sin futuro" (Those Without a Future) by Lewis Gómez stress identity markers such as "niños" (children), "campesino" (peasant), and "colombianos" (Colombians).[55] Both songs refer to a collective subject by employing a plural first person. These texts are representations of collective memory from the perspective of youth. Philosopher Sue Campbell explains that "[c]ollective memory involves experiential memory, but it is more than a collection of individual memories. Collective memory requires the meaning of a group's past to be shared, and to be understood as shared, among at least some group members."[56] On the one hand, the development of a homogeneous social subject has negative effects when one includes all Afro-Colombians in one sole category and, furthermore, when one identifies them as subversive by accusing them of being guerrilla supporters. On the other hand, displaced Afrodescendant communities find comfort in comprising a community that unites in strategic ways, especially drawing from their experience in refugee shelters and in repatriation as a means to resist further displacement or acts of violence against their people and their land. These rap songs indicate identitarian distinctions between IDPs and their aggressors, pillagers, and exploiters.

Conclusion

The songs discussed in this chapter serve not only as emotional expressions but also as social, cultural, and political discourses that legitimate the positions and visions of their composers and singers. These young and displaced Afro-Colombian singers and songwriters utilize the language and traditions of rap; they appropriate this genre and introduce to it their own style and very concrete socio-political content and geographic location. These rappers take hold of music as a tool of resistance by breaking the silence and joining voices to denounce their aggressors and specific forms of violation against them and their land and to demand reparation from the government. "If politics is about making history, then it is also about changing space: political locations are constituted through the struggles that are supposed fixed on them."[57] These songs are a reinterpretation of the events that happened from the time of forced displacement in 1997 until the return to the land. As David Middleton and Derek Edwards explain: "people reinterpret and discover features of the past that become the context for what they will jointly recall and commemorate."[58] In this instance, music is a medium to document history and to re-narrate the experiences of forced internal displacement. It is also a means to reclaim and protect communities' human and land rights and to gain solidarity. Steve Pile explains that "[l]ocation is simultaneously about unity and difference, about definitions of who occupies the same or a similar space and who does not, which do not presume—and, further, undermine the presumption—that there is a sameness to people's location in particular oppressive power relations and a consequent sameness of their struggle."[59] Although these songs date back to 1999 and 2002, the memories of the experiences of forced internal displacement are kept alive through ritual and celebrations, such as the Festival of Memories in Cacarica, which took place from February 25 to March 4, 2019. This was the fourth installment of the festival, and the theme of the festival was "We Are Genesis."[60] The land shapes the songs, and the songs shape the land. The rap songs on both these CDs keep the historic memory alive, which also ensures creating awareness about the atrocities of internal displacement with the hopes to prevent further cases from taking place.

NOTES

1. As Peter Wade reports, "The [2005] census [data] revealed that 79 percent of the population of Chocó Department, which occupies the northern half of the Pacific coastal region, had 'unsatisfied basic needs,' the highest proportion in the country,

while 54 percent of all Afro-Colombians had unsatisfied basic needs (compared to 47 percent of non-Afro-Colombians). Unemployment is higher for Afro-Colombians than non-Afro-Colombians (6 percent versus 3 percent) and poverty is greater (10 percent versus 7 percent)." Peter Wade, "Afro-Colombian Social Movements." In *Comparative Perspectives on Afro-Latin America*, eds. Kwame Dixon and John Burdick (Gainesville: University Press of Florida, 2012), 138.
2. The *Coliseo de Turbo* (sports coliseum) became a camp for some eight hundred and fifty displaced families. The living conditions were overcrowded and unsanitary due to rat problems and rainwater that seeped into the space. In addition, there was constant military surveillance, the lights were on twenty-four hours a day, and the doors were kept locked during the night. Furthermore, there were shortages of water and wood for cooking. Many of the families sheltered in this space remained there three to four years. See Carlos Alberto Giraldo, Jesús Abad Colorado, and Diego Pérez, *Relatos e imágenes: El desplazamiento en Colombia* (Santa Fe de Bogotá: Cinep, 1997), 54.
3. Although the media claimed that 3,500 people (including 234 children) were displaced as a consequence of Operación Génesis (by the military) and Operación Cacarica (by paramilitary units), testimonies by members of displaced communities indicate that over 10,000 people were uprooted and 85 were murdered. Wouters indicates that the bombing in the Salaqui and Cacarica tributaries in the months of January and February 1997, "caused the displacement of ca. 14,000—17,000 inhabitants." Mieke Wouters, "Ethnic Rights under Threat: The Black Peasant Movement Against Armed Groups' Pressure in the Chocó, Colombia," *Bulletin of Latin American Research* 20 (2001): 508.
4. "About 12 percent of all Afro-Colombians are classified as displaced persons. The state estimates that in 2000–2002, the rate of displacement of Afro-Colombians was nearly twice that of non-Afro-Colombians." Wade, "Afro-Colombian Social Movements," 146.
5. Ulrich Oslender, "Tradición oral y memoria colectiva en el Pacífico colombiano: Hacia la construcción de una política cultural negra," *Guaraguao* 20 (2005): 77.
6. "The region is topographically isolated from the rest of the country by the Western Andean Mountain chain, and has been subject to physical and economic marginalisation in relation to Colombia's interior." Ulrich Oslender, "Violence in Development: The Logic of Forced Internal Displacement on Colombia's Pacific Coast," *Development in Practice* 17, no. 6 (2007): 753.
7. Oslender, "Violence in Development," 756.
8. Ibid., 756.
9. According to Ulrich Oslende, the Pacific region of Colombia has 40 percent illiteracy rate, which make oral history and communication a priority. Oslender, "Tradición oral y memoria colectiva," 75.
10. Ibid., 81.
11. The translations are all mine unless otherwise stated. The members of the band Renacientes are Henry Angulo, Onel Martínez, Jefferson Orejuela (Ali), Edison Palacio (Pacho) Jarlenson, and Angulo (Amin). For more information, see "Los Renacientes:

Biography," Last.fm, last modified June 17, 2009, 3:43, https://www.last.fm/music/Los+Renacientes/+wiki.

12. *Vallenato* is currently the emblematic music of Colombia and "is part of a tradition of versification." See Diana Rodríguez Quevedo, "Witnessing Forced Internal Displacement in Colombia through Vallenato Music," in *Song and Social Change in Latin America*, ed. Lauren Shaw (Lanham, MD: Lexington Books, 2013), 130. According to folklorologist Julio Oñate Martínez, this accordion music is a means for storytelling and its history, and it is means for peasants to share their experiences and observations of life. Julio Oñate Martínez, *El ABC del vallenato* (Bogotá: Taurus, 2003), 139. *Chirimía* is a specific Colombian style of music from the Cauca department.

13. A few of these songs are featured in the two following documentaries: *Musiques Rebelles Americas* (*Rebel Musics Americas*, 2004), directed by Marie Boti and Malcolm Guy, and *Nunca más* (*Never Again*, 2001), directed by Marta Rodríguez and Fernando Restrepo Castaña. In the documentaries, the boys perform their rap songs standing outdoors on the bare ground. They sway their bodies and take a few steps forward and backward. The boys are wearing t-shirts and sleeveless shirts and shorts. They don't have any type of accessories or "bling," and they sing a cappella. Other boys sing along to the chorus. All are barefoot. Houses made of wooden planks stand on stilts and pilings in the background. A couple of pigs roam by the area, and roosters are heard as the boys sing.

14. "Many IDPs and their leaders reclaiming land have been subject to criminal acts of intimidation and threats of violence. Threatening displaced land claimants undermines restitution in many ways, including by making victims fearful, discouraging them from pursuing claims, restricting leader's participation in the process, and pushing those who have returned home to flee their land yet again." Max Schoening, *The Risk of Returning Home: Violence and Threats against Displaced People Reclaiming Land in Colombia* (New York: Human Rights Watch, 2013), 22.

15. Songs and oral testimonies that explain the process of empowerment and collective agency in creating a protection mechanism by means of the humanitarian and biodiverse zone that was created in Cacarica were recorded by Contagio Radio. See Ana Sofía Roa and Bernardo Vivas, "Hablemos alguito: Zonas humanas y de biodiversidad en Colombia," *Hablemos alguito*, Radio Contagio, February 13, 2013, accessed March 22, 2013.

16. Stuart Hall, "What is this 'Black' in Black Popular Music?," in *Representing Blackness: Issues in Film and Video*, ed. Valerie Smith (New Brunswick: Rutgers University Press, 1997), 125–29.

17. "El registro único de víctimas del gobierno de Colombia y el observatorio global del desplazamiento interno trabajan juntos para mejorar la comprensión del desplazamiento interno en Colombia," Unidad para la Atención y la Reparación Integral a las Víctimas, May 16, 2018, accessed October 4, 2019, https://www.unidadvictimas.gov.co/es/valoracion-y-registro/el-registro-unico-de-victimas-del-gobierno-de-colombia-y-el-observatorio.

18. Wade explains that "the Pacific coastal region is not home to the majority of Afro-Colombians because of its low population density. Counting Afro-descendants in Colombia has been a difficult matter, as it is in Latin America generally, because of the absence of a widespread consensus about who counts as 'black' (or Afro-Colombian, or whatever other terms are used)." Wade, "Afro-Colombian Social Movements," 137. Between the General Census (*Censo General*) in 2005 and the Population and Housing National Census (CNPU) in 2018, the registered population who self-identifies as Black, Afro-Colombian, Raizal, and Palenquero (NARP) decreased by 30.8 percent. Departamento Administrativo Nacional de Estadísticas (DANE), "Población negra, afrocolombiana, raizal y palenquera: resultados del censo nacional de población y vivienda 2018," Gobierno de Colombia, Departamento Administrativo Nacional de Estadísticas, 2018, accessed September 13, 2019, https://www.dane.gov.co/index.php/estadisticas-por-tema/demografia-y-poblacion/censo-nacional-de-poblacion-y-vivenda-2018.
19. "The grim reality of black communities in the Pacific lowlands of Colombia is but one illustration of how the drive toward capitalist modernity results in placement and violent dispassion. At the same time, this drive toward economic development even in its current globalizing guise reinforces state presence. It is almost a truism to say that the unfolding of such power is inevitably met with resistance. That is, 'local communities' are not unproblematically and completely subsumed by the violent intervention of armed capital. Contemporary struggles for social change not only try to put a brake on the negative forces of capitalist globalization and state power; they also seek alternatives to them." Kiran Asher, *Black and Green: Afro-Colombians, Development, and Nature in the Pacific Lowlands* (Durham: Duke University Press, 2009), 188–89.
20. The United Self-Defense Forces of Colombia (AUC) was a coalition of paramilitary or right-wing death squads. "The AUC signed a peace accord with the government in 2003, and largely demobilized by 2006. New criminal gangs have inherited the paramilitaries' weapons, personnel and modus operandi around the country." See InSight Crime, "AUC," InSight Crime, May 25, 2011, accessed August 30, 2019, https://insightcrime.org/colombia-organized-crime-news/auc-profile/. The Government of Colombia of President Juan Manuel Santos and the guerrilla movement Revolutionary Armed Forces of Colombia (FARC–EP) signed a Peace Accord on November 24, 2016, to end the armed conflict. The Senate and the House of Representative ratified the accord on November 29–30, 2016.
21. Quoted in Wouters, "Ethnic Rights Under Threat," 509.
22. Carlos Rosero, "Los afrodescendientes y el conflicto armado en Colombia: La insistencia en lo propio como alternativa," in *Afrodescendientes en las Américas: Trayectorias sociales e indentitarias: 150 años de la abolición de la esclavitud en Colombia*, eds. Claudia Mosquera, Mauricio Pardo, and Odile Hoffman (Bogotá: Universidad Nacional de Colombia, Icanh, Ird, Ilsa, 2002), 549. Guerrilla and paramilitary groups subsidize their operations through their participation in illegal drug trade. "At the same time, guerrillas and paramilitaries exercise a considerable degree of control over the civilian

population, taking recourse to terror." Wouters, "Ethnic Rights Under Threat," 507.
23. Mabel González Bustelos, "Desterrados: Forced Displacement in Colombia," in *The Dispossessed: Chronicles of the Desterrados of Colombia*, Alfredo Molano, trans. Daniel Bland, (Chicago: Haymarket Books, 2005), 232.
24. Luís Evelis Andrade, "Political Violence, Exclusion and Ethnic Minorities in Colombia," *Ethnicity, Violence and Exclusion in Colombia: The Struggles of Colombia's Indigenous and Afro-Colombian Peoples*, Strong College, York University, Toronto, March 16, 2007.
25. Forrest Hylton, *Evil Hour in Colombia* (London: Verso, 2006), 1–2.
26. Christopher Dennis, *Afro-Colombian Hip-Hop: Globalization, Transcultural Music, and Ethnic Identities* (Plymouth: Lexington Books, 2012), 7.
27. The 2018 census indicates that fewer people were registered as Black, Afro-Colombian, Raizal, and Palenquero compared to the 2005 census because of issues concerning construction of identity, political and organizational awareness, and invisibility of Afrodescendant ethnicity, as well as difficulty reaching certain areas due to safety concerns or because residents did not want to be registered. See DANE, "Población negra, afrocolombiana, raizal y palenquera."
28. S. Craig Watkins, *Hip Hop Matters: Politics, Pop Culture, and the Struggle for the Soul of a Movement* (Boston: Beacon Press, 2005), 9.
29. Cheryl L. Keyes, *Rap Music and Street Consciousness* (Chicago: University of Illinois, 2002), 122.
30. Murray Forman, " 'Represent': Race, Space and Place in Rap Music," in *Cultural Studies: An Anthology*, ed. Michael Ryan (Malden, MA: Blackwell Publishing, 2008), 882.
31. Marie Boti and Malcolm Guy, with Elysee Nouvet and Hind Benchekroun, "Making Rebel Musics: The Films," in *Rebel Musics: Human Rights, Resistant Sounds, and the Politics of Music Making*, eds. Daniel Fischlin and Ajay Heble (Montreal: Black Rose Books, 2003), 81.
32. Forman, " 'Represent,' " 887.
33. Dennis, *Afro-Colombian Hip-Hop*, 47.
34. Andrés Felipe Becerra, "Marcando Territorio, iniciativa artística por la defensa de Buenaventura," *El Pais*, November 30, 2013, accessed June 18, 2021, https://www.elpais.com.co/judicial/marcando-territorio-iniciativa-artistica-por-la-defensa-de-buenaventura.html.
35. Dennis, *Afro-Colombian Hip-Hop*, 145.
36. Steve Pile, "Introduction," in *Geographies of Resistance*, eds. Steve Pile and Michael Keith (London: Routledge, 1997), 29.
37. Renacientes, "Mi tierra querida," *A nuestros mártires. . . comunidades en resistencia del Cacarica Chocó* (CAVIDA, 2002), compact disc.
38. Dennis explains that "[a]lthough slavery in what is now Colombia never reached the same magnitude as it did in places such as Cuba and Brazil, it was significant enough to greatly impact the ethnic-racial landscape of the emerging nation. The need for

slave labor in specific regions greatly contributed to the eventual geo-racial regionalization of modern-day Colombia." Dennis, *Afro-Colombian Hip-Hop*, 3.
39. See Roa and Vivas, "Hablemos alguito."
40. Peter Wade, *Blackness and Race Mixture: The Dynamics of Racial Identity in Colombia* (Baltimore: Johns Hopkins University Press, 1993), 4.
41. Forman, " 'Represent,' " 893.
42. Edward Said, "Reflections on Exile," in *Altogether Elsewhere: Writers in Exile*, ed. Marc Robinson (San Diego: Harcourt Brace and Company, 1994), 174.
43. Renacientes, "Dónde están los mártires." *A nuestros mártires... comunidades en resistencia del Cacarica Chocó* (CAVIDA, 2002), compact disc.
44. Werlin Perea, "No queremos más guerra," *A nuestros mártires... comunidades en resistencia del Cacarica Chocó* (CAVIDA, 2002), compact disc.
45. Former president of Colombia Andrés Pastrana and former president of the United States Bill Clinton conceived Plan Colombia in 1999 as an initiative to provide foreign, military, and diplomatic aid.
46. Henri Lefebvre, *The Production of Space*, trans. Donald Nicholson-Smith (Malden, MA: Blackwell Publishing, 1991), 94.
47. Henry Angulo, "La Guerra," *Óyeme Chocó: Melodías de la esperanza; comunidades en retorno al Cacarica, Chocó* (CAVIDA, 1999), compact disc.
48. Lewis Gómez, "Los sin futuro," *A nuestros mártires... comunidades en resistencia del Cacarica Chocó* (CAVIDA, 2002), compact disc.
49. Robert Harris, interview by Michael Enright, *The Sunday Edition*, Canadian Broadcasting Corporation, Radio Two, CBL-FM, Toronto, March 22, 2009.
50. José Santos Caicedo Cabezas, "Armed Conflict," *Ethnicity, Violence and Exclusion in Colombia: The Struggles of Colombia's Indigenous and Afro-Colombian Peoples*, Strong College, York University, Toronto, March 16, 2007.
51. Marcela Ceballos, *RAP: Entrando al juego de las identidades políticas* (Bogotá: Uniandes, 2001), 21.
52. Pablo Salazar, "Tierra querida," *Óyeme Chocó: Melodías de la esperanza; comunidades en retorno al Cacarica, Chocó* (CAVIDA, 1999), compact disc.
53. Victorien Lavou, "Negro/a no hay tal cosa: una lectura ideológica de la canción 'Me gritaron negra' de Victoria Santa Cruz," in *Afrodescendientes en las Américas: Trayectorias sociales e identitarias; 150 años de la abolición de la esclavitud en Colombia*, eds. Claudia Mosquera, Mauricio Pardo, and Odile Hoffman (Bogotá: Universidad Nacional de Colombia, Icahn, Ird, Ilsa, 2002), 340.
54. Ibid., 334.
55. Angulo, "La Guerra"; and Gómez, "Los sin futuro."
56. Sue Campbell, *Relational Remembering: Rethinking the Memory Wars* (Lanham, MD: Rowman and Littlefield Publishers, 2003), 180.
57. Pile, "Introduction," 28.
58. Quoted in Campbell, *Relational Remembering*, 180.

59. Pile, "Introduction," 28.
60. International Center for Transitional Justice (ICTJ), "Cacarica: 22 Years of Resistance," ICTJ, accessed May 25, 2020. https://www.ictj.org/node/25112.

WORKS CITED

Andrade, Luís Evalis. "Political Violence, Exclusion and Ethnic Minorities in Colombia." *Ethnicity, Violence and Exclusion in Colombia: The Struggles of Colombia's Indigenous and Afro-Colombian Peoples*. Strong College, York University, Toronto. March 16, 2007.

Angulo, Henry. "La Guerra." *Óyeme Chocó: Melodías de la esperanza; comunidades en retorno al Cacarica, Chocó*. CAVIDA, 1999. Compact disc.

———. "Mi tierra natal." *Óyeme Chocó: Melodías de la esperanza; comunidades en retorno al Cacarica, Chocó*. CAVIDA, 1999. Compact disc.

Asher, Kiran. *Black and Green: Afro-Colombians, Development, and Nature in the Pacific Lowlands*. Durham: Duke University Press, 2009.

Becerra, Andrés Felipe. "Marcando Territorio, iniciativa artística por la defensa de Buenaventura." *El Pais*. November 30, 2013. Accessed June 18, 2021. https://www.elpais.com.co/judicial/marcando-territorio-iniciativa-artistica-por-la-defensa-de-buenaventura.html.

Boti, Marie, and Malcolm Guy, dir. *Musiques Rebelles Americas*. Multi-Monde, 2004. DVD.

Boti, Marie, and Malcolm Guy, with Elysee Nouvet and Hind Benchekroun. "Making Rebel Musics: The Films." In *Rebel Musics: Human Rights, Resistant Sounds, and the Politics of Music Making*, edited by Daniel Fischlin and Ajay Heble, 68–87. Montreal: Black Rose Books, 2003.

Bustelos González, Mabel. "Desterrados: Forced Displacement in Colombia." In *The Dispossessed: Chronicles of the Desterrados of Colombia*, by Alfredo Molano, translated by Daniel Bland, 201–260. Chicago: Haymarket Books, 2005.

Caicedo Cabezas, José Santos. "Armed Conflict." *Ethnicity, Violence and Exclusion in Colombia: The Struggles of Colombia's Indigenous and Afro-Colombian Peoples*. Strong College, York University, Toronto. March 16, 2007.

Campbell, Sue. *Relational Remembering: Rethinking the Memory Wars*. Lanham, MD: Rowman and Littlefield Publishers, 2003.

Ceballos, Marcela. *RAP: Entrando al juego de las identidades políticas*. Bogotá: Uniandes, 2001.

Departamento Administrativo Nacional de Estadísticas (DANE). "Población negra, afrocolombiana, raizal y palenquera: Resultados del censo nacional de población y vivienda 2018." Gobierno de Colombia. Departamento Administrativo Nacional de Estadísticas. 2018. Accessed September 13, 2019. https://www.dane.gov.co/index.php/estadisticas-por-tema/demografia-y-poblacion/censo-nacional-de-poblacion-y-vivenda-2018.

Dennis, Christopher. *Afro-Colombian Hip-Hop: Globalization, Transcultural Music, and Ethnic Identities*. Plymouth: Lexington Books, 2012.

Forman, Murray. " 'Represent': Race, Space and Place in Rap Music." In *Cultural Studies: An Anthology*, edited by Michael Ryan, 879–903. Malden, MA: Blackwell Publishing, 2008.
Giraldo, Carlos Alberto, Jesús Abad Colorado, and Diego Pérez. *Relatos e imágenes: El desplazamiento en Colombia*. Santa Fe de Bogotá: Cinep, 1997.
Gómez, Lewis. "Los sin futuro." *A nuestros mártires . . . comunidades en resistencia del Cacarica Chocó*. CAVIDA, 2002. Compact disc.
Hall, Stuart. "What is this 'Black' in Black Popular Music?" In *Representing Blackness: Issues in Film and Video*, edited by Valerie Smith, 123–33. New Brunswick: Rutgers University Press, 1997.
Harris, Robert. Interview by Michael Enright. *The Sunday Edition*. Canadian Broadcasting Corporation. Radio Two. CBL-FM, Toronto. March 22, 2009.
Hylton, Forrest. *Evil Hour in Colombia*. London: Verso, 2006.
InSight Crime. "AUC." InSight Crime. May 25, 2011. Accessed August 30, 2019. https://insightcrime.org/colombia-organized-crime-news/auc-profile/.
International Center for Transitional Justice (ICTJ). "Cacarica: 22 Years of Resistance." ICTJ. Accessed May 25, 2020. https://www.ictj.org/node/25112.
Keyes, Cheryl L. *Rap Music and Street Consciousness*. Chicago: University of Illinois, 2002.
Last FM. "Los Renacientes." www.last.fm/music/Los+Renacientes/+wiki. Web. 30 Aug. 2019.
Lefebvre, Henri. *The Production of Space*. Translated by Donald Nicholson-Smith. Malden, MA: Blackwell Publishing, 1991.
Lavou, Victorien. "Negro/a no hay tal cosa: Una lectura ideológica de la canción 'Me gritaron negra' de Victoria Santa Cruz." In *Afrodescendientes en las Américas: Trayectorias sociales e identitarias; 150 años de la abolición de la esclavitud en Colombia*, edited by Claudia Mosquera, Mauricio Pardo, and Odile Hoffman, 333–47. Bogotá: Universidad Nacional de Colombia, Icahn, Ird, Ilsa, 2002.
Molano, Alfredo. *Desterrados: Crónicas del desarraigo*. Bogotá: El Ancora, 2002.
Oñate Martínez, Julio. *El ABC del vallenato*. Bogotá: Taurus, 2003.
Oslender, Ulrich. "Violence in Development: The Logic of Forced Internal Displacement on Colombia's Pacific Coast." *Development in Practice* 17, no. 6 (2007): 752–64.
———. "Tradición oral y memoria colectiva en el Pacífico colombiano: hacia la construcción de una política cultural negra." *Guaraguao* 20 (2005): 74–104.
Palacio, Edilson, Pablo Salazar, and Henry Angulo. "No queremos más guerra." *Musiques Rebelles Americas*. Directed by Mari Boti and Malcolm Guy. Multi-Monde, 2004. DVD.
Palacios, Marco, and Frank Safford. *Colombia: Fragmented Land, Divided Society*. New York: Oxford University Press, 2002.
Perea, Werlin. "Maldita guerra." *A nuestros mártires . . . comunidades en resistencia del Cacarica Chocó*. CAVIDA, 2002. Compact disc.
———. "No queremos más guerra." *A nuestros mártires . . . comunidades en resistencia del Cacarica Chocó*. CAVIDA, 2002. Compact disc.
Pile, Steve. "Introduction." In *Geographies of Resistance*, edited by Steve Pile and Michael Keith, 1–32. London: Routledge, 1997.

"El registro único de víctimas del gobierno de Colombia y el observatorio global del desplazamiento interno trabajan juntos para mejorar la comprensión del desplazamiento interno en Colombia." Unidad para la Atención y la Reparación Integral a las Víctimas. May 16, 2018. Accessed October 4, 2019. https://www.unidadvictimas.gov.co/es/valoracion-y-registro/el-registro-unico-de-victimas-del-gobierno-de-colombia-y-el-observatorio.

Renacientes. "Dónde están los mártires." *A nuestros mártires... comunidades en resistencia del Cacarica Chocó*. CAVIDA, 2002. Compact disc.

———. "A mi país." *A nuestros mártires... comunidades en resistencia del Cacarica Chocó*. CAVIDA, 2002. Compact disc.

———. "Mi tierra querida." *A nuestros mártires... comunidades en resistencia del Cacarica Chocó*. CAVIDA, 2002. Compact disc.

———. "No queremos seguir llorando." *A nuestros mártires... comunidades en resistencia del Cacarica Chocó*. CAVIDA, 2002. Compact disc.

———. "Venceremos al ratón." *A nuestros mártires... comunidades en resistencia del Cacarica Chocó*. CAVIDA, 2002. Compact disc.

Roa, Ana Sofía, and Bernardo Vivas. "Hablemos alguito: Zonas humanas y de biodiversidad en Colombia." *Hablemos alguito*. Radio Contagio. February 13, 2013. Accessed March 22, 2013.

Rodríguez, Marta, and Fernando Restrepo Castaña, dir. *Nunca más*. Fundación Cine Documental, 2001. Videocassette.

Rodríguez Quevedo, Diana. "Witnessing Forced Internal Displacement in Colombia through Vallenato Music." In *Song and Social Change in Latin America*, edited by Lauren Shaw, 123–50. Lanham, MD: Lexington Books, 2013.

Rosero, Carlos. "Los afrodescendientes y el conflicto armado en Colombia: La insistencia en lo propio como alternativa." In *Afrodescendientes en las Américas: Trayectorias sociales e indentitarias: 150 años de la abolición de la esclavitud en Colombia*, edited by Claudia Mosquera, Mauricio Pardo, and Odile Hoffman, 547–59. Bogotá: Universidad Nacional de Colombia, Icanh, Ird, Ilsa, 2002.

Salazar, Pablo. "Tierra querida." *Óyeme Chocó: Melodías de la esperanza; comunidades en retorno al Cacarica, Chocó*. CAVIDA, 1999. Compact disc.

Said, Edward. "Reflections on Exile." In *Altogether Elsewhere: Writers in Exile*, edited by Marc Robinson, 137–49. San Diego: Harcourt Brace and Company, 1994.

Schoening, Max. *The Risk of Returning Home: Violence and Threats against Displaced People Reclaiming Land in Colombia*. New York: Human Rights Watch, 2013.

Wade, Peter. "Afro-Colombian Social Movements." In *Comparative Perspectives on Afro-Latin America*, edited by Kwame Dixon and John Burdick, 135–55. Gainesville: University Press of Florida, 2012.

———. *Blackness and Race Mixture: The Dynamics of Racial Identity in Colombia*. Baltimore: Johns Hopkins University Press, 1993.

Watkins, S. Craig. *Hip Hop Matters: Politics, Pop Culture, and the Struggle for the Soul of a Movement*. Boston: Beacon Press, 2005.

Wouters, Mieke. "Ethnic Rights under Threat: The Black Peasant Movement against Armed Groups' Pressure in the Chocó, Colombia." *Bulletin of Latin American Research* 20 (2001): 498–519.

◆ AFTERWORD

Racial Encounters in the Americas in Times of Black Lives Matter

Mamadou Badiane

In an interview with Jacqueline Leiner, Aimé Césaire, a founding member of the Négritude movement, affirms that if "Black people were not a people, let's say a vanquished, well, an unhappy people, a humiliated people, etc., reverse history, make them a victorious people, I believe, for my part, that there would be no Négritude."[1] *Améfrica in Letters: Literary Interventions from Mexico to the Southern Cone* thus appears at an opportune moment, when contemporary debates throughout Latin America and the United States have turned to the Black Lives Matter movement and protests against discrimination directed at Native Americans.

From Bolivia to the United States, many Native American groups have organized to protest and fight discrimination and injustice. Believing their religious sites, graves, and water supplies are threatened, Indigenous people have taken action to defend their cultural history and their quality of life. In 2021, for example, Indigenous Bolivians protested to preserve a reservation through which a highway was set to pass. The protest began with strikes and blockades by civic and neighborhood organizations in the cities of El Alto and Potosí. Similarly, the Standing Rock Sioux Tribe in the United States has protested the Dakota Pipeline since 2016.

Meanwhile, Black people in the Americas continue to protest prejudice and injustice, battling against marginalization and identity issues in their host communities. In the United States, a vast number of Black men, women, and children have been shot or brutalized by the police. While the culture of anti-Blackness in policing is pervasive, I will cite a few cases that have had worldwide exposure. In 1997, a Haitian American named Abner Louima was severely brutalized by Justin Volpe, a police officer in the NYPD, who is currently serving a thirty-year sentence but is scheduled for release sometime in 2025. In 1999, Amadou Diallo, a young Guinean who lived peacefully in New York City, was savagely shot, his body ravaged by forty-one bullets, when four NYPD officers mistook him for a serial rapist in the Soundview section of the Bronx. Many other sad cases have followed: Daunte Wright (twenty years old, Minneapolis, Minnesota), Breonna Taylor (twenty-six years old, Louisville, Kentucky), Philando Castile (thirty-two years old, Falcon Heights, Minnesota), Freddie Gray (twenty-five years old, Baltimore, Maryland), Eric Garner (forty-three years old, Staten Island, New York), Tamir Rice (twelve years old, Cleveland, Ohio), Michael Brown (eighteen years old, Ferguson, Missouri), and George Floyd (forty-six years old, Minneapolis Minnesota). Floyd's death at the hands of the police was so egregious that it animated the consciousness of the Black Lives Matter movement, both in the United States and around the world. Following the death of Floyd, activists demanded police reform, including significant changes to how police conduct arrests. Internationally, and in sympathy with Floyd's death, soccer players from the UK professional league have knelt before each match to remember the nine minutes of excruciating pain that Floyd endured. On the first anniversary of Floyd's murder, President Joe Biden proclaimed that "the murder of George Floyd launched a summer of protest that unified people of every race, gender, and generation to say enough of this senseless killing."[2] Compared to the previous administration, Biden's position seems to advocate more for tolerance and justice, which are also needed in many parts of Latin America.

In Brazil, CNN has documented that "um negro é morto pela polícia a cada quatro horas" (a black man is killed by the police every four hours).[3] Another Brazilian source writes that "dados do Monitor da Violência mostram que em 2020 no Brasil 78% dos mortos pela polícia eram negros. O número refere-se às vítimas das polícias militar e civil e significa que quase quatro a cada cinco pessoas mortas pelas polícias em 2020 eram pretas ou pardas" (data from the Violence Monitor show that in 2020 in Brazil, 78 percent of those killed by the police were black. The number refers to victims of the military and civil police and means that almost four out of five people killed by the police in 2020 were black or brown).[4] Finally, the daily *UOL* also writes that "Negros são oito de cada 10 mortos pela polícia no Brasil" (Blacks constitute eight out of ten people killed by police in Brazil).⁵ From these examples, one can easily understand Aimé Césaire's frustration about the "humiliated" and "unhappy" situation of Blacks worldwide.

Améfrica in Letters: Literary Interventions from Mexico to the Southern Cone is an in-depth reflection on the present situation of men and women of color in Latin America and the rise of the Black Lives Matter movement. In the introduction to the book, Jennifer Carolina Gómez Menjívar studies whether "race or class were responsible for the marginalization of Black and Indigenous peoples in Latin America." Cornel West's famous answer to the issue is succinct: Race Matters. For Cornel West, "the urgent problem of black poverty is primarily due to the distribution of wealth, power, and system that denied opportunities to most 'qualified' black people."⁶ *Améfrica in Letters* thus responds to this situation with a clear, organizing focus directed at the difficult situation of Indigenous and Black men and women in different parts of Latin America.

For women, the problem of racial oppression is compounded by sexism and gender-based violence. In Latin America, women continue to be perceived as inferior to their male counterparts. In her contribution to this volume, Paulette A. Ramsay notes that, since the 1960s, attention has increasingly been placed on masculinity and its relationship to language. Studies conducted in the late twentieth century show that men use language differently from women, and these differences in turn project the identity of the speaker. Afro-Mexican *corridos*, for example, are important for the construction of masculinity among Afro-Mexican men. *Corridos* are musical folk-ballads that explore different aspects of Mexican history, particularly the events of the Mexican Revolution. The *corrido* uses language characterized as political to communicate the important political needs of the Afro-Mexican community. Doris A. Graber summarizes the five purposes of political language as information dissemination, agenda-setting, interpretation and linkage, projection for the future and the past, and action stimulation.⁷ Language in the *corrido* fulfills all these purposes. This, coupled with powerful words and ideologies, allows Afro-Mexican men to create an "anti-language" that dismantles the unequal distributions of power.

While these *corridos* are popular in the Black communities of Costa Chica, they contribute to the perception that women's roles in society are somehow less important, less visible, and less meaningful. Interactions in *corridos* demonstrate that women experience the same oppressive systems as Afro-Mexican men, yet they are also marginalized within their own communities. Consequently, Afro-Mexican women experience two forms of marginalization. Ramsay's rhetorical analysis of the Afro-Mexican men in *corridos* shows how they use language to "challenge the status quo, disparage political leadership, and promote themselves as competitive, capable, confident men who are concerned with promoting a culturally nationalist agenda." Thus, they have an arena in which they can assume mastery, however temporarily, over their condition. In addition, some *corridos* depict federal troops (who hold power over Afro-Mexican communities) as weak and, in so doing, bolster the traditionally masculine traits, such as fearlessness and bravery, of the Afro-Mexican protagonists. When in "Pedro el Chicarrón" this blind courage leads to his injury, the protagonist continues to uphold his power and control of the situation, all while writhing in pain. Another important masculine quality that is often depicted in *corridos* is a fierce loyalty to one's community. Unfortunately, women do not yet have a means to achieve these momentary flashes of power and dominance.

The value system of the *corrido* is masculinist, and it is influenced by sexism and patriarchal attitudes, as exposed by the emphasis on male fighting and violence. The writing, production, narration, and acting of *corridos* are all from the male perspective, which is logical when so few women are involved in these aggressive pursuits. The familiar narrative in the *corrido* of homogenic masculinity is powerful, and it simultaneously lionizes Afro-Mexican men while marginalizing Afro-Mexican women. According to Keith Nurse, "Men rarely see themselves as a gender, and society generally treats masculinity as the prototype of human behavior."[8] This fortifies the idea that men act as the brave protectors of helpless and weak women. Most *corridos* establish a correlation between masculinity and self-praise, while also glorifying virility, aggression, and defiance. These characteristics lead to the agenda of masculine validation. This is confirmed by the negative portrayals of women, who are often represented as weeping mothers, disloyal partners, and self-absorbed young girls. According to bell hooks, this reconstruction of masculinity "encourages men to be pathologically narcissistic, infantile, and psychologically dependent on the privileges (however relative) that they receive simply for having been born male."[9] All of this suggests that *corridos* allow men to redefine themselves using powerful language. But this, in turn, often results in a form of male empowerment and masculinity that leads, however passively, to further racism and sexism.

The strong emphasis on race that infiltrates Ramsay's research on female disempowerment and the quest for identity is flipped upside down in Juan Guillermo Sánchez Martínez's research on the introspective writing of Wingston González. According to Sánchez Martínez, Wingston González writes literature that includes an "absent presence of race" designed to undo and challenge fixed definitions of Blackness, Indigeneity, and nationality. González's less emphatic acknowledgment of race allows him to establish a more fluid self-identification as a migrant and artist. Upon deeper inspection, we can see that his poetry distrusts conventional generalizations of race and ethnicity. His attitude derives in part from his unusual heritage. The Garífuna are Black, Indigenous people who are descended from West African slaves who were shipwrecked on the island of St. Vincent in 1635 and the Indigenous people who were living on the island. According to Michelle Ocasio,

> In either 1635 or 1675, a slaving ship bound for the New World sank close to the coast of St. Vincent Island in the Caribbean. The native Indians marveled at the size and musculature of the black-skinned men bound in chains, prompting them to kill the European crew and welcome the Africans into their society. These Africans willingly learned the language and customs of the native St. Vincentians and were gifted with Indian daughters to marry. From this union, a new ethnic group emerged called the Black Carib, or Garífuna.[10]

The Garífuna were exiled from St. Vincent to the Caribbean coast of Central America in 1797 during the British colonial rule. Around five thousand were displaced to the island of Roatán, and, as a result, the Garífuna worldview, belief system, and language spread to Honduras, Belize, Guatemala, and Nicaragua. Currently, there are seventeen thousand people who identify as Garífuna in Central America. The largest group of self-identified Garífuna, around 290,000, live in New York City. Internalized colonization through interracial mixing and liberal multiculturalism has contributed to the whitening and race-denial of these descendants.

Writing on Afrodescendant writers in Latin America, Doris Sommer argues that "a line of literary experimentation can upset the hierarchy of history with new unauthorized authority."[11] Sánchez Martínez argues that González's aesthetic approach is one of freedom and agency. Translators of González's work describe his poetry as messy and playful, and his verses are disrespectful and hostile toward the Spanish language with their use of the Black vernacular. Another explanation for González's untidy verses could be that they reflect the unease of his transitional generation, as cross-cultural identities and the scattered population of Garífuna create many conflicted feelings. Because of this diasporic condition, the Garífuna people are Black, Indigenous, and Latino. Thus, they navigate an even more complex sense of self than their Afro-Hispanic counterparts. According to Sánchez Martínez, "racism and heteropatriarchy have weaponized literacy and literary prestige in Latin America. This has contributed to the oppression of Black and Indigenous peoples and diminished their expressions." González's contemporary poetry challenges the current political system by blurring Western literary genres and by code-switching. His poetry operates in three dimensions at once: Spanish, English, and Garífuna. Following Aida Toledo, Sánchez Martínez writes that "González's poetry separates itself from the conversational poetry of the previous generation." Toledo also asserts that the celebration of the dead in González's poetry is a Garífuna signature. González's inclusion of the Garífuna way of life in his poetry is both an ancient and a postmodern practice. According to Sánchez Martínez, "*cafeína MC* questions univocal identities, homogenous subjectivities, and group labels that want to build walls between oneness and otherness." This sense of fractured identity is particularly acute for Garífuna writers.

Cultural memory is also an important component for Garífuna writers. According to Jennifer Carolina Gómez Menjívar, the Garífuna writer Xiomara Cacho Caballero uses multimodal means to confront the marginality and violence to which Garífuna peoples are subjected on the "narco islands" of Central America. Beginning with an analysis of Cacho Caballero's children's stories, Gómez Menjívar proceeds to discuss her book-length essays, concluding with an analysis of her multilingual poetry. In Gómez Menjívar's assessment, Cacho Caballero views linguistic revitalization as a form of spiritual mending, which, like ceremony and communion with the ancestors, is critical for emerging from a space of violence to a stronger Afro-Indigenous community.

The use of the Garífuna language allows for a richer analysis of logocentric cultural products—such as poetry, short stories, film, music, and even newly written dictionaries—produced by members of the diaspora. By making "the [ancestral] word" dominant, the Garífuna people divest whiteness from the concept of *logos* and invest in its Afro-Indigenous conceptualization. By targeting a young readership, Cacho Caballero defends the need for the youngest members of the Garífuna community to recover their ancestral language. According to Gómez Menjívar, Cacho Caballero understands that when a language is eliminated, the cultural knowledge of a people disappears as well.

Another area of concern for Cacho Caballero is the extent to which the drug trade has altered the land and traditions that the Garífuna peoples have inherited from their ancestors. The Garífuna, like many other Indigenous peoples, have developed healing cultures that emphasize the relationship between the living and the ancestral realms. According to Gómez Menjívar, quantitative socio-medical studies confirm what these authors strive to demonstrate through their poetry, namely that "language is medicine, recognizing that the health of an Indigenous language is reflected in the health of its people, [and] recognizing that using a suppressed ancestral language has health benefits for the individual descendants and their community."[12]

The poetry that Cacho Caballero writes, moving between Garífuna, Spanish, and English, imparts the sense that writing is a ceremony, an offering to the ancestors through a metaphysical connection that is an important element of Indigenous well-being. The act of producing children's stories, essays, poetry, and even cookbooks is the author's ceremonial offering, a gift to her own ancestors and an invocation that they join her in the challenging world of the twenty-first century. By calling them forward, she seeks to challenge the crisis generated by neoliberal globalization, which endangers the language and lives of the Garífuna.

The fractured identity of the Garífuna finds a parallel in the poetry of the Afro-Hispanic writer Antonio Preciado, who has expressed his displeasure with being categorized as either a Black or an Afro poet, which happens to many Afrodescendant writers who find it difficult to identify with African roots and European ancestry at the same time. Consequently, he rejects the value of anthologies dedicated exclusively to Afro writers. He argues that such projects only contribute to the further marginalization of Afro writers with respect to the literary canon. Yet, even though he describes himself as a poet without categories, Preciado adamantly and proudly acknowledges his African heritage. This is a dilemma faced by many Black writers: how to legitimize their intellectual relevance in the literary sphere without minimizing or whitening their racial heritage. I see this as another form of the anxiety shared by Black writers of the diaspora who struggle to answer the ontological question of "who am I?" Aimé Césaire often reflected on his African roots, Glissant developed his Antillean space to stabilize his identity, and Confiant focused on his cultural and linguistic affiliation with the Caribbean. This is a unique reality that Afrodescendants have to face many times. While white Americans mostly know the origins of their ancestors, this is not always the case with Black Americans.

In a poem written on the occasion of contemplating a pre-Columbian archeological artifact, Preciado writes that the Black community is "at war against the historians / against their history / against their silence." This declaration emphasizes the process of resignification and the re-appropriation of multiple identities by Afrodescendants. According to Michael Handelsman in his chapter on Preciado, all thought about Blackness throughout the diaspora begins with enslavement as the origin of social and cultural disconnectedness. In the poems "Sincretismo" and "Desolación," for example, Preciado explores his conflicted status as both an Afrodescendant and a modern Western man. He is torn in different directions and has doubts about the possibility of attaining a state of existential completeness. This leaves him, like so many other Afrodescendants, in a state of incompleteness, which evokes a long history of the suppressed collective memory of Afrodescendants. There can be no doubt that deterritorialization inhibits cultural identity and a sense of belonging. Ancestral territories are "original philosophical constructions, with deep cultural, social, political, spiritual, and religious content" and are thus vital to community growth.[13] For those who are displaced, these spiritual connections must be forged or re-invented. Afrodescendant writers thus question their place in societies that tend to ignore and exclude them from cultural and national identities, as in the case of Antonio Preciado in Ecuador.

The search for home is particularly visible in the case of Costa Rican writer Quincy Duncan who reflects on the acute marginalization of Black in his country. According to Gloria Elizabeth Chacón, the historical, political, and cultural exclusion of Afro-Costa Ricans from the national community has led to the emergence of counternarratives that decisively highlight their essential role and place in the nation. Quince Duncan emerged as the first Afro-Costa Rican author to explore and elucidate this subject, and his work focuses heavily on racial and institutional discrimination in Costa Rica. *Kimbo* indigenizes the vital contributions of the *antillio* (West Indian) population in the nation and creates an Afro-Costa Rican sense of subjectivity. Costa Rica is recognized for its desire to appear more European, democratic, and middle class than its surrounding Central American countries. To achieve this goal, Costa Rica tends to erase any ethnic identities that counter the national discourse, even if this means resorting to violence. *Kimbo* destroys the notion that the Costa Rican government does not utilize state violence and challenges the widespread perception that Blackness is synonymous with criminality. At the same time, it points to the Catholic Church as a powerful source of racial discrimination, thereby dismantling the perception that Costa Rica is an idyllic, peaceful, and democratic country. *Kimbo*'s narrative centers state-sponsored violence and the immorality of the Catholic Church, and it unpacks the societal grouping of races. The eventual murder of Kimbo thus reflects a long history of scapegoating the Afrodescendant population in the Americas. A major concept in *Kimbo* is the role of the *samamfo*, or ancestral spirits, and oral folktales in the cultural collective. Duncan defines *samamfo* as "the collective memory of race-culture that passes from generation to generation and that is updated in the religious-secular rites of the people, in their struggles, in their experiences. The ancestors have never abandoned their heirs."[14] Folktales play an important role in *Kimbo* and in the survival of Afro-Costa Ricans in the narrative of the nation. They are a tool of both power and survival. Thus, a collective belief in *samamfo* affirms African indigeneity in Costa Rica's national corpus.

Like Black Costa Ricans, Afro-Panamanian women fight for recognition in their own country. The scapegoating of Afrodescendants can also be seen as in Panama, where Afro-Panamanian women continue to fight to remain relevant. The fight for female pertinency is at the core of Ángela Castro's research on Melanie Taylor Herrera. Taylor Herrera's *Camino a Mariato*, from 2009, depicts the histories and experiences of Panamanian women as they struggle with contemporary, twenty-first-century themes, such as identity, suicide, silence, and solitude. Although Afro-Panamanian women do not define themselves by race, they cannot escape being demarcated by it. The racial component cannot be disjoined from their identity. What connects the women in Taylor Herrera's collection is their shared historical identity and the physical objects that connect them to each other and to their cultural history. These physical objects prompt the characters to express their deepest thoughts and feelings of abandonment in a society that constantly reminds them of their liminality. The objects also act as metaphors that shift the focus away from racialized themes. Their stories are like a palimpsest drawn over a historical foundation. Following Sara Dillon, Castro describes this palimpsest as an "involuted phenomenon involving otherwise unrelated texts that are entangled and interwoven, interrupting, and inhabiting each other." Similarly, Castro adapts the idea of the palimpsest in postcolonial African novels, which Mercy Ezeala and Almantas Samalavičius describe as a self-reflective "metaphor for understanding the effects of colonialism, the complications of Africa in the colonial enterprise and the need to forge a future that transcends the colonial experiences."[15] The need for introspection is, without doubt, a must in these two cases.

The women in Taylor Herrera's work are depicted from spaces of loneliness, oppression, and abandonment. They work as prostitutes, thieves, and workers in bars. Her opening short story, "Dance with Death," includes a narrative focus on specific objects, such as a coffee cup, a bottle, and high heels. According to Castro, "the hidden discourse of the stories in *Camino a Mariato* conveys the detriment of national racial and social identity. The female characters often finish their journeys discouraged, but this begins a process of internal transformations. All the short stories up to this point consist of unfulfilled situations, which creates a sense of stagnation." In Taylor Herrera's eleventh story, there is a sense of female emancipation rather than stagnation. In the same story, Taylor Herrera unexpectedly uses the words "slave," "Black," and "free woman." Prior to this moment, Taylor Herrera has refrained from explicitly mentioning race when describing the women, but the racial reality seems indispensable on the road to female self-emancipation. While the stories appear to be unrelated, the characters are connected through the destinies they confront. Taylor Herrera's palimpsestic writing warps the continuity of the definition of the Panamanian woman to create a more complete understanding of the women and their history.

In Eliseo Jacob's contribution, the effort to re-cast Black identity is at the heart of Brazil's Black Lives Matter movement. Jacob's efforts illustrate the globalization of this movement after the death of George Floyd. Black Lives Matter in Brazil focuses on various types of violence committed by the Brazilian police against Afro-Brazilians, such as the shocking video recorded in São Paulo of a Black man forced to follow a Military Police motorcycle while handcuffed to the back of the motorcycle. While this event would have led to a massive demonstration in the US, it received little attention in Brazil.[16] Like with Floyd's murder, the incident in Brazil demonstrates the power of personal cell phones in the fight against police brutality. It is well recognized today that many crimes against people of color would have not been prosecuted were it not for the videos recorded by private citizens.

Eliseo Jacob uses the framework of necropolitics to analyze Cidinha da Silva's work, *#Parem de nos matar* (#Stop killing us) and to better understand how Black genocide in Brazil raises questions regarding citizenship for Afro-Brazilians, who continually confront the threat of social and physical death. Da Silva documents the current crisis unfolding in Brazil regarding the high homicide rate of Afro-Brazilians, particularly among young adult males. Of all the stark images tied to the legacy of slavery and racial violence, lynching is a powerful metaphor that da Silva uses when writing about how Black citizens are targeted on Brazil's city streets. Da Silva's decision to label some high-profile cases in Brazil as contemporary instances of "lynching" brings attention to the long history of white individuals and mobs killing Blacks in public spaces with little or no legal consequences. She makes a direct connection between police terror in Brazil's major cities and the interests and policies formulated and enacted by politicians, state institutions, and powerful individuals with direct access to the state. The genocide of Black individuals and groups continues today in Brazil through both material and symbolic violence. However, the use of necropolitics as a theoretical framework to explain how and why these different forms of violence have been directed at a demographic that constitutes over half of the population of the country is key to deconstructing the practice. Ultimately, these theories explain da Silva's use of the image of the police as the "armed hand of the state."

Black women in Brazil confront similar prejudices. They face an aggravated type of banishment from national participation and are not allowed to express their identities fully online or in public for fear of violence or hateful retribution. In many media sources, Black women are seen only as maids or cleaning ladies. Jacob indicates that, while it is not necessarily a problem if Black actresses choose roles as maids or other menial labor positions in film, it is a serious problem if the preponderance of Black characters are those who have no voice at all or who are seen but not heard in scenes, where their function is merely to serve and clean in the background. These Black characters are never able to articulate their own experiences, their feelings, and their lives beyond the white, hegemonic spaces in which they work.

As in Afro-Hispanic literature, there is a strong need to develop a well-built Afro-Brazilian literary archive. Literary paradigms are patterns turned into conventional models that feed into notions of a literary tradition. Only through a historical overview of the formation of Afro-Brazilian literature, from its roots in orature to its poetic and political unfolding, can we begin to envision Afro-Brazilian literary production as part and parcel of its transcontinental diasporic tradition and begin to move it away from Eurocentric ideals. Isis Barra Costa's contribution helps move toward this goal. Her research involves poring through cultural archives that are invisible or of little interest to the Western world. This disregard for archival literature enabled those who were silenced to maintain the power of their civilizations' legacies. These archives reveal a wealth of Afro-Brazilian contributions that rival those of Europeans. For example, we now know that dance was a form of African architecture, with a rich oral, rather than printed, history. To understand the full development of Afro-Brazilian literature, we must contextualize these achievements and discoveries. This effort recalls the critical literary movement that began in the 1970s and that launched a radical questioning of the universalizing postures of Eurocentric canonic literary paradigms. This movement sought to demystify the supposedly apolitical nature of textual reading and production.

T. S. Eliot argues that the process of literary production is not about evolution but rather an awareness that the substance of art is translated in the constant flow and changing outlook of the country represented by the poet. A sense of history leads the poet to express himself not merely within the boundaries of the generation to which he belongs, but also with an attitude in which the totality of European literary production is simultaneously and productively active in the poetics of the present. Interestingly, to get at the Afro-Brazilian archive and the process of literary production, Isis Barra Costa invokes Eliot but places him alongside the Brazilian Antonio Candido. Eliot, like many other writers, cannot be dissociated from his time. Yet Afrodescendant writers face different challenges and, hence, different ways of capturing the cultural, racial, and historical anxieties of their time.

For Afro-Brazilian literary production to be understood not as a modality of the Brazilian canon but as a tradition rooted in its own diasporic forest, with its own epistemological paradigms and worldviews, Isis Barra Costa proposes the delineation of an inclusive hermeneutics emerging from the root of oral literature. Only through these archival contexts can we recognize the poetic forms that African ancestors brought to Brazil. Only then can we weave other paradigms that will allow us to conceptualize the great Afro-Brazilian literary archive within its own literary historical foliage. Only then can we render visible multiple spheres of communication and diasporic convergences. It is thus necessary to first cast out sulfuric paradigms, reconjure what has been silenced, and then enter other forests.

Though the music of Afrodescendants has suffered less than other forms of cultural expression, it is still a point of conflict in many Afro-diasporic communities. In his contribution, Juan Eduardo Wolf examines the music-dance expressions of Afrodescendants, seeking out those perspectives that narratives of modernity have refused to recognize. Wolf takes inspiration in this task from Silvia Rivera Cusicanqui's anti-colonial *ch'ixi* methodology, which assumes that subjects can take part in colonial activities while maintaining an alternate set of values than those presumed by modernity. The Aymara word *ch'ixi* can mean "motley" or "stained," and Rivera Cusicanqui uses it to describe both her understanding of the world and her own mixed, *mestiza* heritage. While the cosmopolitan world might consider Indigenous singing to be a quaint component of staged multicultural folklore, Rivera Cusicanqui notes that music-dance can be cathartic for the struggles of Indigenous peoples, as they often voice their complaints using these artistic expressions. This language-based hermeneutic, then, contributes to a paradigm shift for mainstream understandings of culture, suggesting other ways of dealing with contemporary challenges.

The *morenos de paso* are part of a larger phenomenon of ritual dance-dramas throughout Latin America. In his contribution, Wolf examines the music-dance cultures of *morenos de paso* in northern Chile and *bomba* in Puerto Rico. The *morenos de paso* distinguish themselves within this setting in at least two ways. First, the dancers do not dress exotically, but rather, in what might be considered "business attire." The second way the *morenos de paso* stand out is, as their name suggests, the pacing step they use. Moving from the case of the *morenos de paso* to the *bomba* in Puerto Rico, Wolf considers how music-dance offers linguistic tools for thinking anti-colonially. More *ch'ixi* thinking can be done here: Wolf, for example, teases out the threads of thought from other regions of Africa in the *morenos de paso* and recognizes the values of the Indigenous and European threads in *bomba*. Even with this additional work, however, it is important to remember that these ideas have emerged from two very specific contexts and may not always have value in those contexts today. Whether these alternate perspectives are valuable depends upon whether they resonate with the cultural memory of those who struggle within those contexts and what the society they create ultimately chooses to value. What Juan Eduardo Wolf illustrates, however, is a mode of thinking that may prove useful for those working to dismantle coloniality, both in these and in many other additional contexts. As in the case of Puerto Rico, it is safe to say that *bomba* music has managed to bring many Puerto Ricans together, as Luis Palés Matos envisioned in the first half of the twentieth century. Although he was criticized for his treatment of the female dancer, he managed to use *bomba* to show the different elements that participate in the building of a Puerto Rican cultural identity, one that smartly responds to the Eurocentric vision developed on the island. For Isar Godreau, the recognition of *bomba* in the 1970s "came in response to public pressure from people who already valued the achievement of black and *mulato* musicians."[17] Marginality and violence can be cultural, but most of the time they translate into real ferocity, especially in Central America, where narco-cartels have shown themselves to be very powerful.

Just as poetry is an excellent tool for negotiating elements of cultural identity, rap music is a way to contest imposed identities and create a sense of empowerment for many who decide to challenge elements of their societies. From the *Y'en a marre* group in Senegal to *Patria y vida* in Cuba, music has been used to openly protest the situation of subordinated and marginalized peoples around the globe.[18] This is also the case in rural Chocó. According to Diana Rodríguez Quevedo, many songs produced by Afro-Colombian hip-hop artists function to access personal and collective memory for communities subjected to armed conflict and displacement. Part of this Black musical means of expression is a strategic contestation that incorporates and complements individual identity markers with collective ones. That is to say, the *yo*, or "I," and the *nosotros*, or "we," are highlighted to extend the perception of self beyond the bounds of ethnic identity.

The displacement so often lamented in musical forms is often a function of violence. As the main survivors of racial violence, Afro-Colombian and Indigenous women have been at the forefront of territorial struggles as they are driven to take on leadership roles in their homes and affected communities. Currently, the pressure exerted by the neoliberal model to increase capital circuits has made the process more difficult by introducing factors that change the value of the land. As such, people are not displaced "by violence"; rather, violence is the tool used to expel the population.

The rap songs in the albums *Óyeme Chocó* and *A nuestros mártires* call out specific politicians and denounce the exploitation of natural resources and lack of respect for the people and the wildlife that depend on the land and the waterways. Rap started as an underground musical expression in Colombia, and it continues to be so in many urban settings, although it has become increasingly commercialized (though not to the extent that it has become in the United States). However, the members of the bands *Renacientes* and *Grupo de Rap Infantil* occupy rural spaces, and the songs of these displaced Afro-Colombian young people depict rural spaces as opposed to urban ones. On the one hand, the development of a homogeneous social subject has negative effects when one includes all Afro-Colombians in one sole category, particularly when one identifies them as subversive and accuses them of being guerrilla supporters. On the other hand, displaced communities of Afrodescendants find comfort in a community that unites them in strategic ways, especially when the musicians draw upon their shared experience in refugee shelters and in repatriation complexes. In their music, the members of *Renacientes* and *Grupo de Rap Infantil* call for resisting further displacement or acts of violence against their people and their land. These songs serve not only as emotional expressions but also as social, cultural, and political discourses that legitimize the positions and visions of their composers and singers. These young, displaced Afro-Colombian singers and songwriters utilize the language and traditions of rap; they appropriate this genre to introduce their own style and very concrete socio-political content and geographic locations. The land shapes the songs, and the songs shape the land. The rap songs keep the historical memory alive, creating a continued awareness of the atrocities of internal displacement with the hope of preventing future cases.

While the contributions to *Améfrica in Letters* take up the situations of Black and Indigenous folks in the Americas, they also include methods of modern technology, such as social media. This, too, is a literary innovation. Another highlight of the book is that it turns to those people and places that are generally less discussed in academic research, such as the Afrodescendants of Mexico and Chile, as well as those living Central America. Moreover, the contributors' analyses of linguistics, literature, music, and space promise to encourage solid reflections in the future. For this reason, the literary and socio-political world will benefit from this publication. There is a profound dialogue among the authors and the specialists in the field, and it is particularly interesting to note the close connections they draw across racial, gender, and generational gaps.

The contemporary nature of the studies in *Améfrica in Letters* are perhaps a direct response to the Black Lives Matter movement, and this connection will catch any reader's attention. Whether in Costa Rica, Panama, Brazil, or in Garífuna Land, a common denominator among the contributions is the idea that, at all levels, Black people in general face enormous difficulties. The writing is excellent, and this book will be of interest to those who occupy different social and generational strata. And, because Afrodescendants are increasingly visible and vocal, this book will remain relevant for a very long time.

NOTES

1. "Si les nègres n'étaient pas un peuple, disons de vaincus, enfin, un peuple malheureux, un peuple humilié, etc., renversez l'Histoire, faites d'eux un peuple de vainqueurs, je crois, quant à moi, qu'il n'y aurait pas de Négritude." Aimé Césaire, "Entritien avec Jacqueline Leiner," *Tropics: 1941–1945* (Paris: Jean-Michel Place, 1978), xxi.
2. Joe Biden, "Statement by President Joe Biden on the First Anniversary of George Floyd's Murder," The White House, May 25, 2021, https://www.whitehouse.gov/briefing-room/statements-releases/2021/05/25/statement-by-president-joe-biden-on-the-first-anniversary-of-george-floyds-murder.
3. Lucas Janone and Mylena Guedes, "Um negro é morto pela polícia a cada quatro horas, aponta levantamento," *CNN Brasil*, December 14, 2021, https://www.cnnbrasil.com.br/nacional/um-negro-e-morto-pela-policia-a-cada-quatro-horas-aponta-levantamento.
4. Júlia Pereira, "Segundo pesquisa, 78% dos mortos pela polícia são negros," *Rede Brasil Atual*, April 23, 2021, https://www.redebrasilatual.com.br/cidadania/2021/04/segundo-pesquisa-78-dos-mortos-pela-policia-sao-negros.
5. Paulo Eduardo Dias and Luís Adorno, "Negros são oito de cada 10 mortos pela polícia no Brasil, aponta relatório," *UOL*, October 18, 2020, https://noticias.uol.com.br/cotidiano/ultimas-noticias/2020/10/18/oito-a-cada-10-mortos-pela-policia-no-brasil-sao-negros-aponta-relatorio.htm.
6. Cornel West, *Race Matters* (Boston: Beacon Press, 1993), 93.
7. Doris A. Graber, "Political Languages," in *Handbook of Political Communication*, eds. Daniel Nimmo and Keith R. Sanders (Los Angeles: SAGE Publications), 195.
8. Keith Nurse, "Masculinities in Transition: Gender and the Global Problematique," in *Interrogating Caribbean Masculinities: Theoretical and Empirical Analysis*, ed. Rhoda Reddock (Kingston: University of the West Indies Press, 2004), 5.
9. bell hooks, *Feminism Is for Everybody: Passionate Politics* (Cambridge, MA: South End, 2000), 70.
10. Michelle A. (Forbes) Ocasio, "Proto-Garífuna: The Language of the Kalípona on the Eve of the Africans' Arrival in St. Vincent," *PALARA* no. 15 (2011): 51.
11. Doris Sommer, "Literary Liberties: The Authority of Afrodescendant Authors," in *Afro-Latin American Studies: An Introduction*, eds. Alejandro de la Fuente and George Reid Andrews (Cambridge: Cambridge University Press, 2018), 326.
12. Alice Taff et al., "Indigenous Language Use Impacts Wellness," in *The Oxford Handbook of Endangered Languages*, eds. Kenneth L. Rehg and Lyle Campbell (Oxford: Oxford University Press, 2018), 862.
13. Juan García Salazar and Catherine Walsh, *Pensar sembrando / sembrar pensando con el Abuelo Zenón* (Quito: Universidad Andina Simón Bolívar, Sede Quito, and Abya-Yala, 2017), 53.
14. Quince Duncan, *Kimbo* (San José: Editorial Costa Rica, 1989), 153.
15. Mercy Ezeala and Almantas Samalavičius, "Palimpsest in Postcolonial African Novels," *European Journal of Literature, Language and Linguistics Studies* 2, no. 1 (2018): 84.

16. UOL, "Vídeo mostra homem negro correndo algemado a moto de PM, em São Paulo," YouTube video, 2:09, December 1, 2021, https://www.youtube.com/watch?v=lhM52ufTwY4.
17. Isar Godreau, *Script of Blackness: Race, Cultural Nationalism, and US Colonialism in Puerto Rico* (Urbana: University of Illinois Press, 2015), 187.
18. Ofeiba Quist-Arcton, "'Enough Is Enough,' Say Senegalese Rappers," *NPR*, February 19, 2012, https://www.npr.org/2012/02/19/147113419/enough-is-enough-say-sengalese-rappers; Anamaria Sayre, "Explaining 'Patria Y Vida,' the Song That's Defined the Uprising in Cuba," *NPR*, July 20, 2021, https://www.npr.org/sections/altlatino/2021/07/19/1017887993/explaining-patria-y-vida-the-cuban-song-defying-an-evil-revolution.

WORKS CITED

Bernabé, Jean, Patrick Chamoiseau, and Raphael Confiant. *Eloge de la créolité*. Paris: Gallimard, 1989.
Biden, Joe. "Statement by President Joe Biden on the First Anniversary of George Floyd's Murder." *The White House*. May 25, 2021. https://www.whitehouse.gov/briefing-room/statements-releases/2021/05/25/statement-by-president-joe-biden-on-the-first-anniversary-of-george-floyds-murder.
Césaire, Aimé. "Entritien avec Jacqueline Leiner." *Tropics: 1941–1945*. Paris: Jean-Michel Place, 1978.
Dias, Paulo Eduardo, and Luís Adorno. "Negros são oito de cada 10 mortos pela polícia no Brasil, aponta relatório." *UOL*. October 18, 2020. https://noticias.uol.com.br/cotidiano/ultimas-noticias/2020/10/18/oito-a-cada-10-mortos-pela-policia-no-brasil-sao-negros-aponta-relatorio.htm.
Duncan, Quince. *Kimbo*. San José: Editorial Costa Rica, 1989.
Ezeala, Mercy, and Almantas Samalavičius. "Palimpsest in Postcolonial African Novels." *European Journal of Literature, Language and Linguistics Studies* 2, no. 1 (2018): 84–100.
Figueroa, Victor. *Not at Home in One's Home: Caribbean Self-Fashioning in the Poetry of Luis Palés Matos, Aimé Césaire, and Derek Walcott*. Madison, NJ: Fairleigh Dickinson University Press, 2009.
García Salazar, Juan, and Catherine Walsh. *Pensar sembrando/sembrar pensando con el Abuelo Zenón*. Quito: Universidad Andina Simón Bolívar, Sede Quito and Abya-Yala, 2017.
Glissant, Edouard. *Le discours antillais*. Paris: Seuil, 1981.
Godreau, Isar. *Script of Blackness: Race, Cultural Nationalism, and U.S. Colonialism in Puerto Rico*. Urbana: University of Illinois Press, 2015.
Graber, Doris A. "Political Languages." In *Handbook of Political Communication*, edited by Daniel Nimmo and Keith R. Sanders. Los Angeles: SAGE Publications.
hooks, bell. *Feminism Is for Everybody: Passionate Politics*. Cambridge, MA: South End, 2000.
Janone, Lucas, and Mylena Guedes. "Um negro é morto pela polícia a cada quatro horas,

aponta levantamento." *CNN Brasil.* December 14, 2021. https://www.cnnbrasil.com.br/nacional/um-negro-e-morto-pela-policia-a-cada-quatro-horas-aponta-levantamento.

Nurse, Keith. "Masculinities in Transition: Gender and the Global Problematique." In *Interrogating Caribbean Masculinities: Theoretical and Empirical Analysis*, edited by Rhoda Reddock, 3–33. Kingston: University of the West Indies Press, 2004.

Ocasio, Michelle A. (Forbes). "Proto-Garífuna: The Language of the Kalípona on the Eve of the Africans' Arrival in St. Vincent." *PALARA* no. 15 (2011): 51–65.

Pereira, Júlia. "Segundo pesquisa, 78% dos mortos pela polícia são negros." *Rede Brasil Atual.* April 23, 2021. https://www.redebrasilatual.com.br/cidadania/2021/04/segundo-pesquisa-78-dos-mortos-pela-policia-sao-negros/.

Quist-Arcton, Ofeiba. " 'Enough Is Enough,' Say Senegalese Rappers." *NPR.* February 19, 2012. https://www.npr.org/2012/02/19/147113419/enough-is-enough-say-sengalese-rappers.

Sayre, Anamaria. "Explaining 'Patria Y Vida,' the Song That's Defined the Uprising in Cuba." NPR. July 20, 2021. https://www.npr.org/sections/altlatino/2021/07/19/1017887993/explaining-patria-y-vida-the-cuban-song-defying-an-evil-revolution.

Sommer, Doris. "Literary Liberties: The Authority of Afrodescendant Authors." In *Afro-Latin American Studies: An Introduction*, edited by Alejandro de la Fuente and George Reid Andrews, 319–47. Cambridge: Cambridge University Press, 2018.

Taff, Alice, Melvatha Chee, Jaeci Hall, Millie Yéi Dulitseen Hall, Kawenniyóhstha Nicole Martin, and Annie Johnston. "Indigenous Language Use Impacts Wellness." In *The Oxford Handbook of Endangered Languages*, edited by Kenneth L. Rehg and Lyle Campbell, 862–84. Oxford: Oxford University Press, 2018.

UOL. "Vídeo mostra homem negro correndo algemado a moto de PM, em São Paulo." YouTube video. 2:09. December 1, 2021. https://www.youtube.com/watch?v=lhM52ufTwY4.

West, Cornel. *Race Matters.* Boston: Beacon Press, 1993.

◆   CONTRIBUTORS

BADIANE, MAMADOU, is an associate professor and director of the Afro-Romance Institute at the University of Missouri. He is the former chair of the Department of Romance Languages and Literatures and has published widely on Afro-Caribbean literature, culture, and history. His publications have examined the interconnections between Negrismo and Negritude poets and their interactions with writers of the Harlem Renaissance. His research has also explored the redefinition of national identities in the Caribbean as a direct result of the decolonization movements in Africa. His most recent research focuses on Suzanne Césaire as the unknown mother of Antillanité.

BARRA COSTA, ISIS, is an assistant professor of Contemporary Brazilian Literary and Cultural Studies at The Ohio State University. She is a specialist in Afro-Brazilian orature, cosmology, and performance and is currently working on a manuscript entitled *Imagining the Past and Remembering the Future: Afro-Brazilian Philosophies*. She is the co-author with Eduardo Muslip of *Brasil: Ficciones de argentinos* and *Passo da Guanxuma: Contactos culturales entre Brasil y Argentina*, as well as guest editor with Emanuelle Oliveira-Monte of a special issue of the *Afro-Hispanic Review* on the Afro-Brazilian Diaspora. For the past few decades, she has collectively participated and organized academic symposia and artistic interventions in traditional and digital venues, such as the Afro Digital Museum at the Universidade do Estado Rio de Janeiro, where she serves as member of the Editorial Committee.

CASTRO, ÁNGELA, is an assistant professor at Colorado College. She earned her Master's degree and PhD in Hispanic literatures and cultures at the University of Minnesota. She has published in journals such as the *Journal of Commonwealth and Postcolonial Studies* and contributed to edited volumes such as *Racialized Visions: Haiti and the Spanish Caribbean Imaginary*. Her research focuses on predominant representations of the twentieth-century Afro-Caribbean female body through comparative analysis. She uses the concept of the palimpsest as a means of reconfiguring the Afro-Caribbean female body as a site of empowerment born within the struggles of postcolonial and neocolonial history.

CHACÓN, GLORIA ELIZABETH, is an associate professor in the literature department at the University of California, San Diego. Both her research and teaching focus on Indigenous literatures, questions of autonomy, gender, and philosophy. She is the author of *Indigenous Cosmolectics: Kab'awil and the Making of Maya and Zapotec Literatures* (University of North Carolina Press, 2018). She is currently working on her second book, tentatively titled *Metamestizaje, Indigeneity, and Diasporas*. She is co-editor of *Indigenous Interfaces: Spaces, Technology, and Social Networks in Mexico and Central America* (University of Arizona Press, 2019). Chacón has co-edited a special issue on Indigenous literature for DePaul's University academic journal, *Diálogo*. She has co-edited the anthology *Teaching Central American Literature in a Global Context* for MLA's Teaching Options Series (2022). Chacón's work has appeared in anthologies and journals in Canada, Colombia, Germany, Mexico, and the United States.

GÓMEZ MENJÍVAR, JENNIFER CAROLINA, is an associate professor of media arts at the University of North Texas. Gómez Menjívar's publications have appeared in the *Journal of Pidgin and Creole Languages*, *Applied Linguistics*, *Chasqui*, *Diálogo*, *Hispanófila*, *Transmodernity*, *NAIS Journal*, and *Mesoamérica*, among others. Her books include *Tropical Tongues: Language Ideologies, Endangerment, and Minority Languages in Belize* (University of North Carolina Press, 2018) and *Black in Print: Plotting the Coordinates of Blackness in Central America* (SUNY Press, forthcoming), as well as the co-edited volumes *Indigenous Interfaces: Spaces, Technology, and Social Networks in Mexico and Central America* (University of Arizona Press, 2019) and *Hemispheric Blackness and the Exigencies of Accountability* (University of Pittsburgh Press, 2022).

HANDELSMAN, MICHAEL, is professor emeritus in Hispanic and Latin American studies and distinguished professor emeritus at the University of Tennessee. His book *Leyendo la globalización desde la mitad del mundo: Identidad y resistencias en el Ecuador* (Quito: Editorial El Conejo, 2005) received the "Isabel Tobar Guarderas" Book Award in Quito (2006) and the "A. B. Thomas Book Prize" from the Southeastern Latin American Studies Association in the USA (2006). Among his other books are *Amazonas y artistas: Un estudio de la prosa de la mujer ecuatoriana* (1978), *El modernismo en las revistas literarias del Ecuador: 1895–1930* (1981), *En torno al verdadero Benjamín Carrión* (1989), *Lo afro y la plurinacionalidad: El caso ecuatoriano visto desde su literatura* (1999), *Culture and Customs of Ecuador* (2000), *Género, raza y nación en la literatura ecuatoriana: Hacia una lectura decolonial* (2011), *Guayaquil y sus autores: Un homenaje a algunos clásicos que no se van* (2017), and *Representaciones de lo afro y su recepción en el*

Ecuador: Encuentros y desencuentros en tensión (2019). Handelsman has been a visiting professor at the University of Kentucky, Universidad Católica Santiago de Guayaquil, and Universidad Andina Simón Bolívar de Quito. He is the co-founder of the Asociación de Ecuatorianistas (Estudios de Literatura, Lengua y Cultura). In 2012, the Academia Ecuatoriana de la Lengua, correspondiente a la Real Academia de la Lengua Española, selected him as a Miembro Correspondiente Extranjero.

HERNÁNDEZ NICOLÁS, ALBERTA "BETTY" (ALBERT NICOLÁS), was born on February 24, 1985, in the community of Tamal in the Municipality of Santiago Pinotepa in the Mexican State of Oaxaca. She attended Jardín de Niños Leona Vicario and Benito Juárez Elementary School prior to enrolling in secondary school through the distance learning program at Consejo Nacional de Fomento Educativo (CONAFE). She attended her first painting workshop in fifth grade at the invitation of Father Glynn Gelmo, priest of the El Ciruelo community. The experience reaffirmed her taste and talent for the fine arts. Henceforward, she attended monthly workshops taught by teachers from the fine arts school in El Ciruelo along with other children and young people. The "Rayo de Sol" art contest was organized in the summer of 1999, and she was awarded second place in the painting division. In 2003, at the invitation of Father Glynn, she enrolled at the Universidad Autónoma Benito Juárez de Oaxaca and soon after completed her degree in Visual Arts Education. While studying at the university, she participated in her first collective exhibition with the Centro Cultural Cimarrón. That same year, she had the opportunity to exhibit at the Instituto de Artes Gráficas Oaxaca (IAGO) alongside the work of fellow Mexican painter Cinthya Picazo. In 2008, at the invitation of a colleague, she expanded her skills to include artistic restoration. She has continued to paint and, above all, through her paintings and prints, to express and raise awareness about Afro-Mexican and Indigenous peoples' struggle for recognition.

JACOB, ELISEO, holds a PhD from the University of Texas at Austin with a background in contemporary Latin American and Brazilian literary and cultural productions. As a faculty member in the Department of World Languages and Cultures at Howard University, he teaches courses on Portuguese language and Brazilian popular culture. His recent publications contextualize literary and cultural representations of São Paulo's urban periphery as part of a larger analysis regarding the relationship of the public sphere to marginalized communities of color in Latin America's urban spaces. His current book project, *Masculinidades Marginales: Race, Masculinity, and the City in 21st Century Latin American Literature*, is an examination of writers from Latin America's urban periphery and how their literary representations of marginalized male youth raise urgent questions surrounding citizenship. Additionally, he was recently awarded a Fulbright US Scholar Award for the 2021–22 academic year to Brazil, where he will complete a research project on the *Literatura Periférica* (Peripheral Literature) movement in São Paulo.

RAMSAY, PAULETTE A., is a professor in the Faculty of Humanities and Education, at The University of the West Indies, Mona, Jamaica. She is an interdisciplinary academic, an established writer, and researcher whose interests include language pedagogy, writing theories, and Afro-Hispanic literatures and cultures. She has published many scholarly articles, mainly in the area of Afro-Hispanic literatures and cultures, in international journals such as *The Afro-Hispanic Review, PALARA, Bulletin of Latin American Review, Latin American and Caribbean Ethnic Studies, The Langston Hughes Review, Hispania, Caribbean Quarterly*, and *College Language Association*. Her research draws on broad postcolonial and postmodernist theories, gender studies, feminist studies, and cultural studies, especially as they relate to issues of identity, ethnicity, and nationhood. She is regarded as one of the leading researchers in Afro-Mexican literary and cultural production. She is a writer of fiction and her novel *Aunt Jen* has been translated to German and Italian and is enjoying great popularity. She has also published three anthologies of poems: *Under Basil Leaves* (2010), *October Afternoon* (2012), *and Star Apple Blue and Avocado Green* (2016). She has been the recipient of several awards, including OAS, AECI Fellowships, UWI 60 Under 60 Award for outstanding research, and the Vice Chancellor's Award for Excellence in Research Production.

RODRÍGUEZ QUEVEDO, DIANA, is an associate professor of Spanish at the University of Evansville. She obtained her PhD in Spanish with a specialization in Latin American literature from the University of Toronto. Her research and publications encompass twentieth and twenty-first century Colombian literature relative to issues of race, gender, and space in narratives of forced internal displacement in Colombia, in addition to her scholarship on literary and cultural works by Afro-Latin American authors.

SÁNCHEZ MARTÍNEZ, JUAN GUILLERMO, grew up in Bakatá/Bogotá in the Colombian Andes. He dedicates both his creative and scholarly writing to Indigenous cultural expressions from Abiayala (the Americas.) His book of poetry, *Altamar*, was awarded the National Prize Universidad de Antioquia, Colombia, in 2016. He coordinates the online publication *Siwar Mayu, A River of*

Hummingbirds. He has co-edited "The Five Cardinal Points in Contemporary Indigenous Literatures" (*Dialogo* 19, no. 1, 2016), "K'obéen: Indigenous Subjectivities in Latin American Literature" (*Canadian Magazine of Hispanic Studies*-RCEH 39, no. 1, 2015), "Poetics and Politics of Indigenous America" (*Cuadernos de Literatura* 22, 2007), and the multilingual anthology *Indigenous Message on Water* (Indigenous World Forum on Water and Peace, 2014). His book *Memoria e invención en la poesía de Humberto Ak'abal* (Abya-Yala, 2011) is a journey through the Guatemala highlands through the verses of the K'iche' poet. His most recent works are *Muyurina y el presente profundo: Poéticas andino-amazónicas* (Pakarina, 2019) and "Cinema, Literature and Art against Extractivism in Latin America" (*Dialogo* 22, no. 1, 2019). He is an associate professor of languages and literatures and Native American and Indigenous studies at the University of North Carolina, Asheville.

WOLF, JUAN EDUARDO, is an associate professor of ethnomusicology at the School of Music and Dance at the University of Oregon, where he is also a core faculty member in the Folklore and Public Culture program. He primarily studies the ways that music-dance can perform histories and cultural principles that the forces of coloniality have tried to suppress, especially in the embodied voices of Afrodescendant and Indigenous peoples of the Americas. He is the author of Styling Blackness in Chile: Music and Dance in the African Diaspora (Indiana University Press, 2019) and has contributed to *Theorizing Folklore from the Margins: Critical and Ethical Approaches* (Indiana University Press, 2021).

INDEX

Page numbers in *italic* indicate figures.

Abiayala, 180, 190n29
academy and Afro-Brazilian literature,
    Barra Costa on, 129–49
"A Categoria Político-Cultural de
    Amefricanidade" (Gonzalez), 7–9
Acevedo Leal, Anabella, 57
activism, da Silva and, 111, 121–22
aesthetics
    of cool, 159–60, 164
    González on, 42–67
African culture
    and *bomba*, 161–64
    Brathwaite on, 134–35
    Dawson on, 136
    pluriversality of, 154
Afrodescendants
    activism by, 2
    decade for, 10
    demographics of, 152, 211n18
    erasure of, 4–9, 75–76, 84–85, 102, 136
    Handelsman on, 73–74
    and Indigenous, hooks on, 176
    Preciado and, 68–80
    Rivera Cusicanqui on, 153
    term, 2–3
Afro-realism, Duncan and, 85
Agamben, Giorgio, 111, 115
Agreements on Guatemalan Indigenous
    Peoples and Identities, 56
Aguilar, Yasnaya, 54
Aica, Adolfo, 166n23
Ak'abal, Humberto, 57
Akan people, 92, 155, 162
Aleixo, Ricardo, 109–10, 113

Allende-Gotia, Noel, 160–62
Álvarez, Manuel, 161
Alves, Jaime, 114, 116–17, 122, 123n14
Améfrica, term, 7–9
Amefricanity, Gonzalez on, 8
Ament, Gail, 57–58
Anancy, Duncan and, 85, 91–93
ancestors
    Cacho Caballero on, 180, 182–83, 185
    dügü and, 181
    Duncan on, 85, 89–91
    Garífuna and, 50–52
    Preciado on, 72
    Thompson on, 159
Andrade, Luís Evelis, 197–98
Angulo, Henry, 205, 207, 209n11
anthologies, 7
    Barra Costa on, 132
    Guatemalan, 56–57
    Preciado on, 68
Anthony, Saint, 71–73, 78n12
antillanos
    Cacho Caballero on, 170–93
    Duncan on, 83–96
    Lowe de Goodin on, 98
    term, 94n8
    Wolf on, 162
A nuestros mártires (CD), 195
Araújo, Taís, 118–22, 124n31
Arawak language/people, 172
archive, literary, Afro-Brazilian
    Badiane on, 230
    Barra Costa on, 129–49
Arias, Oscar, 85

arms trafficking, in Chocó region, 197
Arzú, Alvaro, 56
Ashanti people, 162–63
Asher, Kiran, 211n19
Asilo 38, 200
Atrato, Colombia, 197
AUC, 197, 211n20
authenticity, Wolf on, 152
authority
    corridos on, 27–30
    Taylor Herrera on, 105
Aymara, 153, 158–59

Badiane, Mamadou, 219–35
bad-john figure, 27
Báez Lazcano, Cristian Alejandro, 2
bailes religiosos, 150–51, 155–60
Bakhtin, Mikhail, 160
ballads, Ramsay on, 25–41
Bantu language/people
    Pereira on, 138, 140–42
    Wolf on, 155
Barra Costa, Isis, 129–49
Barthes, Roland, 37
Barton, Hablert, 163
becoming, Taylor Herrera on, 97, 101
Beer, June, 6
Bernard, Eulalia, 93
Bernd, Zilá, 136, 145n20
Bhabha, Homi, 37
Biden, Joe, 220
Black letters in Latin America
    Badiane on, 219–35
    development of, 4–9
    Duncan on, 93
    Gómez Menjívar on, 1–22
Black Lives Matter
    Badiane on, 219–20, 227–28
    and Brazil, da Silva and, 109–26
Blackness
    in Chocó, Wade on, 203
    Handelsman on, 70–71, 74–75
    ideas about, movement of, 43

Preciado on, 68, 70–75
    Taylor Herrera on, 97
Bolivia, protests in, 219
bomba, 151–52, 160–64
    Badiane on, 230–31
    term, 161
Bonner, William, 121–22
Borges, Hamilton, 109
Boti, Marie, 199–200, 210n13
Bourdieu, Pierre, 118
Branche, Jerome, 2
Brathwaite, Kamau, 5, 85, 133–35
bravery, and masculine identity, 35
Brazil
    Badiane on, 220–21, 227–30
    Barra Costa on, 129–49
    Bernd on, 136
    concrete poetry, 110
    current conditions in, 132
    da Silva on, 109–26
    Duarte on, 136–37
    and race issues, 1
Brown, Michael, 220

Cacho Caballero, Xiomara, 170–93
    Badiane on, 224–25
cafeína MC (González), 42–67
Caicedo Cabezas, José Santos, 206
Caldwell, Kia Lilly, 119
calypso, 26–27
Camino a Mariato (Taylor Herrera), 97–108
Campbell, Shirley, 94
Campbell, Sue, 207
Campoalegre Septien, Rosa, 10
Candido, Antonio, 140, 146n34, 229
Caño, Daniel, 57
canon, Barra Costa on, 130–31
Carbonell, Walterio, 6
Cardenal, Ernesto, 5
Caribbean
    and Anancy tales, 92
    González on, 53
    music and gender identities in, 26–27

Carib language/people, 172–74
Carneiro, Sueli, 109, 111, 123n2
Casa de las Américas, 5
casa grande image, da Silva on, 119–22
Castile, Philando, 220
Castro, Ángela, 97–108
Castro Rodrigues, Wesley, 116
Catholicism
    Duncan on, 89–91
    Kongolese and, 157
    Pereira on, 138, 140–42
Ceballos, Marcela, 206
"(Celofán)" (González), 52–53
Césaire, Aimé, 219, 225, 233n1
Chacón, Gloria Elizabeth, 83–96
Chakrabarty, Dipesh, 103
Chambers, Veronica, 98
Chau, Lucy Cristina, 98
Chauí, Marilena, 117
Chávez, Rosa, 57
Chicarrón, Pedro el, 27–30, 34
chicharrón, term, 34
Chihuailaf, Elicura, 182
children's books, Cacho Caballero and, 171–76
Chile, Wolf on, 150–69
chirimía music, 195
ch'ixi methodology, 152–55, 164, 230–31
    and *bomba*, 160–62
    and *morenos de paso*, 160
    term, 153
Chocó region, Colombia, 194–217
    Badiane on, 231–32
    Blackness in, Wade on, 203
    characteristics of, 196–97
    current status of, 208n1
Choc Quib Town, 200–202
class
    race and, 1, 8, 11, 221, 226
    stratification, 27, 44, 55, 69, 84, 114–15, 146n33
    Taylor Herrera on, 104
classification, issues in, 54
    Gómez Menjívar on, 173

Lavou on, 207
Preciado on, 69
code-switching, Garifuna and, 49, 223–24
collective memory, Campbell on, 207
Colombia
    demographics of, 198, 211n18
    Pacific coast, characteristics of, 194–95
    Rodríguez Quevedo on, 194–217
    society of, 196–98
colonialism
    Garífunas and, 44
    González on, 55–56
    Ramsay on, 27
    Wolf on, 151–52
    Zenón on, 71
coloniality
    Gómez Menjívar on, 3
    Handelsman on, 69, 74–76
    Preciado on, 75–77
    term, 152
    Wolf on, 150–69
community
    Duncan on, 91
    and masculinity, *corridos* on, 31–35
Compañía de don Andrés Baluarte, 150
Comunidad de Autoderminación, Vida y Dignidad (CAVIDA), 196
concrete objects, Taylor Herrera on, 99–102
concrete poetry, 110
Confiant, Raphaël, 225
Connell, R. W., 31, 37
cool, aesthetic of, 159–60, 164
"corrido de los Zapatistas de San Nicolás, El" 33–34
corridos
    definition of, 26
    Ramsay on, 25–41
cosmology
    and *bomba*, 160–61
    Kongolese, 145n14, 157–58, *158*
Costa Rica, Duncan on, 83–96
Coutinho, Eduardo, 130–31, 137
Coutinho, Maria Júlia, 118–22
COVID-19, 188

creole languages, 172
crônicas
    da Silva and, 109–26
    nature of, 123n1
cross-cultural identities, López Oro on, 48
cross image, Kongolese and, 157
Cú, Maya, 57–58
Cuba
    Afro-Cuban writers, 6
    Revolution, 5–6
culture, African
    and *bomba*, 161–64
    Brathwaite on, 134–35
    Dawson on, 136
    pluriversality of, 154
curriculum, Barra Costa on, 131

da Cunha, Maria Zilda, 130, 143n3
dance
    and healing, 180
    Wolf on, 150–69
"Dance with Death" (Taylor Herrera), 100
Daniel, Yvonne, 155
Darío, Rubén, 3
da Silva, Cidinha, 109–26
    Badiane on, 228
    publications of, 111
da Silva, Tomaz Tadeu, 131
Dawson, Danny, 135–36
death
    corridos on, 33
    Garífuna and, 50–52
décimas, 73–74
decolonization
    de Oto on, 188–89
    González on, 42–67
    Mignolo and Walsh on, 152
    Walsh on, 11
    Wolf on, 150–69
DeCosta-Willis, Miriam, 3
Deficit Model, 136
democracy
    Amefricanity and, 8
    in Brazil, 134–35, 137

    Duncan on, 84, 87–88
    See also racial democracy
Dennis, Christopher, 198, 200–201, 212n38
de Oto, Alejandro, 188–89
Dependency Theory, 1, 17n2
Derrida, Jacques, 146n33
"Desolación" (Preciado), 72–73
deterritorialization
    Badiane on, 225–26
    García Salazar on, 73–74
    See also land
Dewulf, Jeroen, 161–62
Diallo, Amadou, 220
diaspora(s)
    Barra Costa on, 132–34, 144n13
    Brathwaite on, 134–35
    Dawson on, 135
    Duncan on, 91, 93
    Handelsman on, 68
differentiated citizenship, Holston on, 114
digital turn
    Barra Costa on, 132, 144n13
    Gómez Menjívar on, 4, 188
Dillon, Sara, 98–100, 106, 227
"Dimureba-Speak to Us-Alarido" (Cacho Caballero), 185–86
Dios negro: Black Jesus: Búngiu Wuríti (Cacho Caballero), 175–76
do Nascimento, Abdias, 112
"¿Dónde están los mártires?" (Renacientes), 204
"Dream" (Cacho Caballero), 184–85
dress
    Kongolese, 156–57
    for *morenos de paso*, 155–56
drug trade
    Cacho Caballero on, 176–87
    in Chocó region, 197
    current status of, 187–88
    paramilitary groups and, 211n22
drums
    in *bomba*, 151, 160–63
    Cacho Caballero on, 182
    Zapata Olivella on, 68

Duarte, Eduardo de Assis, 132, 136–37
dügü, 180–82, 191n31
Duncan, Quince, 83–96
    Badiane on, 226
Durban Declaration and Programme of Action, 3
Dussel, Enrique, 151

economic issues
    Asher on, 211n19
    Cacho Caballero on, 178–80
    and racism by denial, 60
    and rap, 200
    sulfuric acid analogy and, 139
    Wolf on, 152
Ecuador, Preciado and, 68–80
education
    Cacho Caballero on, 186
    Gómez Menjívar on, 175
    González and, 48–49
Edwards, Derek, 208
Elegba, 71–73, 78n12, 133–34
Eliot, T. S., 138–39, 146n30, 229
ELN (National Liberation Army), 197
empires, Lévi-Strauss on, 139–40, 146n33
enslavement. *See* slavery
erasure of Afrodescendants, 4–9, 75–76, 84–85, 102, 136
Escure, Geneviève, 172
Esmeraldan Blacks, Preciado and, 68–80
essentialism, Preciado and, 69
Esteves, Wilton, 116
ethnicity
    classification issues and, 57–58
    González on, 42–67
ethnic pride, and masculinity, *corridos* on, 31–35
Etnnia, La, 200
Ewe people, 163
extrajudicial killings, in Brazil, 113
Exú, 71–73, 133
Ezeala, Mercy, 98, 227

Fairclough, Norman, 35
Fanon, Frantz, 69

FARC (Revolutionary Armed Forces of Colombia), 197
Ferreira, Claúdia, 121
festivals, rap, 201–2, 208
"(fin de la fiesta, el)" (González), 55–56
Floyd, George, 220
Floyd, Samuel A., Jr., 165n13
folklore
    Duncan on, 85, 226
    Mendoza on, 167n36
    Wolf on, 156
Forbes, Michelle, 174
forest image, Barra Costa on, 129–49
Forman, Murray, 199, 203
Fortaleza, Pablo, 201
Foucault, Michel, 111
Fremont, Cécile, 156–57
Frente Negra Brasiliera, 131
Freyre, Gilberto, 119
funk carioca, 116
futu, term, 134, 145n14

Gallardo, Mario, 50–51
"gallinita, La" (*corrido*), 31–35
"Garáwon-Scream-Tambor" (Cacho Caballero), 182–83
García, Pablo, 57
García Escobar, José, 48
García Salazar, Juan, 73–74
Gargallo, Francesca, 50
Garífuna language/people
    Badiane on, 224
    Cacho Caballero on, 170–93
    children's books for, 171–76
    current condition of, 187–88
    González and, 49–54
    history of, 43–44
    recognition of, 56
    speakers of, 174, *175*
Garner, Eric, 220
gender
    Cacho Caballero on, 179–80
    hooks on, 38–39
    Ramsay on, 25–41
gender identity, language and, 25–26

Generales Rap y Reggae, Los, 200–202
genocide, definition of, 112
genre, González and, 49
Georgina, 102
Ghettos Clan, 200
Glissant, Édouard, 225
Godreau, Isar, 231
Gómez, Lewis, 205, 207
Gómez, Sara, 6
Gómez Menjívar, Jennifer, 1–22, 49, 56, 59, 170–93
González, Gaspar Pedro, 182
Gonzalez, Lélia, 7–8
González, Nancie, 173
González, Wingston, 42–67, 181
    Badiane on, 222–24
    publications of, 42
González Bustelos, Mabel, 197
"(gorriones amados para Sonia)" (González), 51–52
Graber, Davis, 34, 221
graffiti, in rap, 204
Gray, Freddie, 220
Greene, Oliver N., 180
Grupo de Rap Infantil, 195, 202, 205, 231
Guatemala
    peace accords, 56
    Sánchez Martínez on, 42–67
"Guerra, La" (Angulo), 205, 207
Guerriero, Goli, 4, 144n13
Guillén, Nicolás, 3, 5–6
Guillermo Wilson, Carlos "Cubena," 98
Gulf of Guinea, influence of, 154–55
Gutiérrez, Miguel Angel, 26
Guy, Malcolm, 199–200, 210n13

Hall, Gwendolyn Midlo, 154–55
Hall, Stuart, 70, 196
Handelsman, Michael, 7, 68–80
"(hangover all star)" (González), 55
Hanna Meinhof, Ulrike, 25–26, 31
Harjo, Joy, 182
Harris, Robert, 206
Hartman, Saidiya, 89

Harvey-Kattou, Liz, 85
healing
    Cacho Caballero on, 180–81, 191n31
    Wolf on, 161–64
hegemonic masculinity, 36–38
hemispheric Blackness, Gómez Menjívar on, 4. *See also* Améfrica, term
Hernández, Gaspar Octavio, 98, 102
Herrera de Taylor, Isabel, 98
Hijos de Azapa, Los, 156
hip-hop. *See* rap music
Hispanophone Black literature, Jackson on, 7, 74
history
    recovery of, Preciado on, 70–75
    Taylor Herrera on, 104
Holms, John, 172
Holston, James, 114
Honduras, *177*
    Cacho Caballero on, 170–93
hood
    Chocó rap and, 200
    rap and, 204, 206
    term, 199
Hooker, Juliet, 6, 9, 59–60
hooks, bell, 38–39, 176, 187
Howes, Rebecca, 77n2
Hylton, Forrest, 198
Hymes, Dell, 25

identity
    Chocó rap and, 206–7
    Hall on, 70
    Preciado on, 68–69
    Rodríguez Quevedo on, 194–217
    Taylor Herrera on, 98
independence, and erasure of Afrodescendants, 4–9
Indigenous languages, Rivera Cusicanqui on, 153
    linguicide and, 171, 174, 182, 185, 188
Indigenous peoples, and poetry, 182
Indigenous writers, 54–55. *See also* Black letters in Latin America

internally displaced people (IDPs), in Columbia, 194–217
involution, and palimpsest, 99–102, 106
Iser, Wolfgang, 78n8
itinerary, term, 45

Jackson, Richard L., 7, 74
Jackson, Shona N., 95n8
Jacob, Eliseo, 109–26
Jamaica, Duncan on, 83–96
James, C. R., 5
Jarlenson, Edison Palacio (Pacho), 209n11
Jiménez, Blas, 76
Jiménez, Manuel de J., 46
Johnson, Sally, 25–26, 31
Jones, Jennifer A., 43

Kalípona, 172–74. *See also* Garífuna language/people
Kamel, Ali, 120–21
kanga, term, 134, 145n14
Kelley, Robin D. G., 84
Keme, Emil, 190n29
Kempadoo, Kamala, 180
Keyes, Cheryl, 199
Kikongo, 162
kimbo, term, 93
Kimbo (Duncan), 83–96
Kimmell, Michael, 36
King, Tiffany Lethabo, 19n30
knowing, ways of
    Gómez Menjívar on, 3
    King on, 19n30
Kongolese
    and *bomba*, 162
    cosmology, 145n14
    and dress, 156–57
    influence of, 155
    and *morenos de paso*, 156–60, 158

land
    Badiane on, 225–26, 232
    Cacho Caballero on, 182
    Rodríguez Quevedo on, 194–217
    See also deterritorialization

language
    Cacho Caballero and, 170–93
    Duncan and, 85
    gender identity and, 25–26
    González and, 45–50
    and healing, 180–81
    Mufwene and, 187
    Pereira and, 142
    political, purposes of, 34–35, 221
    and power relations, 35–36
    Preciado and, 75
    Ramsay and, 25–41
    Rivera Cisicanqui and, 153
    strategies in, 27
    term, 25–26
Languagui, Antombo, 201
Latin America
    demographics of, 152, 211n18
    See also Black writers in Latin America
Latino, Juan, 102
Lavou, Victorien, 207
Lefebvre, Henri, 204
Lévi-Strauss, Claude, 139–40, 146n33
Lewis, Martin, 7
Lewis, Marvin, 75
linguistic revitalization, Cacho Caballero and, 170–93
literacy, González and, 48–49
literary criticism, Afro-Latin
    Barra Costa on, 138–40
    Eliot and, 146n30
    future directions for, 141
    Gómez Menjívar on, 3
    Sánchez Martínez on, 43
López Oro, Paul Joseph, 43–45, 48
Lorde, Audre, 132
loss
    da Silva on, 116–17
    Preciado on, 72–73
    Rodríguez Quevedo on, 205–6
    Said on, 204
"Los sin futuro" (Gómez), 205, 207
Louima, Abner, 220
Lowe de Goodin, Melva, 98
loyalty, and masculinity, *corridos* on, 31–35

Lucas, Gavin, 104
Lucumi people, 155
Luyaluka, Kiatezua Lubanzadio, 158
lynching
    Badiane on, 228
    da Silva on, 113–14

Machado, Marilyn, 206
Maloney, Gerardo, 93
Mandinka people, 155
Maninka people, 163
maracas
    in *bomba*, 161
    Cacho Caballero on, 175–76
Marcando Territorio, 200–202
marginalization
    Black Indigenous writers and, 16–17
    and masculine identities, 27
    Perreira on, 140
Mariano Beltrame, José, 117
Martín-Barbero, Jesús, 7
Martínez, Onel, 209n11
Martínez Pera, Gloria, 201
Martins, Leda Maria, 141–42, 143n4
martyrdom
    Duncan on, 87
    Renacientes on, 204
masculine identities
    in *corridos*, Ramsay on, 25–41
    Duncan on, 89
material violence, 112
    da Silva on, 113–17
Maya genocide, 64n57
Mbembe, Achille, 111, 115–16, 120
Mbumba, 162
McClintock, Anne, 38
McDonald, Delia, 94
McDonald, John, 26
McDowell, John, 36
McField, David, 6
McKinney, Kitzie, 93
media
    Black women and, in Brazil, 118–22
    empowerment and, 4, 57, 132, 188–89, 232

mainstream, 113, 195–96, 209n3, 228
studies, 3, 123n1, 199
See also digital turn; Wi-Fi diaspora
mediations, 7, 8
Melo, Patricia, 123n14
memory
    collective, 207
    cultural, 153, 165n13
Mendoza, Zoila, 150, 165n2, 167n36
"meninos do Morro da Lagartixa, Os" (da Silva), 115
Messner, Michael, 36
Metáfora, 57
Mexico
    Ramsay on, 25–41
    Revolution, 26
Middleton, David, 208
Mignolo, Walter, 152
military
    corridos on, 34–35
    See also state-sponsored violence
Mills, Alan, 58
"Mi tierra querida" (Renacientes), 202–3
Mobley, Christina, 162
modernity
    Handelsman on, 69, 75–76
    Wolf on, 151
Modestin, Yvette, 98
Monzano, Juan Francisco, 88
Morejón, Nancy, 102
moreno, term, 155
morenos de paso, 150, 152, 155–60, 164
    Badiane on, 230–31
Morin, Edgar, 129
Mosby, Dorothy, 84
Mufwene, Salikoko, 187
Muhammad, Jameelah S., 26
"mula bronco, La" (*corrido*), 37–38
multiculturalism
    López Oro on, 45
    writing against, 9–11
music
    Badiane on, 230–32
    da Silva on, 116–17

González on, 45
Ramsay on, 25–41
Rodríguez Quevedo on, 194–217
Wolf on, 150–69
music-dance
　term, 165n4
　Wolf on, 150–69
Musiques Rebelles Americas (documentary), 199, 202, 210n13

Naranjo, Carmen, 93
Nascimento, Deocleciano, 144n12
nationalism
　and erasure of Afrodescendants, 4–9, 75–76, 84–85, 102
　and gender, 38
　and masculine identities, 27
National Liberation Army (ELN), 197
necropolitics
　da Silva on, 109–26
　term, 111
Négritude, Césaire on, 219
negro, term, 2
negros bozales, 151
　term, 165n5
new Black movements, Gómez Menjívar on, 1, 3
ngoma, term, 161
Nicaragua
　and race issues, 1
　Revolution, 5–7
Nketia, H. H., 163
Noel, Uroyoán, 48
"No queremos más guerra" (Perea), 204–5
nostalgia, hooks on, 187
Nunca más (documentary), 202, 210n13
Nurse, Keith, 36–37, 222

Obama, Michelle, 118
objects, Taylor Herrera on, 99–102
Ocasio, Michelle, 172, 223
odara, term, 119, 125n36
Oñate Martínez, Julio, 210n12
ONEGUA, 44, 59

Operación Génesis, 194, 196–98, 209n3
oral tradition
　Duncan and, 91–92
　Oslender on, 195
　Perreira on, 141
　terminology in, 143n4
Orejuela, Jefferson (Ali), 209n11
Oslender, Ulrich, 195, 209n6, 209n9
Other
　corridos and, 36–37
　Handelsman on, 76
　Wolf on, 155
Oxlaj Cúmez, Miguel Ángel, 181
Óyeme Chocó (CD), 195

Palacio, Joseph O., 181
palimpsest
　Castro on, 97–108
　and involution, 99–102, 106
　nature of, 98
Panama, Castro on, 97–108
paradigms, Barra Costa on, 129–30
#Parem de nos matar (da Silva), 109–26
Paschel, Tianna S., 43
patriarchy
　González and, 46–47, 50
　and identity, 36
Patria y vida, 231
Patterson, William, 112
Payeras, Javier, 48, 50
"Pedro el Chicarrón" (*corrido*), 27–30, 34
Perea, Werlin, 204–5
Pereira, Edimilson de Almeida, 129, 133, 138–43
Pérez, Ana Lilia, 188
Perry, Franklin, 84
pidgin languages, 172
"Piel" (Taylor Herrera), 101
Pile, Steve, 202, 208
pituco, term, 156
poetry
　Cacho Caballero and, 181–87
　da Silva and, 109–26
　González and, 42–67
　Preciado and, 68–80

police violence
    Badiane on, 220–21, 228
    da Silva on, 114–17
    See also state-sponsored violence
Portal Geledés, 123n2
posse, term, 199
postcolonial novels
    palimpsest and, 98
    Taylor Herrera and, 103
poverty
    Afro-Colombian rap and, 200
    Cacho Caballero on, 178
    West on, 221
power relations
    Barra Costa on, 131
    González on, 55–56
    Handelsman on, 69, 74–76
    and language, 35–36
    Ramsay on, 27, 35
    Wolf on, 151–52
Preciado, Antonio, 68–80
    Badiane on, 225–26
Prescott, Laurence, 7
Profetas, 200–201
protest movements, Badiane on, 219–20
Puerto Rico, 165n8
    Wolf on, 150–69

Quechua, 153, 159
Quijano, Aníbal, 165n10
quilombos, 1

race
    González on, 42–67
    Taylor Herrera on, 97
    West on, 221
race discourse, 1–9
    limits on, 6
    See also suppression of discourse on race
racial democracy
    da Silva on, 109–26
    Gómez Menjívar on, 1, 4, 7
    López Oro on, 45
    See also democracy

racism
    da Silva on, 110–11
    by denial, 7–8, 58–61, 64n58, 77
    Duncan on, 85, 89
    Preciado on, 70
radical baroque, 48
Ramchand, Kenneth, 26–27
Ramírez, Sergio, 6
Ramos, Lázaro, 118, 124n31
Ramsay, Paulette A., 7, 25–41, 92
"Rap da Felicidade," 116
rape, Duncan on, 89
rap music
    Badiane on, 231–32
    development of, 198–99
    "Rap da Felicidade," 116
    Rodríguez Quevedo on, 194–217
reader's itinerary, Sánchez Martínez on, 45, 50–58, 61
Reaja ou será morta (React or Die), 109
reception theory, 78n8
Rede Globo, 120–22
reggae, and rap, 200–201
religion
    Barra Costa on, 133–34
    Brathwaite on, 134–35
    Duncan on, 85, 89–91
    Pereira on, 138, 140–42
    Preciado on, 71–73, 78n12
    Sánchez Martínez on, 50–51
    Wolf on, 150, 155–60, 162–63
"Relying" (Cacho Caballero), 185
Renacientes, 195, 202, 209n11, 231
representation, Hall on, 70
resistance
    Barra Costa on, 133–34
    Black Indigenous writers and, 16–17
    González and, 48–49
    land and, 202
Restrepo Castañeda, Fernando, 202, 210n13
Revolutionary Armed Forces of Colombia (FARC), 197
Reyes, Ruben, 186
Rice, Tamir, 220
Risério, Antonio, 130, 141, 147n43

Rivera Cusicanqui, Silvia, 152–53, 162, 166n15, 230
Rivera-Rideau, Petra R., 43
Roa, Ana Sofía, 203
Roatán
    Cacho Caballero on, 170–93
    current status of, 187–88
Rodríguez, Ileana, 9–10
Rodríguez, Marta, 202, 210n13
Rodríguez Castelo, Hernán, 75
Rodríguez Quevedo, Diana, 194–217
Rohlehr, Gordon, 26–27
Roncón, Papá, 69–70, 78n5
rondo, 110
Royal, Kathleen Sawyers, 84

Sabino, Esteban, 57
Said, Edward, 204
Saint Vincent. *See* Yurumein
Salazar, Pablo, 206
Saldaña, Excilia, 102
Samalavičius, Almantas, 98, 227
samamfo
    definition of, 90
    Duncan on, 85, 89–91, 93
Sánchez Martínez, Juan Guillermo, 42–67
Sandinismo, 1, 5–6
Sanjinés, Javier, 76
Schoening, Max, 210n14
"Scream" (Cacho Caballero), 183
self-attribution, Connell on, 31
settler colonialism,
    Chacón on, 83–84
    Gómez Menjívar on, 170, 173
    Handelsman on, 69
    Sánchez Martínez on, 58–60
sexism, Badiane on, 221–22
sex work, Cacho Caballero on, 179–80
silencing
    da Silva on, 117–22
    Preciado on, 70, 73
    Ramírez on, 6
"Sincretismo" (Preciado), 71–72
Skidmore, Thomas, 118

slavery
    Brathwaite on, 134–35
    in Colombia, 212n38
    da Silva on, 119
    Handelsman on, 70–71
    and language, 172
    Taylor Herrera on, 103–6
slave ship, Brathwaite on, 134–35
slave trade
    Mbembe on, 115–16
    Wolf on, 154
Smart, Ian, 7, 94n8
Smith, Claire, 56
Sociedad Religiosa de Morenos Hilario Ayca, 150
Solien González, Nancie L., 50
"Sombra, La" (Taylor Herrera), 102
Sommer, Doris, 4, 47, 223
#SomosTodoMaju, 121
"Speak to Us" (Cacho Caballero), 185–86
spirituality. *See* religion
Standing Rock Sioux Tribe, 219
state of exception, Agamben on, 111, 115
state-sponsored violence
    da Silva on, 109–26
    Duncan on, 87–89
    Mbembe on, 120
    See also police violence
stereotypes, Preciado and, 69
subconscious, González and, 50
subordinate masculinity, 38
    Ramsay on, 36–37
suicide, Taylor Herrera on, 105
sulfuric acid analogy
    Candido on, 140
    Eliot on, 139
suppression of discourse on race
    Costa Rica and, 84–85
    González and, 58–61
    history of, 102
    Taylor Herrera and, 98
    Zapata Olivella on, 75–76
survivance
    Cacho Caballero on, 170–93
    term, 170

symbolic violence, 112
  da Silva on, 117–22
  definition of, 118

tapestry metaphor, Rivera Cusicanqui on, 153
target imagery, Aleixo and, 113
Taylor, Ashley Coleman, 162
Taylor, Breonna, 220
Taylor, Charles, 174
Taylor, Douglas, 171
Taylor Herrera, Melanie, 97–108
  Badiane on, 226–27
terminology, 2–3, 8–9
third diaspora, 4, 144n13. *See also* Wi-Fi diaspora
Thompson, Robert Farris, 136, 159
Thornton, John, 154
"Tierra querida" (Salazar), 206
Tillis, Antonio D., 7
time, Kongolese and, 158
Toledo, Aída, 45, 50, 224
Tolita culture, 78n6
"(tower)" (González), 53–54
tradition
  Barra Costa on, 130
  Candido on, 146n34
  Eliot on, 138
Trinidad, music and gender identities in, 26–27
Tuck, Eve, 59
typography, González on, 45
Tzoc, Manuel, 57

"Uenedu-Dream-Sueño" (Cacho Caballero), 184–85
unemployment
  Cacho Caballero on, 178–79
  Rodríguez Quevedo on, 208n1
United Nations
  definition of genocide, 112
  International Decade for People of African Descent, 10
United Self-Defense Forces of Colombia (AUC), 197, 211n20

United States
  immigration to, 178
  protests in, 220
  racial classification in, 43, 57
  and rap, 199–200
urban environment, and rap, 199, 202
Urriola, José Dolores, 98

Valdés, José Manuel, 102
Valencia Ortiz, Carlos, 201
Vallejo, César, 47
vallenato music, 195, 210n12
Van Kessel, Juan, 150, 158
Vargas, João H. Costa, 115–22
Vega-Drouet, Hector, 162–63
Viaje, pisto, plomo y miedo (Cacho Caballero), 177–87
"Viaje, El" (Taylor Herrera), 103–6
violence
  Badiane on, 221–22, 228
  Cacho Caballero on, 177–87
  and displaced persons, Rodríguez Quevedo on, 194–217
  Duncan on, 87–89
  forms of, 112
  and masculine identity, Ramsay on, 25–41
  See also police violence; state-sponsored violence
Virgen de las Peñas, 150
visionary masculinity, hooks on, 38–39
visual arts, in Brazil, Barra Costa on, 132
Vivas, Bernardo, 203
Vizenor, Gerald, 170
Volpe, Justin, 220
Voodoo Souldjahs, 200–201
"Voyage, The" (Taylor Herrera), 102–3

Wade, Peter, 43, 60, 64n58, 173, 208n1, 211n18
Wafien and his Maracas (Cacho Caballero), 175–76
Walsh, Catherine, 10–11, 152
Ward, Grame K., 56
Watson, Sonja Stephenson, 97–99, 101–2

"Wayuna-Relying-Ancestor" (Cacho Caballero), 185
weaving, Van Kessel on, 158
well-being, Indigenous conceptions of, 180–81
West, Cornel, 221
West Africa, influence of, 154–55
white supremacy, da Silva on, 114–15
Wi-Fi diaspora, 132
    term, 144n13
Williams, Lorna, 7
Wolf, Juan Eduardo, 150–69
Wolfe, Patrick, 84
women
    Badiane on, 221–22, 227–28
    Cacho Caballero on, 179–80
    Castro on, 97–108
    corridos and, 36–39
    da Silva on, 117–22
    Rodríguez on, 9–10
Wright, Daunte, 220
writing, Lévi-Strauss on, 139–40, 146n33

Xinca, recognition of, 56
Xiquín, Calixta Gabriel, 181

Yang, K. Wayne, 59
Yen a marre, 231
Yoruba people
    Perreira on, 141
    religion, 133–34
youth
    Cacho Caballero on, 178–79
    Rodríguez Quevedo on, 194–217
    violence against, in Brazil, 113–16, 123n14
yowa, 157–58, *158*
Yurumein
    Cacho Caballero on, 170–93
    González and, 50–55

Zanatón, El, 33–34
Zapata Olivella, Manuel, 68, 72–73, 75–76, 93
Zenón, Abuelo, 69, 71, 77n3

◆ VOLUMES IN THE HISPANIC ISSUES SERIES

46 *Améfrica in Letters: Literary Interventions from Mexico to the Southern Cone*, edited by Jennifer Carolina Gómez Menjívar
45 *Rite, Flesh, and Stone: Cultures of Death in Contemporary Spain, 1959–2021*, edited by Antonio Córdoba and Daniel García-Donoso
44 *Iberian Empires and the Roots of Globalization*, edited by Ivonne del Valle, Anna More, and Rachel Sarah O'Toole
43 *Cartographies of Madrid*, edited by Silvia Bermúdez and Anthony L. Geist
42 *Ethics of Life: Contemporary Iberian Debates*, edited by Katarzyna Beilin and William Viestenz
41 *In and Of the Mediterranean: Medieval and Early Modern Iberian Studies*, edited by Michelle M. Hamilton and Núria Silleras-Fernández
40 *Coloniality, Religion, and the Law in the Early Iberian World*, edited by Santa Arias and Raúl Marrero-Fente
39 *Poiesis and Modernity in the Old and New Worlds*, edited by Anthony J. Cascardi and Leah Middlebrook
38 *Spectacle and Topophilia: Reading Early (and Post-) Modern Hispanic Cultures*, edited by David R. Castillo and Bradley J. Nelson
37 *New Spain, New Literatures*, edited by Luis Martín-Estudillo and Nicholas Spadaccini
36 *Latin American Jewish Cultural Production*, edited by David William Foster
35 *Post-Authoritarian Cultures: Spain and Latin America's Southern Cone*, edited by Luis Martín-Estudillo and Roberto Ampuero
34 *Spanish and Empire*, edited by Nelsy Echávez-Solano and Kenya C. Dworkin y Méndez
33 *Generation X Rocks: Contemporary Peninsular Fiction, Film, and Rock Culture*, edited by Christine Henseler and Randolph D. Pope
32 *Reason and Its Others: Italy, Spain, and the New World*, edited by David Castillo and Massimo Lollini

31 *Hispanic Baroques: Reading Cultures in Context*, edited by Nicholas Spadaccini and Luis Martín-Estudillo
30 *Ideologies of Hispanism*, edited by Mabel Moraña
29 *The State of Latino Theater in the United States: Hybridity, Transculturation, and Identity*, edited by Luis A. Ramos-García
28 *Latin America Writes Back: Postmodernity in the Periphery (An Interdisciplinary Perspective)*, edited by Emil Volek
27 *Women's Narrative and Film in Twentieth-Century Spain: A World of Difference(s)*, edited by Ofelia Ferrán and Kathleen M. Glenn
26 *Marriage and Sexuality in Medieval and Early Modern Iberia*, edited by Eukene Lacarra Lanz
25 *Pablo Neruda and the U.S. Culture Industry*, edited by Teresa Longo
24 *Iberian Cities*, edited by Joan Ramon Resina
23 *National Identities and Sociopolitical Changes in Latin America*, edited by Mercedes F. Durán-Cogan and Antonio Gómez-Moriana

www.ingramcontent.com/pod-product-compliance
Lightning Source LLC
Chambersburg PA
CBHW030533230426
43665CB00010B/880